97th Congress
2d Session

COMMITTEE PRINT

THE RIGHT TO KEEP AND BEAR ARMS

REPORT

OF THE

SUBCOMMITTEE ON THE CONSTITUTION

OF THE

COMMITTEE ON THE JUDICIARY

UNITED STATES SENATE

NINETY-SEVENTH CONGRESS

SECOND SESSION

FEBRUARY 1982

Printed for the use of the Committee on the Judiciary

U.S. GOVERNMENT PRINTING OFFICE
88-618 O WASHINGTON : 1982

For sale by the Superintendent of Documents, U. S. Government Printing Office
Washington, D.C. 20402

CONTENTS

PREFACE

"To preserve liberty, it is essential that the whole body of the people always possess arms, and be taught alike, especially when young, how to use them." (Richard Henry Lee, Virginia delegate to the Continental Congress, initiator of the Declaration of Independence, and member of the first Senate, which passed the Bill of Rights.)

"The great object is that every man be armed . . . Everyone who is able may have a gun." (Patrick Henry, in the Virginia Convention on the ratification of the Constitution.)

"The advantage of being armed . . . the Americans possess over the people of all other nations . . . Notwithstanding the military establishments in the several Kingdoms of Europe, which are carried as far as the public resources will bear, the governments are afraid to trust the people with arms." (James Madison, author of the Bill of Rights, in his Federalist Paper No. 26.)

"A well regulated Militia, being necessary to the security of a free State, the right of the people to keep and bear Arms, shall not be infringed." (Second Amendment to the Constitution.)

In my studies as an attorney and as a United States Senator, I have constantly been amazed by the indifference or even hostility shown the Second Amendment by courts, legislatures, and commentators. James Madison would be startled to hear that his recognition of a right to keep and bear arms, which passed the House by a voice vote without objection and hardly a debate, has since been construed in but a single, and most ambiguous, Supreme Court decision, whereas his proposals for freedom of religion, which he made reluctantly out of fear that they would be rejected or narrowed beyond use, and those for freedom of assembly, which passed only after a lengthy and bitter debate, are the subject of scores of detailed and favorable decisions. Thomas Jefferson, who kept a veritable armory of pistols, rifles and shotguns at Monticello, and advised his nephew to forsake other sports in favor of hunting, would be astounded to hear supposed civil libertarians claim firearm ownership should be restricted. Samuel Adams, a handgun owner who pressed for an amendment stating that the "Constitution shall never be construed . . . to prevent the people of the United States who are peaceable citizens from keeping their own arms," would be shocked to hear that his native state today imposes a year's sentence, without probation or parole, for carrying a firearm without a police permit.

This is not to imply that courts have totally ignored the impact of the Second Amendment in the Bill of Rights. No fewer than twenty-one decisions by the courts of our states have recognized an individual right to keep and bear arms, and a majority of these have not only recognized the right but invalidated laws or regulations which abridged it. Yet in all too many instances, courts or commentators have sought, for reasons only tangentially related to constitutional history, to construe this right out of existence. They argue that the Second Amendment's words "right of the people" mean "a right of the state"—apparently overlooking the impact of those same words when used in the First and Fourth Amendments. The "right of the people" to assemble or to be free from unreasonable searches and seizures is not contested as an individual guarantee. Still they ignore consistency and claim that the right to "bear arms" relates only to military uses. This not only violates a consistent constitutional reading of "right of the people" but also ignores that the second amendment protects a right to "keep" arms. These commentators contend instead that the amendment's preamble regarding the necessity of a "well regulated militia . . . to a free state" means that the right to keep and bear arms applies only to a National Guard. Such a reading fails to note that the Framers used the term "militia" to relate to every citizen capable of bearing arms, and that Congress has established the present National Guard under its power to raise armies, expressly stating that it was not doing so under its power to organize and arm the militia.

When the first Congress convened for the purpose of drafting a Bill of Rights, it delegated the task to James Madison. Madison did not write upon a blank tablet. Instead, he obtained a pamphlet listing the State proposals for a bill of rights and sought to produce a briefer version incorporating all the vital proposals of these. His purpose was to incorporate, not distinguish by technical changes, proposals such as that of the Pennsylvania minority, Sam Adams, or the New Hampshire delegates. Madison proposed among other rights that "That right of the people to keep and bear arms shall not be infringed; a well armed and well regulated militia being the best security of a free country; but no person religiously scrupulous of bearing arms shall be compelled to render military service in person." In the House, this was initially modified so that the militia clause came before the proposal recognizing the right. The proposals for the Bill of Rights were then trimmed in the interests of brevity. The conscientious objector clause was removed following objections by Elbridge Gerry, who complained that future Congresses might abuse the exemption to excuse everyone from military service.

The proposal finally passed the House in its present form: "A well regulated militia, being necessary to the security of a free state, the right of the people to keep and bear arms, shall not be infringed.:" In this form it was submitted into the Senate, which passed it the following day. The Senate in the process indicated its intent that the right be an individual one, for private purposes, by rejecting an amendment which would have limited the keeping and bearing of arms to bearing "For the common defense".

The earliest American constitutional commentators concurred in giving this broad reading to the amendment. When St. George   Tucker, later Chief Justice of the Virginia Supreme Court, in 1803 published an edition of Blackstone annotated to American law, he followed Blackstone's citation of the right of the subject "of having arms suitable to their condition and degree, and such as are allowed by law" with a citation to the Second Amendment, "And this without any qualification as to their condition or degree, as is the case in the British government." William Rawle's "View of the Constitution" published in Philadelphia in 1825 noted that under the Second Amendment: "The prohibition is general. No clause in the Constitution could by a rule of construction be conceived to give to Congress a power to disarm the people. Such a flagitious attempt could only be made under some general pretense by a state legislature. But if in blind pursuit of inordinate power, either should attempt it, this amendment may be appealed to as a restraint on both." The Jefferson papers in the Library of Congress show that both Tucker and Rawle were friends of, and corresponded with, Thomas Jefferson. Their views are those of contemporaries of Jefferson, Madison and others, and are entitled to special weight. A few years later, Joseph Story in his "Commentaries on the Constitution" considered the right to keep and bear arms as "the palladium of the liberties of the republic", which deterred tyranny and enabled the citizenry at large to overthrow it should it come to pass.

Subsequent legislation in the second Congress likewise supports the interpretation of the Second Amendment that creates an individual right. In the Militia Act of 1792, the second Congress defined "militia of the United States" to include almost every free adult male in the United States. These persons were obligated by law to possess a firearm and a minimum supply of ammunition and military equipment. This statute, incidentally, remained in effect into the early years of the present century as a legal requirement of gun ownership for most of the population of the United States. There can be little doubt from this that when the Congress and the people spoke of a "militia", they had reference to the traditional concept of the entire populace capable of bearing arms, and not to any formal group such as what is today called the National Guard. The purpose was to create an armed citizenry, which the political theorists at the time considered essential to ward off tyranny. From this militia, appropriate measures might create a "well regulated militia" of individuals trained in their duties and responsibilities as citizens and owners of firearms.

If gun laws in fact worked, the sponsors of this type of legislation should have no difficulty drawing upon long lists of examples of crime rates reduced by such legislation. That they cannot do so after a century and a half of trying—that they must sweep under the rug the southern attempts at gun control in the 1870-1910 period, the northeastern attempts in the 1920-1939 period, the attempts at both Federal and State levels in 1965-1976—establishes the repeated, complete and inevitable failure of gun laws to control serious crime.

Immediately upon assuming chairmanship of the Subcommittee on the Constitution, I sponsored the report which follows as an effort to study, rather than ignore, the history of the controversy over the right to keep and bear arms. Utilizing the research capabilities   of the Subcommittee on the Constitution, the resources of the Library of Congress, and the assistance of constitutional scholars such as Mary Kaaren Jolly, Steven Halbrook, and David T. Hardy, the subcommittee has managed to uncover information on the right to keep and bear arms which documents quite clearly its status as a major individual right of American citizens. We did not guess at the purpose of the British 1689 Declaration of Rights; we located the Journals of the House of Commons and private notes of the Declaration's sponsors, now dead for two centuries. We did not make suppositions as to colonial interpretations of that Declaration's right to keep arms; we examined colonial newspapers which discussed it. We did not speculate as to the intent of the framers of the second amendment; we examined James Madison's drafts for it, his handwritten outlines of speeches upon the Bill of Rights, and discussions of the second amendment by early scholars who were personal friends of Madison, Jefferson, and Washington and wrote while these still lived. What the Subcommittee on the Constitution uncovered was clear—and long-lost—proof that the second amendment to our Constitution was intended as an individual right of the American citizen to keep and carry arms in a peaceful manner, for protection of himself, his family, and his freedoms. The summary of our research and findings forms the first portion of this report.

In the interest of fairness and the presentation of a complete picture, we also invited groups which were likely to oppose this recognition of freedoms to submit their views. The statements of two associations who replied are reproduced here following the report of the Subcommittee. The Subcommittee also invited statements by Messrs. Halbrook and Hardy, and by the National Rifle Association, whose statements likewise follow our report.

When I became chairman of the Subcommittee on the Constitution, I hoped that I would be able to assist in the protection of the constitutional rights of American citizens, rights which have too often been eroded in the belief that government could be relied upon for quick solutions to difficult problems.

Both as an American citizen and as a United States Senator I repudiate this view. I likewise repudiate the approach of those who believe to solve American problems you simply become something other than American. To my mind, the uniqueness of our free institutions, the fact that an American citizen can boast freedoms unknown in any other land, is all the more reason to resist any erosion of our individual rights. When our ancestors forged a land "conceived in liberty", they did so with musket and rifle. When they reacted to attempts to dissolve their free institutions, and established their identity as a free nation, they did so as a nation of armed freemen. When they sought to record forever a guarantee of their rights, they devoted one full amendment out of ten to nothing but the protection of their right to keep and bear arms against government interference. Under my chairmanship the Subcommittee on the Constitution will concern itself with a proper recognition of, and respect for, this right most valued by free men.

ORRIN G. HATCH,
Chairman,
Subcommittee on the Constitution.

JANUARY 20, 1982.

The right to bear arms is a tradition with deep roots in American society. Thomas Jefferson proposed that "no free man shall ever be debarred the use of arms," and Samuel Adams called for an amendment banning any law "to prevent the people of the United States who are peaceable citizens from keeping their own arms." The Constitution of the State of Arizona, for example, recognizes the "right of an individual citizen to bear arms in defense of himself or the State."

Even though the tradition has deep roots, its application to modern America is the subject of intense controversy. Indeed, it is a controversy into which the Congress is beginning, once again, to immerse itself. I have personally been disappointed that so important an issue should have generally been so thinly researched and so minimally debated both in Congress and the courts. Our Supreme Court has but once touched on its meaning at the Federal level and that decision, now nearly a half-century old, is so ambiguous that any school of thought can find some support in it. All Supreme Court decisions on the second amendment's application to the States came in the last century, when constitutional law was far different than it is today. As ranking minority member of the Subcommittee on the Constitution, I, therefore, welcome the effort which led to this report—a report based not only upon the independent research of the subcommittee staff, but also upon full and fair presentation of the cases by all interested groups and individual scholars.

I personally believe that it is necessary for the Congress to amend the Gun Control Act of 1968. I welcome the opportunity to introduce this discussion of how best these amendments might be made.

The Constitution subcommittee staff has prepared this monograph bringing together proponents of both sides of the debate over the 1968 Act. I believe that the statements contained herein present the arguments fairly and thoroughly. I commend Senator Hatch, chairman of the subcommittee, for having this excellent reference work prepared. I am sure that it will be of great assistance to the Congress as it debates the second amendment and considers legislation to amend the Gun Control Act.

DENNIS DECONCINI,
Ranking Minority Member,
Subcommittee On the Constitution.

JANUARY 20, 1982.

The right to keep and bear arms as a part of English and American law antedates not only the Constitution, but also the discovery of firearms. Under the laws of Alfred the Great, whose reign began in 872 A.D., all English citizens from the nobility to the peasants were obliged to privately purchase weapons and be available for military duty.[1] This was in sharp contrast to the feudal system as it evolved in Europe, under which armament and military duties were concentrated in the nobility. The body of armed citizens were known as the "fyrd".

While a great many of the Saxon rights were abridged following the Norman conquest, the right and duty of arms possession was retained. Under the Assize of Arms of 1181, "the whole community of freemen" between the ages of 15 and 40 were required by law to possess certain arms, which were arranged in proportion to their possessions.[2] They were required twice a year to demonstrate to Royal Officials that they were appropriately armed. In 1253, another Assize of Arms expanded the duty of armament to include not only freeman, but also villeins, who were the English equivalent of serfs. Now all "citizens, burgesses, free tenants, villeins and others from 15 to 60 years of age" were obliged to be armed.[3] While on the Continent the villeins were regarded as little more than animals hungering for rebellion, the English legal system not only permitted, but affirmatively required them, to be armed.

The thirteenth century saw further definitions of this right as the long bow, a formidable armor-piercing weapon, became increasingly the mainstay of British national policy. In 1285, Edward I commanded that all persons comply with the earlier Assizes and added that "anyone else who can afford them shall keep bows and arrows".[4] The right of armament was subject only to narrow limitations. In 1279, it was ordered that those appearing in Parliament or other public assemblies "shall come without all force and armor, well and peaceably".[5] In 1328, the statute of Northampton ordered that no one use their arms in "affray of the peace, nor to go nor ride armed by day or by night in fairs, markets, nor in the presence of the justices or other ministers".[6] English courts construed this ban consistently with the general right of private armament as applying only to wearing of arms "accompanied with such circumstances as are apt to terrify the people".[7] In 1369, the King ordered that the sheriffs of London require all citizens "at leisure time on holidays" to "use in their recreation bowes and arrows" and to stop all other games which might distract them from this practice.[8]

The Tudor kings experimented with limits upon specialized weapons—mainly crossbows and the then-new firearms. These measures were not intended to disarm the citizenry, but on the contrary, to prevent their being diverted from longbow practice by (pg.2) sport with other weapons which were considered less effective. Even these narrow measures were shortlived. In 1503, Henry VII limited shooting (but not possession) of crossbows to those with land worth 200 marks annual rental, but provided an exception for those who "shote owt of a howse for the lawefull defens of the same".[9] In 1511, Henry VIII increased the property requirement to 300 marks. He also expanded the requirement of longbow ownership, requiring all citizens to "use and exercyse shootyng in longbowes, and also have a bowe and arrowes contynually" in the house.[10] Fathers were required by law to purchase bows and arrows for their sons between the age of 7 and 14 and to train them in longbow use.

In 1514 the ban on crossbows was extended to include firearms.[11] But in 1533, Henry reduced the property qualification to 100 pounds per year; in 1541 he limited it to possession of small firearms ("of the length of one hole yard" for some firearms and "thre quarters of a yarde" for others)[12] and eventually he repealed the entire statute by proclamation.[13] The later Tudor monarchs continued the system and Elizabeth added to it by creating what came to be known as "train bands", selected portions of the citizenry chosen for special training. These trained bands were distinguished from the "militia", which term was first used during the Spanish Armada crisis to designate the entire of the armed citizenry.[14]

The militia continued to be a pivotal force in the English political system. The British historian Charles Oman considers the existence of the armed citizenry to be a major reason for the moderation of monarchical rule in Great Britain; "More than once he [Henry VIII] had to restrain himself, when he discovered that the general feeling of his subjects was against him.... His 'gentlemen pensioners' and his yeomen of the guard were but a handful, and bills or bows were in every farm and cottage".[15]

When civil war broke out in 1642, the critical issue was whether the King or Parliament had the right to control the militia.[16] The aftermath of the civil war saw England in temporary control of a military government, which repeatedly dissolved Parliament and authorized its officers to "search for, and seize all arms" owned by Catholics, opponents of the government, "or any other person whom the commissioners had judged dangerous to the peace of this Commonwealth".[17]

The military government ended with the restoration of Charles II. Charles in turn opened his reign with a variety of repressive legislation, expanding the definition of treason, establishing press censorship and ordering his supporters to form their own troops, "the officers to be numerous, disaffected persons watched and not allowed to assemble, and their arms seized".[18] In 1662, a Militia Act was enacted empowering officials "to search for and seize all arms in the custody or possession of any person or persons whom the said lieutenants or any two or more of their deputies shall judge dangerous to the peace of the kingdom".[19] Gunsmiths were ordered to deliver to the government lists of all purchasers.[20] These confiscations were continued under James II, who directed them particularly against the Irish population: "Although the   country was infested by predatory bands, a Protestant gentleman could scarcely obtain permission to keep a brace of pistols."[21]

In 1668, the government of James was overturned in a peaceful uprising which came to be known as "The Glorious Revolution". Parliament resolved that James had abdicated and promulgated a Declaration of Rights, later enacted as the Bill of Rights. Before coronation, his successor William of Orange, was required to swear to respect these rights. The debates in the House of Commons over this Declaration of Rights focused largely upon the disarmament under the 1662 Militia Act. One member complained that "an act of Parliament was made to disarm all Englishmen, who the lieutenant should suspect, by day or night, by force or otherwise—this was done in Ireland for the sake of putting arms into Irish hands." The speech of another is summarized as "militia bill—power to disarm all England—now done in Ireland." A third complained "Arbitrary power exercised by the ministry.... Militia—imprisoning without reason; disarming—himself disarmed." Yet another summarized his complaints "Militia Act—an abominable thing to disarm the nation...."[22]

The Bill of Rights, as drafted in the House of Commons, simply provided that "the acts concerning the militia are grievous to the subject" and that "it is necessary for the public Safety that the Subjects, which are Protestants, should provide and keep arms for the common defense; And that the Arms which have been seized, and taken from them, be restored."[23] The House of Lords changed this to make it a more positive declaration of an individual right under English law: "That the subjects which are Protestant may have arms for their defense suitable to their conditions and as allowed by law."[24] The only limitation was on ownership by Catholics, who at that time composed only a few percent of the British population and were subject to a wide variety of punitive legislation. The Parliament subsequently made clear what it meant by "suitable to their conditions and as allowed by law". The poorer citizens had been restricted from owning firearms, as well as traps and other commodities useful for hunting, by the 1671 Game Act. Following the Bill of Rights, Parliament reenacted that statute, leaving its operative parts unchanged with one exception—which removed the word "guns" from the list of items forbidden to the poorer citizens.[25] The right to keep and bear arms would henceforth belong to all English subjects, rich and poor alike.

In the colonies, availability of hunting and need for defense led to armament statues comparable to those of the early Saxon times. In 1623, Virginia forbade its colonists to travel unless they were "well armed"; in 1631 it required colonists to engage in target practice on Sunday and to "bring their peeces to church."[26] In 1658 it required every householder to have a functioning firearm within his house and in 1673 its laws provided that a citizen who claimed he was too poor to purchase a firearm would have one purchased for him by the government, which would then require him to pay a reasonable price when able to do so.[27] In Massachusetts, the first session of the legislature ordered that not only freemen, but also indentured servants own firearms and in 1644 it imposed a stern 6 shilling fine upon any citizen who was not armed.[28]

When the British government began to increase its military presence in the colonies in the mid-eighteenth century, Massachusetts responded by calling upon its citizens to arm themselves in defense. One colonial newspaper argued that it was impossible to complain that this act was illegal since they were "British subjects, to whom the privilege of possessing arms is expressly recognized by the Bill of Rights" while another argued that this "is a natural right which the people have reserved to themselves, confirmed by the Bill of Rights, to keep arms for their own defense".[29] The newspaper cited Blackstone's commentaries on the laws of England, which had listed the "having and using arms for self preservation and defense" among the "absolute rights of individuals." The colonists felt they had an absolute right at common law to own firearms.

Together with freedom of the press, the right to keep and bear arms became one of the individual rights most prized by the colonists. When British troops seized a militia arsenal in September, 1774, and incorrect rumors that colonists had been killed spread through Massachusetts, 60,000 citizens took up arms.[30] A few months later, when Patrick Henry delivered his famed "Give me liberty or give me death" speech, he spoke in support of a proposition "that a well regulated militia, composed of gentlemen and freemen, is the natural strength and only security of a free government...." Throughout the following revolution, formal and informal units of armed citizens obstructed British communication, cut off foraging parties, and harassed the thinly stretched regular forces. When seven states adopted state "bills of rights" following the Declaration of Independence, each of those bills of rights provided either for protection of the concept of a militia or for an express right to keep and bear arms.[31]

Following the revolution but previous to the adoption of the Constitution, debates over militia proposals occupied a large part of the political scene. A variety of plans were put forth by figures ranging from George Washington to Baron von Steuben.[32] All of the proposals called for a general duty of all citizens to be armed, although some proposals (most notably von Steuben's) also emphasized a "select militia" which would be paid for its services and given special training. In this respect, this "select militia" was the successor of the "trained bands" and the predecessor of what is today the "national guard". In the debates over the Constitution, von Steubon's proposals were criticized as undemocratic. In Connecticut one writer complained of a proposal that "this looks too much like Baron von Steubon's militia, by which a standing army was meant and intended."[33] In Pennsylvania, a delegate argued "Congress may give us a select militia which will, in fact, be a standing army—or Congress, afraid of a general militia, may say there will be no militia at all. When a select militia is formed, the people in general may be disarmed."[34] Richard Henry Lee, in his widely read pamphlet "Letters from the Federal Farmer to the Republican" worried that the people might be disarmed "by modelling the militia. Should one fifth or one eighth part of the people capable of bearing arms be made into a select militia, as has been proposed, and those the young and ardent parts of the community, possessed of little or no property, the former will answer all the purposes of an army, while the latter will be defenseless." He   proposed that "the Constitution ought to secure a genuine, and guard against a select militia," adding that "to preserve liberty, it is essential that the whole body of the people always possess arms and be taught alike, especially when young, how to use them."[35]

The suspicion of select militia units expressed in these passages is a clear indication that the framers of the Constitution did not seek to guarantee a State right to maintain formed groups similar to the National Guard, but rather to protect the right of individual citizens to keep and bear arms. Lee, in particular, sat in the Senate which approved the Bill of Rights. He would hardly have meant the second amendment to apply only to the select militias he so feared and disliked.

Other figures of the period were of like mind. In the Virginia convention, George Mason, drafter of the Virginia Bill of Rights, accused the British of having plotted "to disarm the people—that was the best and most effective way to enslave them", while Patrick Henry observed that "The great object is that every man be armed" and "everyone who is able may have a gun".[36]

Nor were the antifederalist, to whom we owe credit for a Bill of Rights, alone on this account. Federalist arguments also provide a source of support for an individual rights view. Their arguments in favor of the proposed Constitution also relied heavily upon universal armament. The proposed Constitution had been heavily criticized for its failure to ban or even limit standing armies. Unable to deny this omission, the Constitution's supporters frequently argued to the people that the universal armament of Americans made such limitations unnecessary. A pamphlet written by Noah Webster, aimed at swaying Pennsylvania toward ratification, observed

> Before a standing army can rule, the people must be disarmed; as they are in almost every kingdom in Europe. The supreme power in America cannot enforce unjust laws by the sword, because the whole body of the people are armed, and constitute a force superior to any band of regular troops that can be, on any pretense, raised in the United States.[37]

In the Massachusetts convention, Sedgwick echoed the same thought, rhetorically asking if an oppressive army could be formed or "if raised, whether they could subdue a Nation of freemen, who know how to prize liberty, and who have arms in their hands?"[38] In Federalist Paper 46, Madison, later author of the Second Amendment, mentioned "The advantage of being armed, which the Americans possess over the people of all other countries" and that "notwithstanding the military establishments in the several kingdoms of Europe, which are carried as far as the public resources will bear, the governments are afraid to trust the people with arms."

A third and even more compelling case for an individual rights perspective on the Second Amendment comes from the State demands for a bill of rights. Numerous state ratifications called for adoption of a Bill of Rights as a part of the Constitution. The first such call came from a group of Pennsylvania delegates. Their proposals, which were not adopted but had a critical effect on future debates, proposed among other rights that "the people have   a right to bear arms for the defense of themselves and their own state, or the United States, or for the purpose of killing game; and no law shall be passed for disarming the people or any of them, unless for crimes committed, or a real danger of public injury from individuals."[39] In Massachusetts, Sam Adams unsuccessfully pushed for a ratification conditioned on adoption of a Bill of Rights, beginning with a guarantee "That the said Constitution shall never be construed to authorize Congress to infringe the just liberty of the press or the rights of conscience; or to prevent the people of the United States who are peaceable citizens from keeping their own arms...."[40] When New Hampshire gave the Constitution the ninth vote needed for its passing into effect, it called for adoption of a Bill of Rights which included the provision that "Congress shall never disarm any citizen unless such as are or have been in actual rebellion".[41] Virginia and North Carolina thereafter called for a provision "that the people have the right to keep and bear arms; that a well regulated militia composed of the body of the people trained to arms is the proper, natural and safe defense of a free state."[42]

When the first Congress convened for the purpose of drafting a Bill of Rights, it delegated the task to James Madison. Madison did not write upon a blank tablet. Instead, he obtained a pamphlet listing the State proposals for a Bill of Rights and sought to produce a briefer version incorporating all the vital proposals of these. His purpose was to incorporate, not distinguish by technical changes, proposals such as that of the Pennsylvania minority, Sam Adams, and the New Hampshire delegates. Madison proposed among other rights that:

> "The right of the people to keep and bear arms shall not be infringed; a well armed and well regulated militia being the best security of a free country; but no person religiously scrupulous of bearing arms shall be compelled to render military service in person."[43]

In the House, this was initially modified so that the militia clause came before the proposal recognizing the right. The proposals for the Bill of Rights were then trimmed in the interests of brevity. The conscientious objector clause was removed following objections by Elbridge Gerry, who complained that future Congresses might abuse the exemption for the scrupulous to excuse everyone from militia service.

The proposal finally passed the House in its present form: "A well regulated militia, being necessary to the security of a free state, the right of the people to keep and bear arms, shall not be infringed." In this form it was submitted into the Senate, which passed it the following day. The Senate in the process indicated its intent that the right be an individual one, for private purposes, by rejecting an amendment which would have limited the keeping and bearing of arms to bearing "for the common defense".

The earliest American constitutional commentators concurred in giving this broad reading to the amendment. When St. George Tucker, later Chief Justice of the Virginia Supreme Court, in 1803 published an edition of Blackstone annotated to American law, he followed Blackstone's citation of the right of the subject "of having   arms suitable to their condition and degree, and such as are allowed by law" with a citation to the Second Amendment, "And this without any qualification as to their condition or degree, as is the case in the British government".[44] William Rawle's "View of the Constitution" published in Philadelphia in 1825 noted that under the Second Amendment

> The prohibition is general. No clause in the Constitution could by a rule of construction be conceived to give to Congress a power to disarm the people. Such a flagitious attempt could only be made under some general pretense by a state

legislature. But if in blind pursuit of inordinate power, either should attempt it, this amendment may be appealed to as a restraint on both."[45]

The Jefferson papers in the Library of Congress show that both Tucker and Rawle were friends of, and corresponded with Thomas Jefferson. This suggests that their assessment, as contemporaries of the Constitution's drafters, should be afforded special consideration.

Later commentators agreed with Tucker and Rawle. For instance, Joseph Story in his "Commentaries on the Constitution" considered the right to keep and bear arms as "the palladium of the liberties of the republic", which deterred tyranny and enabled the citizenry at large to overthrow it should it come to pass.[46]

Subsequent legislation in the Second Congress likewise supports the interpretation of the second amendment that creates an individual right. In the Militia Act of 1792, the second Congress defined "militia of the United States" to include almost every free adult male in the United States. These persons were obliged by law to possess a firearm and a minimum supply of ammunition and military equipment.[47] This statute, incidentally remained in effect into the early years of the present century as a legal requirement of gun ownership for most of the population of the United States. There can be little doubt from this that when the Congress and the people spoke of a "militia", they had reference to the traditional concept of the entire populace capable of bearing arms, and not to any formal group such as what is today called the National Guard. The purpose was to create an armed citizenry, such as the political theorists at the time considered essential to ward off tyranny. From this militia, appropriate measures might create a "well regulated militia" of individuals trained in their duties and responsibilities as citizens and owners of firearms.

The Second Amendment as such was rarely litigated prior to the passage of the Fourteenth Amendment. Prior to that time, most courts accepted that the commands of the federal Bill of Rights did not apply to the states. Since there was no federal firearms legislation at this time, there was no legislation which was directly subject to the Second Amendment, if the accepted interpretations were followed. However, a broad variety of state legislation was struck down under state guarantees of the right to keep and bear arms and even in a few cases, under the Second Amendment, when it came before courts which considered the federal protections applicable to the states. Kentucky in 1813 enacted the first carrying concealed weapon statute in the United States; in 1822 the Kentucky Court of Appeals struck down the law as a violation of the state constitutional protection of the right to keep and bear arms: "And can there be entertained a reasonable doubt but the provisions of that act import a restraint on the right of the citizen to bear arms? The court apprehends it not. The right existed at the adoption of the Constitution; it then had no limit short of the moral power of the citizens to exercise it, and in fact consisted of nothing else but the liberty of the citizen to bear arms."[48] On the other hand, a similar measure was sustained in Indiana, not upon the grounds that a right to keep and bear arms did not apply, but rather upon the notion that a statute banning only concealed carrying still permitted the carrying of arms and merely regulated one possible way of carrying them.[49] A few years later, the Supreme Court of Alabama upheld a similar statute but added "We do not desire to be understood as maintaining, that in regulating the manner of wearing arms, the legislature has no other limit than its own discretion. A statute which, under the pretense of regulation, amounts to a destruction of that right, or which requires arms to be so borne as to render them wholly useless for the purpose of defense, would be clearly unconstitutional."[50] When the Arkansas Supreme Court in 1842 upheld a carrying concealed weapons statute, the chief justice explained that the statute would not "detract anything from the power of the people to defend their free state and the established institutions of the country. It prohibits only the wearing of certain arms concealed. This is simply a regulation as to the manner of bearing such arms as are specified", while the dissenting justice proclaimed "I deny that any just or free government upon earth has the power to disarm its citizens.[51]

Sometimes courts went farther. When in 1837, Georgia totally banned the sale of pistols (excepting the larger pistols "known and used as horsemen's pistols") and other weapons, the Georgia Supreme Court in *Nunn v. State* held the statute unconstitutional under the Second Amendment to the federal Constitution. The court held that the Bill of Rights protected natural rights which were fully as capable of infringement by states as by the federal government and that the Second Amendment provided "the right of the whole people, old and young, men, women and boys, and not militia only, to keep and bear arms of every description, and not merely such as are used by the militia, shall not be infringed, curtailed, or broken in on, in the slightest degree; and all this for the important end to be attained: the rearing up and qualifying of a well regulated militia, so vitally necessary to the security of a free state."[52] Prior to the Civil War, the Supreme Court of the United States likewise indicated that the privileges of citizenship included the individual right to own and carry firearms. In the notorious *Dred Scott* case, the court held that black Americans were not citizens and could not be made such by any state. This decision, which by striking down the Missouri Compromise did so much to bring on the Civil War, listed what the Supreme Court considered the rights of American citizens by way of illustrating what rights would have to be given to black Americans if the Court were to recognize them as full fledged citizens:

> It would give to persons of the negro race, who are recognized as citizens in any one state of the Union, the right to enter every other state, whenever they pleased.... and it would give them full liberty of speech in public and in private upon all subjects upon which its own citizens might meet; to hold public meetings upon political affairs, and to keep and carry arms wherever they went.[53]

Following the Civil War, the legislative efforts which gave us three amendments to the Constitution and our earliest civil rights acts likewise recognized the right to keep and bear arms as an existing constitutional right of the individual citizen and as a right specifically singled out as one protected by the civil rights acts and by the Fourteenth Amendment to the Constitution, against infringement by state authorities. Much of the reconstruction effort in the South had been hinged upon the creation of "black militias" composed of the armed and newly freed blacks, officered largely by black veterans of the Union Army. In the months after the Civil War, the existing southern governments struck at these units with the enactment of "black codes" which either outlawed gun ownership by blacks entirely, or imposed permit systems for them, and permitted the confiscation of firearms owned by blacks. When the Civil Rights Act of 1866 was debated members both of the Senate and the House referred to the disarmament of blacks as a major consideration.[54] Senator Trumbull cited provisions outlawing ownership of arms by blacks as among those which the Civil Rights Act would prevent;[55] Senator Sulsbury complained on the other hand that if the act were to be passed it would prevent his own state from enforcing a law banning gun ownership by individual free blacks.[56] Similar arguments were advanced during the debates over the "anti-KKK act"; its sponsor at one point explained that a section making it a federal crime to deprive a person of "arms or weapons he may have in his house or possession for the defense of his person, family or property" was "intended to enforce the well-known constitutional provisions guaranteeing the right in the citizen to 'keep and bear arms'."[57] Likewise, the debates over the Fourteenth Amendment

Congress frequently referred to the Second Amendment as one of the rights which it intended to guarantee against state action.[58]

Following adoption of the Fourteenth Amendment, however, the Supreme Court held that that Amendment's prohibition against states depriving any persons of their federal "privileges and immunities" was to be given a narrow construction. In particular, the "privileges and immunities" under the Constitution would refer only to those rights which were not felt to exist as a process of natural right, but which were created solely by the Constitution. These might refer to rights such as voting in federal elections and of interstate travel, which would clearly not exist except by virtue of the existence of a federal government and which could not be said to be "natural rights".[59] This paradoxically meant that the rights which most persons would accept as the most important—those flowing from concepts of natural justice—were devalued at the expense of more technical rights. Thus when individuals were charged with having deprived black citizens of their right to freedom

of assembly and to keep and bear arms, by violently breaking up a peaceable assembly of black citizens, the Supreme Court in *United States v. Cruikshank*[60] held that no indictment could be properly brought since the right "of bearing arms for a lawful purpose" is "not a right granted by the Constitution. Neither is it in any manner dependent upon that instrument for its existence." Nor, in the view of the Court, was the right to peacefully assemble a right protected by the Fourteenth Amendment: "The right of the people peaceably to assemble for lawful purposes existed long before the adoption of the Constitution of the United States. In fact, it is and has always been one of the attributes of citizenship under a free government.... It was not, therefore, a right granted to the people by the Constitution." Thus the very importance of the rights protected by the First and Second Amendment was used as the basis for the argument that they did not apply to the states under the Fourteenth Amendment. In later opinions, chiefly *Presser v. Illinois*[61] and *Miller v. Texas*,[62] the Supreme Court adhered to the view. *Cruikshank* has clearly been superseded by twentieth century opinions which hold that portions of the Bill of Rights—and in particular the right to assembly with which *Cruikshank* dealt in addition to the Second Amendment—are binding upon the state governments. Given the legislative history of the Civil Rights Acts and the Fourteenth Amendment, and the more expanded views of incorporation which have become accepted in our own century, it is clear that the right to keep and bear arms was meant to be and should be protected under the civil rights statutes and the Fourteenth Amendment against infringement by officials acting under color of state law.

Within our own century, the only occasion upon which the Second Amendment has reached the Supreme Court came in *United States v. Miller*.[63] There, a prosecution for carrying a sawed off shotgun was dismissed before trial on Second Amendment grounds. In doing so, the court took no evidence as to the nature of the firearm or indeed any other factual matter. The Supreme Court reversed on procedural grounds, holding that the trial court could not take judicial notice of the relationship between a firearm and the Second Amendment, but must receive some manner of evidence. It did not formulate a test nor state precisely what relationship might be required. The court's statement that the amendment was adopted "to assure the continuation and render possible the effectiveness of such [militia] forces" and "must be interpreted and applied with that end in view", when combined with the court's statement that all constitutional sources "show plainly enough that the militia comprised all males physically capable of acting in concert for the common defense.... these men were expected to appear bearing arms supplied by themselves and of the kind in common use at the time,"[64] suggests that at the very least private ownership by a person capable of self defense and using an ordinary privately owned firearm must be protected by the Second Amendment. What the Court did not do in *Miller* is even more striking: It did not suggest that the lower court take evidence on whether Miller belonged to the National Guard or a similar group. The hearing was to be on the nature of the firearm, not on the nature of its use; nor is there a single suggestion that National Guard status is relevant to the case.

The Second Amendment right to keep and bear arms therefore, is a right of the individual citizen to privately posses and carry in a peaceful manner firearms and similar arms. Such an "individual rights" interpretation is in full accord with the history of the right to keep and bear arms, as previously discussed. It is moreover in accord with contemporaneous statements and formulations of the right by such founders of this nation as Thomas Jefferson and Samuel Adams, and accurately reflects the majority of the proposals which led up to the Bill of Rights itself. A number of state constitutions, adopted prior to or contemporaneously with the federal Constitution and Bill of Rights, similarly provided for a right of the people to keep and bear arms. If in fact this language creates a right protecting the states only, there might be a reason for it to be inserted in the federal Constitution but no reason for it to be inserted in state constitutions. State bills of rights necessarily protect only against action by the state, and by definition a state cannot infringe its own rights; to attempt to protect a right belonging to the state by inserting it in a limitation of the state's own powers would create an absurdity. The fact that the contemporaries of the framers did insert these words into several state constitutions would indicate clearly that they viewed the right as belonging to the individual citizen, thereby making it a right which could be infringed either by state or federal government and which must be protected against infringement by both.

Finally, the individual rights interpretation gives full meaning to the words chosen by the first Congress to reflect the right to keep and bear arms. The framers of the Bill of Rights consistently used the words "right of the people" to reflect individual rights—as when these words were used to recognize the "right of the people" to peaceably assemble, and the "right of the people" against unreasonable searches and seizures. They distinguished between the rights of the people and of the state in the Tenth Amendment. As discussed earlier, the "militia" itself referred to a concept of a universally armed people, not to any specifically organized unit. When the framers referred to the equivalent of our National Guard, they uniformly used the term "select militia" and distinguished this from "militia". Indeed, the debates over the Constitution constantly referred to organized militia units as a threat to freedom comparable to that of a standing army, and stressed that such organized units did not constitute, and indeed were philosophically opposed to, the concept of a militia.

That the National Guard is not the "Militia" referred to in the second amendment is even clearer today. Congress has organized the National Guard under its power to "raise and support armies" and not its power to "Provide for organizing, arming and disciplining the Militia".[65] This Congress chose to do in the interests of organizing reserve military units which were not limited in deployment by the strictures of our power over the constitutional militia, which can be called forth only "to execute the laws of the Union, suppress insurrections and repel invasions." The modern National Guard was specifically intended to avoid status as the constitutional militia, a distinction recognized by 10 U.S.C. Sec 311(a).

The conclusion is thus inescapable that the history, concept, and wording of the second amendment to the Constitution of the United States, as well as its interpretation by every major commentator and court in the first half-century after its ratification, indicates that what is protected is an individual right of a private citizen to own and carry firearms in a peaceful manner.

REFERENCES

1. Charles Hollister, Anglo-Saxon Military Institutions 11-42 (Oxford University Press 1962); Francis Grose, Military Antiquities Respecting a History of the British Army, Vol. I at 1-2 (London, 1812).

2. Grose, supra, at 9-11; Bruce Lyon, A Constitutional and Legal History of Medieval England 273 (2d. ed. New York 1980).

3. J. J. Bagley and P. B. Rowley, A Documentary History of England 1066-1540, Vol. 1 at 155-56 (New York 1965).

4. Statute of Winchester (13 Edw. I c. 6). See also Bagley and Rowley, supra at 158.

5. 7 Ed. I c. 2 (1279).

6. Statute of Northampton (2 Edw. III c. 3).

7. Rex v. Knight, 90 Eng. Rep. 330; 87 Eng. Rep. 75 (King's Bench, 1686).

8. E. G. Heath, The Grey Goose Wing 109 (London, 1971).

9. 19 Hen. VII c. 4 (1503).

10. 3 Hen. VIII c. 13 (1511).

11. 64 Hen. VIII c. 13 (1514).

12. 33 Hen. VIII c. 6 (1514).

13. Noel Perrin, Giving Up the Gun 59-60 (Boston, 1979).

14. Jim Hill, The Minuteman in War and Peace 26-27 (Harrisburg, 1968).

15. Charles Oman, A History of the Art of War in the Sixteenth Century 288 (New York, 1937).

16. William Blackstone, Commentaries, Vol. 2 at 412 (St. George Tucker, ed., Philadelphia 1803).

17. "An Act for Settling the Militia," Ordinances and Acts of the Interregnum, Vol. 2 1320 (London, HMSO 1911).

18. 8 Calendar of State Papers (Domestic), Charles II, No. 188, p. 150.

19. 14 Car. II c. 3 (1662).

20. Joyce Malcolm, Disarmed: The Loss of the Right to Bear Arms in Restoration England, at 11 (Mary Ingraham Bunting Institute, Radcliffe College 1980).

21. Thomas Macaulay, The History of England from the Accession of Charles II, Vol. II at 137 (London, 1856).

22. Phillip, Earl of Hardwicke, Miscellaneous State Papers from 1501-1726, vol. 2 at 407-17 (London, 1778).

23. J. R. Western, Monarchy and Revolution: The English State in the 1680's, at 339 (Totowa, N.J., 1972).

24. Journal of the House of Commons from December 26, 1688, to October 26, 1693, at 29. (London, 1742). The Bill of Rights was ultimately enacted in this form. 1 Gul. and Mar., Sess. 2, c. 2 (1689).

25. Joyce Malcolm, supra, at 16.

26. William Hening, The Statutes at Large: Being a Collection of All the Laws of Virginia from the First Session of the Legislature in 1619, at pp. 127, 173-74 (New York, 1823).

27. Id.

28. William Brigham, The Compact with the Charter and Laws of the Colony of New Plymouth, 31, 76 (Boston, 1836).

29. Oliver Dickerson, ed., Boston Under Military Rule, 61, 79, (Boston, 1936).

30. Steven Patterson, Political Parties in Revolutionary Massachusetts, at 103 (Univ. of Wisconsin Press, 1973).

31. See Sprecher, The Lost Amendment, 51 A.B.A.J. 554, 665 (1965).

32. The most extensive studies of these militia proposals are John McAuley Palmer, Washington, Lincoln, Wilson: Three War Statesmen (New York, 1930); Frederick Stern, Citizen Army (New York, 1957); John Mahon, The American Militia: Decade of Decision 1789-1800 (Univ of Florida, 1960).

33. Merrill Jensen, ed., The Documentary of History of the Ratification of the Constitution, vol. 3 at 378 (Madison, Wisc.).

34. Id., vol. 2 at 508.

35. Walter Bennett, ed., Letters from the Federal Farmer to the Republican, at 21, 22, 124 (Univ. of Alabama Press, 1975).

36. Debates and other Proceedings of the Convention of Virginia, . . . taken in shorthand by David Robertson of Petersburg, at 271, 275 (2d ed. Richmond, 1805).

37. Noah Webster, "An Examination into the Leading Principles of the Federal Constitution . . .", in Paul Ford, ed., Pamphlets on the Constitution of the United States, at 56 (New York, 1888).

38. Johnathan Elliott, ed., Debates in the Several State Conventions on the Adoption of the Federal Constitution, vol. 2 at 97 (2d ed., 1888).

39. Merrill Jensen, supra, vol. 2 at 597-98.

40. Debates and Proceedings in the Convention of the Commonwealth of Massachusetts, at 86-87 (Peirce & Hale, eds., Boston, 1850); 2 B. Schwartz, the Bill of Rights 675 (1971).

41. Documents Illustrative of the Formation of the Union of the American States, at 1026 (Washington, D.C.: GPO, 1927).

42. Id. at 1030.

43. Annals of Congress 434 (1789).

44. St. George Tucker, ed., Blackstone's Commentaries, Volume 1 at 143 n. 40, 41 (Philadelphia, 1803).

45. William Rawle, A View of the Constitution 125-6 (2d ed., Philadelphia, 1803).

46.   Joseph Story, Commentaries on the Constitution, vol. 2 at 746 (1833).
47.   Act of May 8, 1792; Second Cong., First Session, ch. 33.
48.   Bliss v. Commonwealth, 12 Ken. (2 Litt.) 90, 92 (1822).
49.   State v. Mitchell, (3 Black.) 229.
50.   State v. Reid, 1 Ala. 612, 35 Am. Dec. 44 (1840).
51.   State v. Buzzard, 4 Ark. 18, 27, 36 (1842). The Arkansas Constitutional provision at issue was narrower than the second amendment, as it protected keeping and bearing arms "for the common defense." Id. at 34.
52.   Nunn v. State, 1 Ga. 243, 251 (1846).
53.   Dred Scott v. Sandford, 60 U.S. 691, 705.
54.   The most comprehensive work in this field of constitutional law is Steven Halbrook, the Jurisprudence of the Second and Fourteenth Amendments (Institute for Humane Studies, Menlo Park, California, 1979), reprinted in 4 George Mason L. Rev. 1 (1981).
55.   Cong. Globe, 39th Congress, 1st Sess., pt. 1, p. 474 (Jan. 29, 1866).
56.   Id. at 478.
57.   H.R. Rep. No. 37, 41st Cong., 3d sess., p. 3 (1871).
58.   See generally Halbrook, supra, at 42-62.
59.   Slaughterhouse Cases, 83 U.S. 36 (L873).
60.   United States v. Cruikshank, 92 U.S. 542 (1876).
61.   Presser v. Illinois, 116 U.S. 252 (1886).
62.   Miller v. Texas, 153 U.S. 535 (1894).
63.   United States v. Miller, 307 U.S. 175 (1939).
64.   Id. at 178, 179.
65.   H.R. Report No. 141, 73d Cong., 1st sess. at 2-5 (1933).

APPENDIX

CASE LAW

The United States Supreme Court has only three times commented upon the meaning of the second amendment to our constitution. The first comment, in *Dred Scott*, indicated strongly that the right to keep and bear arms was an individual right; the Court noted that, were it to hold free blacks to be entitled to equality of citizenship, they would be entitled to keep and carry arms wherever they went. The second, in *Miller*, indicated that a court cannot take judicial notice that a short-barrelled shotgun is covered by the second amendment—but the Court did not indicate that National Guard status is in any way required for protection by that amendment, and indeed defined "militia" to include all citizens able to bear arms. The third, a footnote in *Lewis v. United States*, indicated only that "these legislative restrictions on the use of firearms"—a ban on possession by felons—were permissable. But since felons may constitutionally be deprived of many of the rights of citizens, including that of voting, this dicta reveals little. These three comments constitute all significant explanations of the scope of the second amendment advanced by our Supreme Court. The case of *Adam v. Williams* has been cited as contrary to the principle that the second amendment is an individual right. In fact, that reading of the opinion comes only in Justice Douglas's dissent from the majority ruling of the Court.

The appendix which follows represents a listing of twenty-one American decisions, spanning the period from 1822 to 1981, which have analysed right to keep and bear arms provisions in the light of statutes ranging from complete bans on handgun sales to bans on carrying of weapons to regulation of carrying by permit systems. Those decisions not only explained the nature of such a right, but also struck down legislative restrictions as violative of it, are designated by asterisks.

20th century cases

1. * *State v. Blocker*, 291 Or. 255, — — — P.2d — — — (1981).
"The statute is written as a total proscription of the mere possession of certain weapons, and that mere possession, insofar as a billy is concerned, is constitutionally protected."
"In these circumstances, we conclude that it is proper for us to consider defendant's 'overbreadth' attack to mean that the statute swept so broadly as to infringe rights that it could not reach, which in this setting means the right to possess arms guaranteed by sec 27."
2. * *State v. Kessler*, 289 Or. 359, 614 P.2d 94, at 95, at 98 (1980).
"We are not unmindful that there is current controversy over the wisdom of a right to bear arms, and that the original motivations for such a provision might not seem compelling if debated as a new issue. Our task, however, in construing a constitutional provision is to respect the principles given the status of constitutional guarantees and limitations by the drafters; it is not to abandon these principles when this fits the needs of the moment."
"Therefore, the term 'arms' as used by the drafters of the constitutions probably was intended to include those weapons used by settlers for both personal and military defense. The term 'arms' was not limited to firearms, but included several handcarried weapons commonly used for defense. The term 'arms' would not have included cannon or other heavy ordnance not kept by militia-men or private citizens."

3. *Motley v. Kellogg*, 409 N.E.2d 1207, at 1210 (Ind. App. 1980) (motion to transfer denied 1-27-1981).

"[N]ot making applications available at the chief's office effectively denied members of the community the opportunity to obtain a gun permit and bear arms for their self-defense."

4. *Schubert v. DeBard*, 398 N.E.2d 1339, at 1341 (Ind. App. 1980) (motion to transfer denied 8-28-1980).

"We think it clear that our constitution provides our citizenry the right to bear arms for their self-defense."

5. *Taylor v. McNeal*, 523 S.W.2d 148, at 150 (Mo. App. 1975).

"The pistols in question are not contraband. * * * Under Art. I, sec 23, Mo. Const. 1945, V.A.M.S., every citizen has the right to keep and bear arms in defense of his home, person and property, with the limitation that this section shall not justify the wearing of concealed arms."

6. * *City of Lakewood v. Pillow*, 180 Colo. 20, 501 P.2d 744, at 745 (en banc 1972).

"As an example, we note that this ordinance would prohibit gunsmiths, pawnbrokers and sporting goods stores from carrying on a substantial part of their business. Also, the ordinance appears to prohibit individuals from transporting guns to and from such places of business. Furthermore, it makes it unlawful for a person to possess a firearm in a vehicle or in a place of business for the purpose of self-defense. Several of these activities are constitutionally protected. Colo. Const. art. II, sec 13."

7. * *City of Las Vegas v. Moberg*, 82 N.M. 626, 485 P.2d 737, at 738 (N.M. App. 1971).

"It is our opinion that an ordinance may not deny the people the constitutionally guaranteed right to bear arms, and to that extent the ordinance under consideration is void."

8. *State v. Nickerson*, 126 Mt. 157, 247 P.2d 188, at 192 (1952).

"The law of this jurisdiction accords to the defendant the right to keep and bear arms and to use same in defense of his own home, his person and property."

9. *People v. Liss*, 406 Ill. 419, 94 N.E. 2d 320, at 323 (1950).

"The second amendment to the constitution of the United States provides the right of the people to keep and bear arms shall not be infringed. This of course does not prevent the enactment of a law against carrying concealed weapons, but it does indicate it should be kept in mind, in the construction of a statute of such character, that it is aimed at persons of criminal instincts, and for the prevention of crime, and not against use in the protection of person or property."

10. * *People v. Nakamura*, 99 Colo. 262, at 264, 62 P.2d 246 (en banc 1936).

"It is equally clear that the act wholly disarms aliens for all purposes. The state ... cannot disarm any class of persons or deprive them of the right guaranteed under section 13, article II of the Constitution, to bear arms in defense of home, person and property. The guaranty thus extended is meaningless if any person is denied the right to posses arms for such protection."

11. * *Glasscock v. City of Chattanooga*, 157 Tenn. 518, at 520, 11 S.W. 2d 678 (1928).

"There is no qualifications of the prohibition against the carrying of a pistol in the city ordinance before us but it is made unlawful 'to carry on or about the person any pistol,' that is, any sort of pistol in any sort of manner. *** [W]e must accordingly hold the provision of this ordinance as to the carrying of a pistol invalid."

12. * *People v. Zerillo*, 219 Mich. 635, 189 N.W. 927, at 928 (1922).

"The provision in the Constitution granting the right to all persons to bear arms is a limitation upon the power of the Legislature to enact any law to the contrary. The exercise of a right guaranteed by the Constitution cannot be made subject to the will of the sheriff."

13 * *State v. Kerner*, 181 N.C. 574, 107 S.E. 222, at 224 (1921).

"We are of the opinion, however, that 'pistol' ex vi termini is properly included within the word 'arms,' and that the right to bear such arms cannot be infringed. The historical use of pistols as 'arms' of offense and defense is beyond controversy."

"The maintenance of the right to bear arms is a most essential one to every free people and should not be whittled down by technical constructions."

14. * *State v. Rosenthal*, 75 VT. 295, 55 A. 610, at 611 (1903).

"The people of the state have a right to bear arms for the defense of themselves and the state. *** The result is that Ordinance No. 10, so far as it relates to the carrying of a pistol, is inconsistent with and repugnant to the Constitution and the laws of the state, and it is therefore to that extent, void."

15. * In re *Brickey*, 8 Ida. 597, at 598-99, 70 p. 609 (1902).

"The second amendment to the federal constitution is in the following language: 'A well-regulated militia, being necessary to the security of a free state, the right of the people to keep and bear arms, shall not be infringed.' The language of section 11, article I of the constitution of Idaho, is as follows: 'The people have the right to bear arms for their security and defense, but the legislature shall regulate the exercise of this right by law.' Under these constitutional provisions, the legislature has no power to prohibit a citizen from bearing arms in any portion of the state of Idaho, whether within or without the corporate limits of cities, towns, and villages."

19th century cases

16. * *Wilson v. State*, 33 Ark. 557, at 560, 34 Am. Rep. 52, at 54 (1878).

"If cowardly and dishonorable men sometimes shoot unarmed men with army pistols or guns, the evil must be prevented by the ⸳ penitentiary and gallows, and not by a general deprivation of constitutional privilege."

17. * *Jennings v. State*, 5 Tex. Crim. App. 298, at 300-01 (1878).

"We believe that portion of the act which provides that, in case of conviction, the defendant shall forfeit to the county the weapon or weapons so found on or about his person is not within the scope of legislative authority. * * * One of his most sacred rights is that of having arms for his own defence and that of the State. This right is one of the surest safeguards of liberty and self-preservation."

18. * *Andrews v. State*, 50 Tenn. 165, 8 Am. Rep. 8, at 17 (1871).

"The passage from Story shows clearly that this right was intended, as we have maintained in this opinion, and was guaranteed to and to be exercised and enjoyed by the citizen as such, and not by him as a soldier, or in defense solely of his political rights."

19. * *Nunn v. State*, 1 Ga. (1 Kel.) 243, at 251 (1846).

"'The right of the people to bear arms shall not be infringed.' The right of the whole people, old and young, men, women and boys, and not militia only, to keep and bear arms of every description, and not such merely as are used by the militia, shall not be infringed, curtailed, or broken in upon, in the smallest degree; and all this for the important end to be attained: the rearing up and qualifying a well-regulated militia, so vitally necessary to the security of a free State."

20. *Simpson v. State*, 13 Tenn. 356, at 359-60 (1833).

"But suppose it to be assumed on any ground, that our ancestors adopted and brought over with them this English statute, [the statute of Northampton,] or portion of the common law, our constitution has completely abrogated it; it says, 'that the freemen of this State have a right to keep and bear arms for their common defence.' Article II, sec. 26. * * * By this clause of the constitution, an express power is given and secured to all the free citizens of the State to keep and bear arms for their defence, without any qualification whatever as to their kind or nature; and it is conceived, that it would be going much too far, to impair by construction or abridgement a constitutional privilege, which is so declared; neither, after so solumn an instrument hath said the people may carry arms, can we be permitted to impute to the acts thus licensed, such a necessarily consequent operation as terror to the people to be incurred thereby; we must attribute to the framers of it, the absence of such a view."

21. *Bliss v. Commonwealth*, 12 Ky. (2 Litt.) 90, at 92, and 93, 13 Am. Dec. 251 (1822).

"For, in principle, there is no difference between a law prohibiting the wearing concealed arms, and a law forbidding the wearing such as are exposed; and if the former be unconstitutional, the latter must be so likewise."

"But it should not be forgotten, that it is not only a part of the right that is secured by the constitution; it is the right entire and complete, as it existed at the adoption of the constitution; and if any portion of that right be impaired, immaterial how small the part may be, and immaterial the order of time at which it be done, it is equally forbidden by the constitution."

The following represents a list of twelve scholarly articles which have dealt with the subject of the right to keep and bear arms as reflected in the second amendment to the Constitution of the United States. The scholars who have undertaken this research range from professors of law, history and philosophy to a United States Senator. All have concluded that the second amendment is an individual right protecting American citizens in their peaceful use of firearms.

BIBLIOGRAPHY

Hays, THE RIGHT TO BEAR ARMS, A STUDY IN JUDICIAL MISINTERPRETATION, 2 Wm. & Mary L. R. 381 (1960)

Sprecher, THE LOST AMENDMENT, 51 Am. Bar Assn. J. 554 & 665 (2 parts) (1965)

Comment, THE RIGHT TO KEEP AND BEAR ARMS; A NECESSARY CONSTITUTIONAL GUARANTEE OR AN OUTMODED PROVISION OF THE BILL OF RIGHTS? 31 Albany L. R. 74 (1967)

Levine & Saxe, THE SECOND AMENDMENT: THE RIGHT TO BEAR ARMS, 7 Houston L. R. 1 (1969)

McClure, FIREARMS AND FEDERALISM, 7 Idaho L. R. 197 (1970)

Hardy & Stompoly, OF ARMS AND THE LAW, 51 Chi.-Kent L. R. 62 (1974)

Weiss, A REPLY TO ADVOCATES OF GUN CONTROL LAW, 52 Jour. Urban Law 577 (1974)

Whisker, HISTORICAL DEVELOPMENT AND SUBSEQUENT EROSION OF THE RIGHT TO KEEP AND BEAR ARMS, 78 W. Va. L. R. 171 (1976)

Caplan, RESTORING THE BALANCE: THE SECOND AMENDMENT REVISITED, 5 Fordham Urban L. J. 31 (1976)

Caplan, HANDGUN CONTROL: CONSTITUTIONAL OR UNCONSTITUTIONAL?, 10 N.C. Central L. J. 53 (1979)

Cantrell, THE RIGHT TO BEAR ARMS, 53 Wis. Bar Bull. 21 (Oct. 1980)

Halbrook, THE JURISPRUDENCE OF THE SECOND AND FOURTEENTH AMENDMENTS, 4 Geo. Mason L. Rev. 1 (1981)

Enforcement of Federal Firearms Laws From the Perspective of the Second Amendment

Federal involvement in firearms possession and transfer was not significant prior to 1934, when the National Firearms Act was adopted. The National Firearms Act as adopted covered only fully automatic weapons (machine guns and submachine guns) and rifles and shotguns whose barrel length or overall length fell below certain limits. Since the Act was adopted under the revenue power, sale of these firearms was not made subject to a ban or permit system. Instead, each transfer was made subject to a $200 excise tax, which must be paid prior to transfer; the identification of the parties to the transfer indirectly accomplished a registration purpose.

The 1934 Act was followed by the Federal Firearms Act of 1938, which placed some limitations upon sale of ordinary firearms. Persons engaged in the business of selling those firearms in interstate commerce were required to obtain a Federal Firearms License, at an annual cost of $1, and to maintain records of the name and address of persons to whom they sold firearms. Sales to persons convicted of violent felonies were prohibited, as were interstate shipments to persons who lacked the permits required by the law of their state.

Thirty years after adoption of the Federal Firearms Act, the Gun Control Act of 1968 worked a major revision of federal law. The Gun Control Act was actually a composite of two statutes. The first of these, adopted as portions of the Omnibus Crime and Safe Streets Act, imposed limitations upon imported firearms, expanded the requirement of dealer licensing to cover anyone "engaged in the business of dealing" in firearms, whether in interstate or local commerce, and expanded the recordkeeping obligations for dealers. It also imposed a variety of direct limitations upon sales of handguns. No transfers were to be permitted between residents of different states (unless the recipient was a federally licensed dealer), even where the transfer was by gift rather than sale and even where the recipient was subject to no state law which could have been evaded. The category of persons to whom dealers could not sell was expanded to cover persons convicted of any felony (other than certain business-related felonies such as antitrust violations), persons subject to a mental commitment order or finding of mental incompetence, persons who were users of marijuana and other drugs, and a number of other categories. Another title of the Act defined persons who were banned from possessing firearms. Paradoxically, these classes were not identical with the list of classes prohibited from purchasing or receiving firearms.

The Omnibus Crime and Safe Streets Act was passed on June 5, 1968, and set to take effect in December of that year. Barely two weeks after its passage, Senator Robert F. Kennedy was assassinated while campaigning for the presidency. Less than a week after his death, the second bill which would form part of the Gun Control Act of 1968 was introduced in the House. It was reported out of Judiciary ten days later, out of Rules Committee two weeks after that, and was on the floor barely a month after its introduction. the second bill worked a variety of changes upon the original Gun Control Act. Most significantly, it extended to rifles and shotguns the controls which had been imposed solely on handguns, extended the class of persons prohibited from possessing firearms to include those who were users of marijuana and certain other drugs, expanded judicial review of dealer license revocations by mandating a de novo hearing once an appeal was taken, and permitted interstate sales of rifles and shotguns only where the parties resided in contiguous states, both of which had enacted legislation permitting such sales. Similar legislation was passed by the Senate and a conference of the Houses produced a bill which was essentially a modification of the

House statute. This became law before the Omnibus Crime Control and Safe Streets Act, and was therefore set for the same effective date.

Enforcement of the 1968 Act was delegated to the Department of the Treasury, which had been responsible for enforcing the earlier gun legislation. This responsibility was in turn given to the Alcohol and Tobacco Tax Division of the Internal Revenu Service. This division had traditionally devoted itself to the pursuit of illegal producers of alcohol; at the time of enactment of the Gun Control Act, only 8.3 percent of its arrests were for firearms violations. Following enactment of the Gun Control Act the Alcohol and Tobacco Tax Division was retitled the Alcohol, Tobacco and Firearms Division of the IRS. By July, 1972 it had nearly doubled in size and became a complete Treasury bureau under the name of Bureau of Alcohol, Tobacco and Firearms.

The mid-1970's saw rapid increases in sugar prices, and these in turn drove the bulk of the "moonshiners" out of business. Over 15,000 illegal distilleries had been raided in 1956; but by 1976 this had fallen to a mere 609. The BATF thus began to devote the bulk of its efforts to the area of firearms law enforcement.

Complaints regarding the techniques used by the Bureau in an effort to generate firearms cases led to hearings before the Subcommittee on Treasury, Post Office, and General Appropriations of the Senate Appropriations Committee in July 1979 and April 1980, and before the Subcommittee on the Constitution of the Senate Judiciary Committee in October 1980. At these hearings evidence was received from various citizens who had been charged by BATF, from experts who had studied the BATF, and from officials of the Bureau itself.

Based upon these hearings, it is apparent that enforcement tactics made possible by current federal firearms laws are constitutionally, legally, and practically reprehensible. Although Congress adopted the Gun Control Act with the primary object of limiting access of felons and high-risk groups to firearms, the overbreadth of the law has led to neglect of precisely this area of enforcement. For example the Subcommittee on the Constitution received correspondence from two members of the Illinois Judiciary, dated in 1980, indicating that they had been totally unable to persuade BATF to accept cases against felons who were in possession of   firearms including sawed-off shotguns. The Bureau's own figures demonstrate that in recent years the percentage of its arrests devoted to felons in possession and persons knowingly selling to them have dropped from 14 percent down to 10 percent of their firearms cases. To be sure, genuine criminals are sometimes prosecuted under other sections of the law. Yet, subsequent to these hearings, BATF stated that 55 percent of its gun law prosecutions overall involve persons with no record of a felony conviction, and a third involve citizens with no prior police contact at all.

The Subcommittee received evidence that BATF has primarily devoted its firearms enforcement efforts to the apprehension, upon technical malum prohibitum charges, of individuals who lack all criminal intent and knowledge. Agents anxious to generate an impressive arrest and gun confiscation quota have repeatedly enticed gun collectors into making a small number of sales—often as few as four—from their personal collections. Although each of the sales was completely legal under state and federal law, the agents then charged the collector with having "engaged in the business" of dealing in guns without the required license. Since existing law permits a felony conviction upon these charges even where the individual has no criminal knowledge or intent numerous collectors have been ruined by a felony record carrying a potential sentence of five years in federal prison. Even in cases where the collectors secured acquittal, or grand juries failed to indict, or prosecutors refused to file criminal charges, agents of the Bureau have generally confiscated the entire collection of the potential defendant upon the ground that he intended to use it in that violation of the law. In several cases, the agents have refused to return the collection even after acquittal by jury.

The defendant, under existing law is not entitled to an award of attorney's fees, therefore, should he secure return of his collection, an individual who has already spent thousands of dollars establishing his innocence of the criminal charges is required to spend thousands more to civilly prove his innocence of the same acts, without hope of securing any redress. This, of course, has given the enforcing agency enormous bargaining power in refusing to return confiscated firearms. Evidence received by the Subcommittee on the Constitution demonstrated that Bureau agents have tended to concentrate upon collector's items rather than "criminal street guns". One witness appearing before the Subcommittee related the confiscation of a shotgun valued at $7,000. Even the Bureau's own valuations indicate that the value of firearms confiscated by their agents is over twice the value which the Bureau has claimed is typical of "street guns" used in crime. In recent months, the average value has increased rather than decreased, indicating that the reforms announced by the Bureau have not in fact redirected their agents away from collector's items and toward guns used in crime.

The Subcommittee on the Constitution has also obtained evidence of a variety of other misdirected conduct by agents and supervisors of the Bureau. In several cases, the Bureau has sought conviction for supposed technical violations based upon policies and interpretations of law which the Bureau had not published in the Federal Register, as required by 5 U.S.C. § 552. For instance, beginning in 1975, Bureau officials apparently reached a judgment that   a dealer who sells to a legitimate purchaser may nonetheless be subject to prosecution or license revocation if he knows that that individual intends to transfer the firearm to a nonresident or other unqualified purchaser. This position was never published in the Federal Register and is indeed contrary to indications which Bureau officials had given Congress, that such sales were not in violation of existing law. Moreover, BATF had informed dealers that an adult purchaser could legally buy for a minor, barred by his age from purchasing a gun on his own. BATF made no effort to suggest that this was applicable only where the barrier was one of age. Rather than informing the dealers of this distinction, Bureau agents set out to produce mass arrests upon these "straw man" sale charges, sending out undercover agents to entice dealers into transfers of this type. The first major use of these charges, in South Carolina in 1975, led to 37 dealers being driven from business, many convicted on felony charges. When one of the judges informed Bureau officials that he felt dealers had not been fairly treated and given information of the policies they were expected to follow, and refused to permit further prosecutions until they were informed, Bureau officials were careful to inform only the dealers in that one state and even then complained in internal memoranda that this was interfering with the creation of the cases. When BATF was later requested to place a warning to dealers on the front of the Form 4473, which each dealer executes when a sale is made, it instead chose to place the warning in fine print upon the back of the form, thus further concealing it from the dealer's sight.

The Constitution Subcommittee also received evidence that the Bureau has formulated a requirement, of which dealers were not informed that requires a dealer to keep official records of sales even from his private collection. BATF has gone farther than merely failing to publish this requirement. At one point, even as it was prosecuting a dealer on this charge (admitting that he had no criminal intent), the Director of the Bureau wrote Senator S. I. Hayakawa to indicate that there was no such legal requirement and it was completely lawful for a dealer to sell from his collection without recording it. Since that date, the Director of the Bureau has stated that that is not the Bureau's position and that such sales are completely illegal; after making that statement, however, he was quoted in an interview for a magazine read primarily by licensed firearms dealers as stating that such sales were in fact legal and permitted by the Bureau. In these and similar areas, the Bureau has violated not only the dictates of common sense, but of 5 U.S.C. Sec 552, which was intended to prevent "secret lawmaking" by administrative bodies.

These practices, amply documented in hearings before this Subcommittee, leave little doubt that the Bureau has disregarded rights guaranteed by the constitution and laws of the United States.

It has trampled upon the second amendment by chilling exercise of the right to keep and bear arms by law-abiding citizens.

It has offended the fourth amendment by unreasonably searching and seizing private property.

It has ignored the Fifth Amendment by taking private property without just compensation and by entrapping honest citizens without regard for their right to due process of law.

The rebuttal presented to the Subcommittee by the Bureau was utterly unconvincing. Richard Davis, speaking on behalf of the Treasury Department, asserted vaguely that the Bureau's priorities were aimed at prosecuting willful violators, particularly felons illegally in possession, and at confiscating only guns actually likely to be used in crime. He also asserted that the Bureau has recently made great strides toward achieving these priorities. No documentation was offered for either of these assertions. In hearings before BATF's Appropriations Subcommittee, however, expert evidence was submitted establishing that approximately 75 percent of BATF gun prosecutions were aimed at ordinary citizens who had neither criminal intent nor knowledge, but were enticed by agents into unknowing technical violations. (In one case, in fact, the individual was being prosecuted for an act which the Bureau's acting director had stated was perfectly lawful.) In those hearings, moreover, BATF conceded that in fact (1) only 9.8 percent of their firearm arrests were brought on felons in illicit possession charges; (2) the average value of guns seized was $116, whereas BATF had claimed that "crime guns" were priced at less than half that figure; (3) in the months following the announcement of their new "priorities", the percentage of gun prosecutions aimed at felons had in fact fallen by a third, and the value of confiscated guns had risen. All this indicates that the Bureau's vague claims, both of focus upon gun-using criminals and of recent reforms, are empty words.

In light of this evidence, reform of federal firearm laws is necessary to protect the most vital rights of American citizens. Such legislation is embodied in S. 1030. That legislation would require proof of a willful violation as an element of a federal gun prosecution, forcing enforcing agencies to ignore the easier technical cases and aim solely at the intentional breaches. It would restrict confiscation of firearms to those actually used in an offense, and require their return should the owner be acquitted of the charges. By providing for award of attorney's fees in confiscation cases, or in other cases if the judge finds charges were brought without just basis or from improper motives, this proposal would be largely self-enforcing. S. 1030 would enhance vital protection of constitutional and civil liberties of those Americans who choose to exercise their Second Amendment right to keep and bear arms.

OTHER VIEWS OF THE SECOND AMENDMENT

DOES THE SECOND AMENDMENT MEAN WHAT IT SAYS?

by DAVID J. STEINBERG
Executive Director
National Council for a Responsible Firearms Policy

"A well-regulated militia being necessary to the security of a free state, the right of the people to keep and bear arms shall not be infringed."

— Second Amendment, the U.S. Constitution

The "right of the people to keep and bear arms" is part of the Bill of Rights. It stands alongside the First Amendment's rights of freedom of speech, press, religion, and assembly. Opponents of strict or any regulation of private possession of firearms regard the Second Amendment as no less important than the First, indeed as a defense against a tyrannical government that would deprive the people of the basic rights for which a revolution was fought and an independent nation founded. Regardless of the degree of gun control any of us may prefer, it is essential that the meaning and intent of the Second Amendment be clearly understood, and its mandate carried out.

100 Years of Court Decisions

Although a lively debate has raged over the purpose of the Second Amendment, the nation's courts—federal and state alike—have been in basic agreement on this subject for as long as judicial judgments have been made on contentions that the Second Amendment establishes a personal right to have firearms, free from government regulation. Such decisions go back more than 100 years. The Supreme Court's first decision in this field was in 1875 in *United States v. Cruikshank.* Here the Court found that

the right to keep and bear arms was not a right granted by the Constitution, was not dependent on the Constitution for its existence, was protected only against infringement by the federal government, and in any case its application to personal rights was only in the context of the freedom of the states to have their own militias. That is, the right of the individual to have firearms was given constitutional protection only to the extent that the right of the particular individual to have a gun was essential to the ability of the state to have an effective militia.

The significance of this relationship of the individual to the organized militia is better understood when one recalls the nature of the armed forces (pg.25) (i.e., the land forces) in the early years of the nation's history.

Bone and Muscle of the Infantry

There was no national standing army at the time the Second Amend ment became law (1791) and there would be none of any consequence for over 100 years. The state militias were the bone and muscle of the nation's infantry both during and after the Revolution. Fear of a national standing army with any real strength permeated attention to the military powers of the national government and the various state governments. The basic Constitution, in Article I, Section 8, empowered Congress to provide for "calling forth the militia to execute the laws of the union, suppress insurrections, and repel invasions," and for "organizing, arming, and disciplining the militia." The state militias were by no means regarded as the sole instrument of national defense. They were, however, regarded, not only as a vital national resource, but as the sole defense of the states against national encroachment.

At that time, and for about another hundred years, the firearms used in the state militias were mostly those brought into such service by the citizen soldiers themselves. If these men didn't have guns, the militias could hardly be effective. Thus, the "right of the people to keep and bear arms" was essential to the viability of the "well-regulated militia," which in turn was "necessary to the security of a free state."

Those who interpret the Second Amendment as providing only for a state's right to have a militia see only half the picture, omitting the Amendment's implication that private possession of guns is basic to the existence of such militias (at the time the Amendment was adopted and for many years thereafter). Those who interpret the Second Amendment as providing or protecting the individual's personal right to have firearms see only the other half of the picture, omitting the component that the individual's right to have a gun must be shown to be essential to the formation of an effective militia.

If, as now and indeed ever since Congress in 1903 established state militias known as the National Guard, the arms used by the state militias are entirely provided by the government, the right of the people to keep and bear arms appears to lose whatever meaning it once had as an individual right protected by the Constitution. The 1903 act also provided for a reserve militia consisting of all able-bodied men between 18 and 45 who were not members' of the organized militia. But no firearms were issued to them in this reserve status. Nor are reservists expected or required to have and bring their own.

Title 10, Section 311

Many opponents of gun control make much, in fact too much, of Title 10, Section 311 of the United States (pg.26) Code in their attempt to prove that the militia is not limited to the National Guard—namely, that there is an "unorganized militia" and that under the Second Amendment every member of it has a constitutional right to have firearms. Title 10, Section 311, states that "the militia of the United States consists of all able-bodied males at least 17 years of age and ... under 45 years of age who are, or who have made a declaration of intention to become, citizens of the United States."

Those who cite that regulation in the debate on gun control interpret it to mean that every such person, in fact every adult citizen, has a Second Amendment right to a gun to protect himself or herself against violent harm to themselves, their families and their communities. The police, they contend, are not always available. When widespread violence occurs, the National Guard and other military forces may be preoccupied elsewhere. In this light, the National Rifle Association sees the armed citizen as "a potential community stabilizer" whether as a civilian member of an organized posse or simply as a member of the "unorganized militia." In some renditions of the right to keep and bear arms, the armed citizen is seen as "a vital last line of defense against crime, federal tyranny, and foreign invasion"—the people's "ultimate check against abuses by their government," including abuse of power by a militia.

"Well Regulated" Militia

Whatever the merits of such notions about personal and national security (they are, to say the least, highly questionable in this day and age), it is important to note that the only kind of militia the Second Amendment expressly regards as consistent with security is a "well-regulated" militia. One may rationally and reasonably conclude that this applies both to an organized militia and an unorganized one. Otherwise, an armed citizenry consisting of men and women using guns for presumed high purpose according to their respective dictates of personal whim and political fancy is the stuff from which anarchy could result, and in turn the tyranny against which the private possession of guns is supposed to protect Americans.

The right to keep and bear arms (a term that connotes a military purpose) stems from the English common law right of self-defense. However, the possession of guns in the mother country of the common law was never an absolute right. Various conditions were imposed. Britain today has one of the strictest gun laws in the world.

There is nothing absolute about the freedoms in our own Bill of Rights. Freedom of speech is not freedom to shout "fire" in a crowded theater. Freedom of religion is not freedom to have multiple spouses, or sacrifice a lamb in the local park, as religiously sanctioned practices. Similarly, whatever right the Second Amendment protects regarding the private possession of guns, for whatever definition of "militia," is not an absolute right. It must serve the overall public interest, including (from the preamble of the US Constitution) the need to "insure domestic tranquility, provide for the common defense and promote the general welfare." Whatever right there is to possess firearms is no less important than the right of every American, gun owners included, to protection against the possession of guns by persons who by any reasonable standard lack the crucial credentials for responsible gun ownership.

[Originally published as Report of the Subcommittee on the Constitution of the Committee on the Judiciary, United States Senate, 97th Cong., 2d Sess., The Right to Keep and Bear Arms, 27-44 (1982) ("Other Views"). Reproduced in the 1982 Senate Report, pg. 27-44.]

JUNE 26, 1981

NATIONAL COALITION TO BAN HANDGUNS

STATEMENT

ON THE

SECOND AMENDMENT

By: Michael K. Beard,
Executive Director

and

Samuel S. Fields,
Legal Affairs
Coordinator

John Levin. "The Right to Bear Arms:
The Development of the American Ex-
perience." Chicago - Kent Law Review,
Fall-Winter 1971.

1975 American Bar Association Gun
Control Policy

Standing Armies and Armed Citizens:
An Historical Analysis of the Second
Amendment

Gun Control Legislation
By The Committee on Federal Legislation

There is probably less agreement, more misinformation, and less understanding of the right to keep and bear arms than any other current controversial constitutional issue. The crux of the controversy is the construction of the Second Amendment to the Constitution, which reads: "A well-regulated militia, being necessary to the security of a free State, the right to keep and bear arms shall not be infringed." In addition to the five decisions in which the Supreme Court has construed the Amendment, every Federal court decision involving the Amendment has given the Amendment a collective, militia interpretation and/or held that firearms control laws enacted under a state's police power are constitutional. Thus arguments premised upon the Federal Second Amendment, or the similar provisions in the thirty-seven state constitutions, have never prevented regulation of firearms.

--American Bar Association
Background Report on
Firearms Control

The Union agrees with the Supreme Court's long-standing interpretation of the Second Amendment that the individual's right to keep and bear arms applies only to the preservation or efficiency of a "well-regulated militia." Except for lawful police and military purposes, the possession of weapons by individuals is not constitutionally protected.

--American Civil Liberties Union
Policy #43

The Second Amendment to the United States Constitution says: "A well regulated militia being necessary to the security of a free state, the right of the people to keep and bear arms, shall not be infringed." While NRA takes the firm stand that law-abiding Americans are constitutionally entitled to the legal ownership and use of firearms, the Second Amendment has not prevented firearms regulation on national and state levels. Also, the few federal court decisions involving the Second Amendment have largely given the Amendment a collective, militia interpretation and have limited the application of the Amendment to the Federal Government.

--National Rifle Association
"NRA Fact Book on Firearms Control"

YOU DO NOT HAVE A CONSTITUTIONAL RIGHT TO OWN A HANDGUN.

The Second Amendment to the U.S. Constitution states: "A well-regulated militia, being necessary to the security of a free State, the right of the people to keep and bear arms, shall not be infringed." Some people claim that this amendment prohibits the federal government from interfering with their private "right to bear arms." However, in every instance where the Supreme Court has ruled on the Second Amendment or discussed it in a footnote or dicta their position has been uniformly in favor of interpreting the Second Amendment as a collective right of the several states and not as an individual right.

While the American "right to bear arms" developed at the time of the revolution, it grew out of the duty imposed on the early colonists to keep arms for the defense of their isolated and endangered communities. This duty was limited, however, by the colonial governments in order to prevent the use of firearms for harmful purposes. To prevent civil disturbances the colonial governments were careful to keep arms from falling into the "wrong hands" and passed regulations concerning the conditions under which arms could be used.

Following the revolution the founders of the nation lacked confidence in the newly formed federation. Having just waged a revolution against an oppressive colonial ruler, they felt the need to protect their collective right to rise up and defend themselves against the new federal government. The founding fathers wanted to be sure that a people's militia could continue to exist in case the states needed to protect themselves from abuses by the new federal government.

Records of the debates over the passage of the Second Amendment clearly show that the intent of Congress was to prevent the federal government from destroying the state militias. The "right to bear arms" was a corporate right used to insure that a balance between liberty and authority within the union would be maintained. Personal self-protection was not the issue. While some attempts were made to include a personal right to have arms in the Bill of Rights, these provisions were never adopted.

Many court decisions and virtually every leading legal scholar and constitutional expert in the country agree that the intent, wording and meaning of the Second Amendment in its full context, refer only to the people's collective right to bear arms as members of a well-regulated and authorized militia. Moreover, no serious student of law believes that the amendment prevents the reasonable regulation of firearms. This is evidenced by the many unchallenged laws on the books which require licenses and permits or prohibit the carrying of concealed weapons.

While the Second Amendment does not guarantee an individual a right to bear arms, the rights and responsibilities of self-protection are implicit in much of the constitution and in the vast body of law that rules our political and social life. Members of the pro-handgun lobby sometimes cite common law to support their arguments against handgun control. According to these arguments the individual has a Common Law right to keep and bear arms for self-defense and to defend one's country. It should be noted, however, that England, the country which is the source of all U.S. Common Law, has enacted some of the most stringent handgun control laws in the world and thus does not feel that they are in violation of Common Law rights.

Attached to this submission are four scholarly articles on the origins and meaning of the Second Amendment. An analysis by the U.S. Federal Courts follows immediately.

What the Courts Say

The "right to bear arms" question has been brought into the courts many times since the Constitution was written. The courts have consistently ruled that the Second Amendment does not guarantee a personal right to own firearms.

Supreme Court decisions on the "right to bear arms" have repeatedly stated that the Second Amendment was conceived of as a restraint on the power of the federal government over the state militias. In U.S. v. Cruikshank, 95 U.S. 542 (1874), the Court held that while there may be an individual right to possess arms, it existed independently of the Second Amendment.

Subsequent decisions elaborated on the scope of the Second Amendment's guarantee. In Presser v. Illinois, 116 U.S. 252 (1886), the Court upheld an Illinois statute forbidding bodies of men to associate in military organizations or to drill or parade with arms in cities or towns. The court also ruled (pg. 33) that the states had the power to regulated firearms as was necessary for the common good.

The third and least important of the Second Amendment cases was <u>Miller v. Texas</u>, 153 U.S. 535 (1894), in which a convicted murderer asserted that the state had violated his Second and Fourth Amendment rights. The Supreme Court unanimously dismissed the claim saying that the Second Amendment did not apply to the states citing, <u>Cruikshank</u> and other cases.

The most frequently discussed case on the issue of the Second Amendment is <u>U.S. v. Miller</u> 307 U.S. 174, 59 S. Ct. 816, 83 L.Ed. 1206 (1939). At issue is the so-called "ordinary military equipment" question. Proponents of the Second Amendment as an individual right insist that the <u>Miller</u> Court was attempting to dichotomize "militia" and "non-militia" weapons, the latter being subject to legislative control while the former is not. The argument then goes on to state that the court was unaware that Miller's weapon, a sawed-off shotgun, had in fact been used in World War I. Therefore, the argument continues, if the Court had only been made aware of this historical fact it would have overturned Miller's conviction and ruled the 1934 National Firearm Act unconstitutional.

The problem with this argument is twofold. First, the Court was not creating the "militia" versus "non-militia" dichotomy for the purposes of identifying individual right versus collective right weapons. Second, and probably more important, the Court was probably <u>not</u> attempting to formulate a rule at all. See: <u>Cases v. U.S.</u> 131 F.2d 916 (1 CCA, 1942) cert. denied 319 U.S. 770, 63 S. Ct. 1431, 87 L.Ed. 1718 (1942). [**Note:** in the certiorari denial the defendant is referred to as <u>Velazquez v. U.S.</u> His full name was Jose Cases Velazquez, hence, this has been a source of some confusion.]

In rejecting the military character of the shotgun the <u>Miller</u> court wrote:

> In the absence of any evidence tending show that possession or use of a "shotgun having a barrel of less than eighteen inches in length" at this time has some reasonable relationship to the preservation or efficiency of a <u>well regulated militia</u>, we cannot say that the Second Amendment guarantees for the right to keep and bear such an instrument [emphasis added].

What we have then is two tiered test: first for the weapon and second for the weapon holder. Even assuming that clear convincing proof had shown that sawed-off shotguns were not merely part of the military arsenal but in fact were standard issue as common as K-rations and helmets and furthermore it was a court martial offense to be found without it, it still would not have done Mr. Miller a whit of good. Mr. Miller fails miserably in the weapon holder test. He was not acting in the role of the member of "militia," much less a "regulated militia," and least of all the "well regulated militia," described by the Court and the Second Amendment.

The most that can be said for whose right emerged in <u>Miller</u> is that of the state militia's and their own arsenals. But even here common sense tells us there are clear parameters on state militia arsenals. If not, it would logically follow that the several states could, at will, establish independent nuclear strike forces. If nothing else, such a development would certainly enliven the annual Governor's conference.

But, of course, shortly after the <u>Miller</u> court ruled, the idea of a "militia/non-militia" test was put to a well needed rest. In <u>Cases</u> [a.k.a. <u>Velazquez</u>] the Court of Appeals not only rejected the idea that individuals were part of the militia/non-militia weapons dichotomy but insisted that no such dichotomy was intended:

we do not feel that the Supreme Court in this case was attempting to formulate a general rule applicable to all cases. The rule which it laid down was adequate to dispose of the case before it and that we think was as far as the Supreme Court intended to go.

Since Miller the Supreme Court has on at least two occasions spoken on the subject of the Second Amendment. In E. Adams v. Williams 407 U.S. 143, 92 S. Ct. 1921, 322 Ed. 612 (1972) Justice Douglas discussing search and seizure problems wrote:

> A powerful lobby dins into the ears of our citizenry that these gun purchases are constitutional rights protected by the Second Amendment, which reads, "A well regulated Militia, being necessary to the security of a free State, the right of the people to keep and bear Arms, shall not be infringed."
>
> There is under our decisions no reason why stiff state laws governing the purchase and possession of pistols may not be enacted. There is no reason why pistols may not be barred from anyone with a police record. There is no reason why a state may not require a purchaser of a pistol to pass a psychiatric test. There is no reason why all pistols   should not be barred to everyone except the police.
>
> The leading case is United States v. Miller, 307 U.S. 174, 59 S.Ct . 816, 83 L.Ed. 1206, upholding a federal law making criminal the shipment in interstate commerce of a sawed-off shotgun. The law was upheld, there being no evidence that a sawed-off shotgun had "some reasonable relationship to the preservation or efficiency of a well regulated militia." Id., at 178, 59 S.Ct. at 818. The Second Amendment, it was held, "must be interpreted and applied" with the view of maintaining a "militia."
>
> "The Militia which the States were expected to maintain and train is set in contrast with Troops which they were forbidden to keep without the consent of Congress. The sentiment of the time strongly disfavored standing armies: the common view was that adequate defense of country and laws could be secured through the Militia—civilians primarily, soldiers on occasion." Id., at 178-179, 59 S.Ct., at 818.
>
> Critics say that proposals like this water down the Second Amendment. Our decisions belie that argument, for the Second Amendment, as noted, was designed to keep alive the militia.

Douglas and Marshall's opinion on the Second Amendment is unequivocally clear: the Amendment is a collective right of the state.

Most recently in Lewis v. United States 445 U.S. 95, 100 S. Ct. 915 __ L.Ed. ____ (1980) Justice Blackmun, writing for the majority, upheld the 1968 Gun Control Act and noted in a critical footnote:

> 8. These legislative restrictions on the use of firearms are neither based upon constitutionally suspect criteria, nor do they trench upon any constitutionally protected liberties. See United States v. Miller, 307 U.S. 174, 178, 59 S. Ct. 816, 818, 83 L.Ed. 1206 (1939) (the Second Amendment guarantees no right to keep and bear a firearm that does   not have some reasonable relationship to the preservation or

efficiency of a well regulated militia"); <u>United States v. Three Winchester 30-30 Caliber Lever Action Carbines</u>, 504 F.2d 1288, 1290, n. 5 (CA7 1975); <u>United States v. Johnson</u>, 497 F.2d 548 (CA4 1974); <u>Cody v. United States</u>, 460 F.2d 34 (CA8), cert. denied, 490 U.S. 1010, 93 S.Ct. 454, 34 L.Ed.2d 303 (1972) (the latter three cases holding, respectively, that Sec. 1202(a)(1), Sec. 922(g), and Sec. 922(a)(6) do not violate the Second Amendment).

The <u>Miller</u> standard has once again been vindicated to be a collective right of "a well regulated militia."

The Court of Appeals on Various Aspects of the Second Amendment

U.S. v. Wilbur 545 F.2d 7641 (1st 1976)
In prosecution for violation of the Gun Control Act of 1968, trial court action in curtailing defense counsel's argument on Second Amendment was proper as preventing confusion lest jury believe that United States Constitution provided defendants with legal defense.

Eckert v. City of Philadelphia 477 F.2d 610 (3rd 1973)
Appellant's theory in the district court which he now repeats is that by the Second Amendment to the United States Constitution he is entitled to bear arms. Appellant is completely wrong about that.

U.S. v. King 532 F.2d 505 (3rd 1976)
We firmly disagree with the argument that the statute violates appellant's right to keep and bear arms. He was   neither charged with nor convicted of keeping and bearing arms. He was charged with and convicted of engaging without a license in the business of dealing in firearms and of conspiring with others so to do.

U.S. v. Graves 554 F.2d 65 (3rd 1977)
The courts consistently have found no conflict between federal gun laws and the Second Amendment, narrowly construing the latter to guarantee the right to bear arms as a member of a militia. Graves has not attempted to invoke the Second Amendment as a defense in the present prosecution. Even if he had, we would deem controlling the interpretation adopted in <u>Miller</u> and the cases following it.

U.S. v. Johnson 497 F.2d 548 (4th 1974)
The statute prohibiting the transportation of a firearm in interstate commerce after having been convicted of a felony is not unconstitutional as violative of defendant's Second Amendment right to keep and bear arms since the Second Amendment only confers a collective right of keeping and bearing arms which must bear a reasonable relationship to the presentation or efficiency of a well-regulated militia.

U.S. v. Snider 502 F.2d 645 (4th 1974)
Dissent (not in conflict with the majority view on this issue):

Although thousand of perfectly well intentioned persons doubtless believe with all sincerity that the Second Amendment protection of the right to bear arms is violated by the Gun Law e.g. 18 U.S.C. Appendix (201 et seq.), such a contention would be frivolous.

U.S. v. Johnson 441 F.2d 1134 (5th 1971)
Appellant's remaining contention, that his constitutional right to bear arms has been infringed by the Act, misconstrues the Second Amendment. The Supreme Court dealt with such a constitutional attack directed against the National Firearms Act of 1934 in U.S. v. Miller.

U.S. v. Williams 446 F.2d 4b (5th 1971)
Statutes proscribing offense of and penalty for possession of an unregistered firearm are not violative of the right to bear arms as guaranteed by Second Amendment.

McKnight v. U.S. 507 F.2d 1034 (5th 1975)
Appeals Court upholds lower court's rejection of defendant's motion for relief on the basis that the firearms charge under which he was convicted violated his Second Amendment rights.(pg.40)

U.S. v. Forgett 349 F.2d 601 (6th 1965)
Upholds Miller ruling regarding the National Firearms Act as not violating the Second Amendment.

Stevens v. U.S. 440 F.2d 144 (6th 1971)
Constitutional right to keep and bear arms applies only to the right of the state to maintain militia and not to individuals' rights to bear arms. Congress had authority under commerce clause to prohibit possession of firearms by convicted felons, based upon congressional finding that such possession passes threat to interstate commerce.

U.S. v. Day 476 F.2d 562 (6th 1973)
As to the alleged right to bear arms, Day's claim is meritless. There is no absolute constitutional right of an individual to possess a firearm.

U.S. v. Birmley 529 F.2d 103 (6th 1976)
Statute under which defendants were convicted of possession of unregistered firearms did not violate defendants' right to bear arms.

U.S. v. Warin 530 F.2d 103 (6th 1976)
It is clear that the Second Amendment guarantees a collective rather than an individual right. The fact that the defendant Warin, in common with all adult residents and citizens of Ohio, is subject to enrollment in the militia of the state confers on him no right to possess the submachine gun in question.

U.S. v. Pruner 606 F.2d 871 (6th 1979)
Upholds Justice Douglas' concurring and dissenting discussion on the proposition that the purchase of guns is a constitutional right protected by the Second Amendment in Adams v. Williams.

Witherspoon v. U.S. 633 F.2d 1247 (6th 1980)

Appellant contended that the Second Amendment afforded him protection from the federal firearms statutes because he was on his own business premises. There is, of course, no such specific proviso in the Second Amendment nor is there any Supreme Court interpretation to that effect.

U.S. v. Lauchli 444 F.2d 1037 (7th 1971)

We reject defendant's argument that the Gun Control Act of 1968 is violative of the Second Amendment guarantee of the right to bear arms.

U.S. v. McCutcheon 446 F.2d 133 (7th 1971)

Statute requiring one who makes firearm to file with Secretary of Treasury or his delegate written application to make and register firearm and pay any applicable tax thereon and   statute requiring registration of such firearm by maker thereof did not infringe Second Amendment right to keep and bear arms.

U.S. v. Three Winchester 30-30 Caliber Lever Action Carbines 504 F.2d 1288 (7th 1974)

Statute prohibiting possession of firearms by previously convicted felon does not infringe on Second Amendment's protection of right to bear arms.

U.S. v. Synnes 438 F.2d 764 (8th 1971)

While the Court in Miller dealt with the prohibited possession of a sawed-off shotgun, the reasoning and conclusion of that case has carried forward to other federal gun legislation. We think it is also applicable here. Although Sec. 1202(a) is the broadest federal gun legislation to date, we see no conflict between it and the Second Amendment since there is no showing that prohibiting possession of firearms by felons the maintenance of a "well regulated militia."

U.S. v. Decker 446 F.2d 164 (8th 1971)

The record-keeping requirements at issue here bear an even more tenuous relationship to the Second Amendment than did the statute involved in Miller. Thus, in light of the defendants failure to present any evidence indicating a conflict between the requirements of Secs. 922(m) and 923(g) and the maintenance of a well-regulated militia. We decline to hold that the statute violates the Second Amendment.

Cody v. U.S. 460 F.2d 34 (8th 1972)

Second Amendment right to bear arms is not an absolute bar to Congressional regulation of the use or possession of firearms and its guarantee extends only to use or possession which has some reasonable relationship to the presentation or efficiency of a well-regulated militia.

U.S. v. Turcotte 558 F.2d 893 (8th 1977)

We find no reason to reconsider the decision in Cody that the prohibition of section 922 does not obstruct the maintenance of a well-regulated militia, and therefore is not violative of the Second Amendment.

U.S. v. Wynde 579 F.2d 1088 (8th 1978)

Upholds U.S. v. Turcotte, which declared that Sec. 922(h) does not violate the Second Amendment right to bear arms.

<u>U.S.</u> <u>v.</u> <u>Tomlin</u> <u>454</u> <u>F.2d</u> <u>17b</u> <u>(9th</u> <u>1972)</u>
       Statutes requiring registration of firearms and making it unlawful for any person to receive or possess unregistered firearms are not unconstitutional as infringing on right to bear arms under Second Amendment.

<u>U.S.</u> <u>v.</u> <u>Oakes</u> <u>564</u> <u>F.2d</u> <u>384</u> <u>(10th</u> <u>1977)</u>
       Purpose of the Second Amendment guaranteeing the right of the people to keep and bear arms, was to preserve the (pg.44) effectiveness and assure the continuation of the state militia. To apply the Second Amendment so as to guarantee defendant's right to keep an unregistered firearm which was not shown to have any connection to the militia, merely because defendant was technically a member of the Kansas militia, would be unjustified in terms of either logic or policy; and his membership in "Posse Comitatus," an apparently non-governmental organization.

[Originally published as Report of the Subcommittee on the Constitution of the Committee on the Judiciary, United States Senate, 97th Cong., 2d Sess., The Right to Keep and Bear Arms, 45-67 (1982) ("Other Views"). Reproduced in the 1982 Senate Report, pg. 45-67.]

HISTORICAL BASES OF THE RIGHT TO KEEP AND BEAR ARMS

by David T. Hardy,* Partner in the Law Firm Sando & Hardy

In analyzing the right to keep and bear arms, we must constantly keep in mind that it is one of the few rights in the Constitution which can claim any considerable antiquity. Freedom of the press, for instance, had little ancestry at common law: statutes requiring a government license to publish any works on political or religious matters were in effect in England until 1695, when they were allowed to expire for economic, not libertarian, reasons.[1] Long after that date, prosecutions after-the-fact for seditious libel were common. In the Colonies, these and similar statutes were likewise enforced and offending religious material was burned in Massachusetts as late as 1723.[2] Protests against general search warrants did not become common until after 1760, and the invalidity of such warrants at common law was not recognized until the eve of the American Revolution.[3]

In contrast to these rights, the right to keep and bear arms can claim an ancestry stretching for well over a millennium. The antiquity of the right is so great that it is all but impossible to document its actual beginning. It is fairly clear that its origin lay in the customs of Germanic tribes, under which arms bearing was a right and a duty of free men; in fact, the ceremony for giving freedom to a slave required that the former slave be presented with the armament of a free man.[4] He then acquired the duty to serve in an equivalent of a citizen army. These customs were brought into England by the earliest Saxons. The first mention of the citizen army, or the "fyrd" is found in documents dating to 690 A.D., but scholars have concluded that the duty to serve in such with personal armament "is older than our oldest records." (Not knowing of the earlier records, 18th century legal historians including the great Blackstone attributed the origin of the English system to Alfred the Great, who ruled in the late 9th century A.D.)[5]

This viewpoint of individual armament and duty differed greatly from the feudal system which were coming into existence in Europe. The feudal system presupposed that the vast bulk of fighting duties would fall to a small warrior caste, composed primarily of the mounted knight. These individuals held the primary political and military power. Thus peasant armament was a threat to the political status quo. In England, on the other hand, a system evolved whereby peasant armament became the great underpinning of the status quo and individual armament became viewed as a right rather than a threat.

This in turn significantly changed the evolution of political systems in Britain. Since so much military power lay with the private citizen, the traditional monarchy was necessarily much more a limited monarchy than an absolute one. Even after the Norman Conquest of 1066, which brought feudal systems into Britain, kings regularly appealed to the people for assistance. William Rufus, second Norman king of England, was driven to appeal to the citizenry to put down a rebellion of feudal barons. To obtain the assistance of the individual armed citizen, he promised the people of England to provide better laws then had ever been made, to rescind all new taxes instituted during his reign, and to annul the hated forest laws which imposed draconian punishments; inspired by his promises, the citizenry rose with their arms and defended his government against the rebels.[6] After his death, his brother, Henry I, often drilled the citizen units in person, seeking to appeal to the individual members. In short, kingship in Britain became a far more democratic affair than it would ever become on the Continent, due in major part to the individual armament of the British citizen.

The Angevin monarchs expanded this still farther. Henry II, who is considered the father of the common law, promulgated the Assize of Arms in 1181. This required all British citizens between 15 and 40 to purchase and keep arms. The type of arms required varied with wealth; the wealthiest had to provide themselves with full armor, sword, dagger, and war horse, while even the poorest citizens, "the whole community of freemen", must have leather armor, helmet and a lance.[7] Twice a year all citizens were to be inspected by the king's officials to insure that they possessed the necessary arms. Conversely, the English made it quite clear that the king was to be expected to depend exclusively upon his armed freemen. When rebellious barons forced John I to sign the Magna Carta in 1215, they inserted in its prohibitions a requirement that he "expel from the kingdom all foreign knights, crossbowmen, sergeants, and mercenaries, who have come with horses and weapons to the harm of the realm."

Henry III continued this tradition. In his 1253 Assize of Arms he expanded the age categories to include everyone between 15 and 60 years of age, and made a further modification which bordered on the revolutionary. Now, not only were freemen to be armed, but even villeins, who were little more than serfs and were bound to the land. Now all "citizens, burgesses, free tenants, villeins and others from 15 to 60 years of age" were legally required to be armed.[8] Even the poorest classes of these were required to have a halberd (a pole arm with an axe and spike head) and a knife, plus a bow if they owned lands worth over two pounds sterling.

The role of the armed citizen expanded under the rule of the four Edwards. During civil wars in Wales, Edward I discovered the utility of the Welsh longbow, an extremely potent bow (its pull was estimated to have been between 100-200 pounds, whereas today a 60-pound bow is considered extremely powerful) which could penetrate the heaviest armor. Unlike the crossbow (and to an even greater extent, the armor and horse of the mounted knight) the longbow could be made cheaply enough and maintained easily enough to become the universal armament of all citizens. While on the Continent so deadly a weapon was considered a threat to the rule of the armored knight, in Britain its use was encouraged by the monarch. At Crecy, Poitiers and Agincourt, the longbow in the hands of British commoners decimated the French armored   knights. By 1369 Edward III was ordering the sheriffs of London to require "everyone of said city stronge in body, at leisure time on holidays" to "use in their recreation bowes and arrows."[9] He hardly needed the encouragement; the archery ranges outside London were so constantly swamped with arrows that no grass would grow upon them. Edward IV continued this policy, commanding that "every Englishman or Irishman dwelling in England must have a bow of his own height", and commanding that each town build and maintain an archery range upon which every citizen must practice on feast days.[10] In 1470 he banned games of dice, horseshoes, and tennis in order to force citizens to use nothing but the bow for sport.[11] He imposed price controls on bows in order to ensure that bows would be inexpensive enough for even the poorest citizen to purchase them.[12]

While the common law sought to force all commoners to possess what was then the most deadly military weapon, it also imposed only the most minimal restraints upon use of that weapon. These focused purely upon criminal misuse of the weapon or its transportation into certain highly protected areas. In 1279, for instance, those coming before the royal courts were required to "come without all force and armor".[13] The Statute of Arms, whose date of enactment is uncertain, required that spectators at tournaments attend without armament and that those participating in the tournament carry swords without points.[14] The 1328 Statute of Northampton prohibited anyone, other than the king's servants or citizens attempting to keep the peace, from coming before the king's ministers "with force and arms", or acting "in affray of the peace", and from going or riding "armed by night or by day in fairs, markets, nor in the presence of the justices or other ministers nor in no part elsewhere...."[15] In light of the common law preference for individual armament, however, English courts construed this to mean that only carrying of arms in a threatening or terrifying manner was prohibited. In the words of William Hawkins in his "Pleas of the Crown", "no wearing of arms is within the meaning of the statute, unless it be accompanied with such circumstances as are apt to terrify the people; from which it seems to follow, that persons of quality are in no danger of offending against the statute by wearing common weapons...."[16] Thus the sole common law restraints upon use of armament in this period focused either upon carrying into specially protected areas or upon what today would be considered assault with a deadly weapon.

While firearms had been invented sometime before, only in the 16th century did they become truly portable with the invention of the wheellock. This breakthrough inspired a number of attempts in Europe and England to control weaponry. The Emperor Maximilian attempted to impose bans upon wheellock manufacture throughout his empire on the Continent; the French imposed strict controls both upon manufacture and sale of firearms and upon assembly of ammunition and making of powder.[17] The English briefly experimented with such but found them repugnant to their institutions. Henry VII had in 1503 banned the shooting of crossbows upon an extremely limited basis.[18] First, only shooting and not possession was outlawed, and that only without a license or "placarde" from the king. Secondly, an exception was made for those who shot in   defense of a residence ("but if he shote aw of a howse for the lawefull defen of the same") and for lords who owned land worth 200 marks per year. Third, as might be surmised from the ban upon shooting rather than upon ownership, the purpose was to force citizens to use the longbow, which was considered a much deadlier weapon.

His successor Henry VIII was a great devotee of the longbow and early in his reign attempted to push its use by still more vigorous means. In 1511 he enacted "an act concerning shooting in longe bowes" which banned games, required fathers to purchase bows for sons between the ages of 7 and 14 and to "lern theym and bryng theym up in shootyng". From age 14 until 40 each non-disabled citizen was obliged to practice longbow shooting and also to have bow and arrows "contynually in hys house." Anyone who failed to own and use a longbow was subject to a fine. The ban upon crossbows was renewed and the property requirement for such was raised to 300 marks.[19]

In 1514 Henry extended the ban upon crossbows to include "handgonnes" (which at that time meant any firearm carried by hand, as opposed to cannons, rather than what are today called "pistols"), and to extend the ban to possession as well as shooting.[20] Once again the intent was to force ownership and use of the longbow in place of the less efficient firearms of the time.

Unlike his continental equivalents, Henry was soon forced to give up his attempt at gun control. In 1523 the property qualification was lowered from 300 pounds sterling to only 100 pounds, and the penalty was reduced from imprisonment and fine to a fine only.[21] In 1541 the statute was again amended (adding in its preface a protest that despite the earlier law people "have used and yet doe daylie ryde and go in the King's highwayes and elsewhere, having with them crosbowes and little handguns") to permit ownership of the longer arms (over three-quarters of a yard or one yard in total length, depending upon type) by any citizen, and ownership of the shorter arms by citizens with over 100 pounds' worth of land.[22] It also prohibited shooting within a quarter of a mile of a town except upon a range "or for defense of his person or house", and provided that "it shal be laufull from henceforth to all gentlemen, yoemen and servingemen ... and to all the inhabitants of citties, boroughes and markett townes of this realme of Englande to shote with any handgune, demyhake or hagbutt at anye butt or bank of earth ... to have and kepe in everie of their houses any such handgune or handgunes ... with the intent to use and shote the same at a but or bank of earth ... this present act or anythinge therein conteyned to the contrarie notwithstandinge." Eventually Henry gave up the entire effort and simply rescinded his firearm laws by proclamation.[23] Weapons control—at least that which limited armament rather than required it—was recognized as repugnant to the English system. Indeed, the Tudor legal commentator Sir John Fortescue would comment (in his comparison between the happy state of peasants in England, with its limited monarchy, and the unhappy state of peasants in France, with absolute monarchy) that the French peasants were so poorly off that they not only starved but could not have any "Wepen" or the means to obtain it.[24] The consciousness of English as a weapons   owning and using people, in contrast to the French and other Continentals, was beginning to take form.

Under Elizabeth the English militia system developed still farther; indeed, it was during her reign that the phrase "militia" was first used to describe the concept of a universally armed people ready to stand in defense of their nation.[25] The militia were now mustered by county lieutenants and called to formal musters to display and practice with their weapons.[26] Elizabeth also sought the creation of "trained bands" or "train bands", which were small militia units given special training and provided with governmentally purchased arms.[27]

Her efforts largely decayed under her successor James I, who permitted repeal of some of the most important militia statutes. His successor, Charles I, paid the price. Increasing hostility from Parliament, which was now beginning to assert itself as a distinct legislative body, brought the kingdom to the brink of civil war. The king compromised, sending his best advisor to the scaffold, but when Parliament asked for control over the militia he exploded. "By God, not for an hour, you have asked that of me in this, which was never asked of a king,"[28] he replied. An unsuccessful attempt to arrest five members of Parliament on charges of treason led to the final breach. The five members were protected by the London militia, and the king was forced to flee the city and attempt to muster his own army.

As the civil war wore on, Parliament was at length driven to create the "New Model Army", a standing body of veteran troops who were predominantly Puritan.[29] These were rigorously disciplined under the leadership of Oliver Cromwell, who eventually rose to head the army, and with their aid Parliament ended as the victor in the civil war. But in July 1647 the New Model Army (alienated by a failure of pay and by the anti-Puritan measures of the Parliament) marched on London and took over the government. On December 6, 1648 troops, acting on Cromwell's orders, surrounded the Parliament building and drove off over 140 members. The remainder formed what became known as "the Rump Parliament". By 1653 even the Rump was an impediment to Cromwell and he used his troops to totally shut down parliamentary government; the army officers then selected a new Parliament composed largely of Puritan elders. A short time later Cromwell pressured its dissolution and in 1654 he replaced it with yet another Parliament, in whose election only those whose land was worth over 200 pounds sterling could vote. This Parliament in turn named Cromwell "Lord Protector" and king of England in all but name. Yet a year later Cromwell dissolved even this Parliament and established a military dictatorship, dividing the nation into eleven districts, each headed by a major general whose duties included political surveillance, censorship of publications, and influencing future elections.[30] A major factor in the dissolution of several of these parliaments was their attempt to adopt new militia statutes; Cromwell, who controlled by the new model army, had little interest in permitting Parliament to reorganize the militia.

Following Cromwell's death, the English were more than happy to accept back the son of the late Charles, Charles II, as monarch. Charles II promptly dissolved the army, offering full pay plus a   bonus from his own finances, and guaranteeing work on public works projects for the demobilized troops.[31] He also sought to secure himself by a variety of legislation which people in Parliament, in their haste to welcome the end of Puritan rule, did not recognize as dictatorial. In 1661 and 1662 he expanded the definition of treason, imposed press censorship, restricted practice of religion by Puritans and others and leveled the protective walls of many towns which had sided with Parliament.[32] Instructions were also issued to the lord's lieutenant to form special militia units out of volunteers of favorable political views, "the officers to be numerous, disaffected persons watched and not allowed to assemble, and their arms seized...."[33] The excessive searches for arms under that order led to Parliamentary resistance and refusal to grant a militia bill in the sessions of 1660 and 1661.[34] Only in 1662 was Charles able to obtain a militia statute pleasing to him. The 1662 statute permitted the King to appoint Lieutenants for each county and major city; these lieutenants could charge persons with the responsibility of equipping and paying a militia man. But not every Englishman was required to be armed or serve, and those who were required could always hire a substitute to appear for them. The lieutenants were moreover empowered to hire persons "to search for and seize all arms in the custody or possession of any person or persons whom the said lieutenant or any two or more of their deputies shall judge dangerous to the peace of the kingdom...."[35] The Calendar of State Papers for the period is filled with reports of confiscations of weapons from suspicious persons and religious independents.[36] Charles also by proclamation ordered gunsmiths to produce records of all firearms sold; importation of firearms from overseas was banned; and carriers throughout the realm were forbidden to transport firearms without first obtaining a license. (The resemblance between these measures and the American 1968 Gun Control Act is astonishing).

In 1671 this was followed with an amendment to the Hunting Act. Hunting was restricted to those who owned lands worth 100 pounds and, most importantly, those who could not hunt (who formed the vast bulk of the kingdom) were "declared to be persons by the laws of this realm, not allowed to have or keep for themselves, or any other person or persons, any guns, bows, greyhounds...."[37] "Guns" were an addition to the list: all but the wealthiest land-owners could be disarmed. As Charles' reign wore on he encountered increasing opposition from Parliament and from what was becoming the Whig party. This he met by such drastic measures as moving the sitting of Parliament from London (which was quite favorable to the Whigs) to Oxford, and by arresting and executing several Whig leaders on charges of treason. Charles survived, but it was a close race.

James II, Charles' brother and successor, would not be so lucky. He continued to enforce the laws on disarmament, directing them with increasing force against Puritans and his political opponents. Moreover he used his "dispensing power" to permit Catholic officers to stay with the army. He sought to obtain permission to expand the standing army complaining that during rebellion the militia "is not sufficient for such occasions, and that there is nothing but a good force of well disciplined troops in constant pay that   can defend us...."[38] Parliament refused, but James kept a limited standing army on foot from his own resources. In 1686 he issued orders to six lord lieutenants complaining that "a great many persons not qualified by law, under pretense of shooting matches, keep muskets or other guns in their houses," and that he desired them to "cause strict search to be made for such muskets or guns and to seize and safely keep them until further order."[39] In Ireland he ordered General Tyrconnel to disarm the populace:

A royal order came from Whitehall for disarming the population. This order Tyrconnel strictly executed as he respected the English. Although the country was infested by predatory bands, a Protestant gentleman could scarcely obtain permission to keep a brace of pistols.[40]

These measures did James little good; in 1688 his son-in-law and daughter, William of Orange and Mary entered the nation in a supposed "invasion" which came to be known as the "the Glorious Revolution". After defection of a number of his nobility and refusal of the militia to fight, James fled to the Continent.

This left Parliament with an interesting question: was James king and, if not, how did they go about putting William and Mary on the throne? They approached this problem by promulgating a Declaration of Rights, which listed complaints against James and argued that these had forfeited him the right to rule. After William accepted this Declaration as definitive of the rights of Englishmen, he was permitted to assume the throne and call a Parliament, which then reenacted the Declaration as the Bill of Rights.[41]

The Declaration and Bill of Rights were later said to be "the essence of the revolution";[42] only a year before the adoption of the American Bill of Rights, the great English jurist Edmund Burke would refer to the Declaration as "the cornerstone of our Constitution."[43] The Declaration listed a variety of civil liberties which James was accused of infringing. Prominent among these was the right to keep and bear arms. The form finally adopted complained that James had violated the liberties of the kingdom by keeping a standing army and moreover by causing his Protestant subjects "to be disarmed at the same time when Papists were both armed and employed contrary to law." It accordingly resolved that "the subjects which are Protestant may have arms for their defense suitable to their conditions and as allowed by law."[44] Since only slightly over one percent of the population was then Catholic, this amounted to a general right to own arms applicable to virtually all Englishmen. The possible restriction—that they be arms "as allowed by law"—was clarified by prompt amendment of the Hunting Act to remove the word "guns" from items which even the poorest Englishman was not permitted to own. Now all Englishmen could own arms "for their defense suitable to their conditions and as allowed by law" in the form of whatever firearms they desired.[45]

A few modern writers, none of whom cite any historical evidence, have claimed that the Bill of Rights was directed not so much at disarmament as at the fact that Catholics were permitted to be armed while the Protestants had been disarmed.[46] The statutory history of the Declaration of Rights proves beyond any doubt that this is totally incorrect. The debates in the House of Commons, as recorded by Lord Somers, the principal draftsman of the Declaration, show that the Members focused on the confiscation of private arms collections under the 1662 Militia Act. Sergeant Maynard, for instance, complains of James: "Can he sell or give away his subjects; an act of Parliament was made to disarm all Englishmen, whom the lieutenant should suspect, by day or by night, by force or otherwise—this was done in Ireland for the sake of putting arms into Irish hands." Somers condensed a speech by Sir Richard Temple to "Militia bill—power to disarm all England—now done in Ireland." A Mr. Boscawen complained of "arbitrary power exercised by the ministry—militia—imprisoning without reason; disarming—himself disarmed...." Sergeant Maynard complained of the "Militia Act—an abominable thing to disarm the nation...."[47]

The Lords felt even more strongly about the issue. The Commons originally passed a declaration simply declaring that "the acts concerning the militia are grievous to the subject" and that "it is necessary for the public safety that the subjects which are Protestant should provide and keep arms for the common defense; and that the arms which have been seized and taken from them be restored."[48] The Lords apparently felt this did not state the individual rights strongly enough and completely omitted the language regarding the common defense, substituting the final version: "The subjects which are Protestant may have arms for their defense suitable to their conditions and as allowed by law."[49] The language referring to the fact that Catholics were armed while the disarmaments were proceeding was added only at conference, with the Lords suggesting that it was a "further aggravation" to the underlying illegality and therefore "fit to be mentioned."[50] Indeed, the modern British historian J. R. Western complains that the modifications by the House of Lords created too much of an individual right: "The original wording implied that everyone had a duty to be ready to appear in arms whenever the state was threatened. The revised wording suggested only that it was lawful to keep a blunderbuss to repel burglars."[51]

The "Glorious Revolution" also gave birth to the political philosophy which underlay the American Revolution less than a century later. The two major British parties, the Whigs and the Tories, had achieved both their essence and their names during the fight under Charles II to exclude his brother James II from the succession to the throne. One of the major points of the Whig philosophy was the need for a true militia, in the sense which England had had it during the Tudor years, and the scrapping of the standing army. All the major Whig authors stressed this point; Algernon Sidney counseled that "no state can be said to stand on a steady foundation, except those whose whole strength is in their own soldiery, and the body of their own people;"[52] Robert Molesworth advised that with standing armies "the people are contributors to their own misery; and their purses are drained in order to their misery,"[53] while attacking disarmament under the game laws with the argument that "I hope no wise man will put a hare or a partridge in balance with the safety and liberties of Englishmen".[54]   These and other Whig authors were to be found in the library of every American political thinker during the years before the Revolution;[55] John Adams himself would estimate that ninety percent of Americans were at that time Whigs by sentiment.[56]

Notwithstanding this growing support for a true militia, the use of the militia system in Britain steadily declined. By 1757 when a new Militia Act was adopted, only 32,000 men, a very small part of the population, were to serve.[57] The officers were to be chosen from the more wealthy of the gentry; property qualifications were imposed for all commissioned officers. The government would issue the arms to the militia, which were to be kept under lock and key, and could be seized by the lieutenant or deputy lieutenant of the county whenever he "shall adjudge it necessary to the peace of the kingdom".[58] "The Whigs considered this "select militia" as little better than a standing army: it was hardly a true "militia", an armed citizenry. In the debates over the Scottish militia act, the Lord Mayor of London argued to the Commons that the militia "could not longer be deemed a constitutional defense, under the immediate control and direction of the people; for by that bill they were rendered a standing army for all intents and purpose."[59] This background—that of a tradition of an armed citizenry met with recent infringements upon the traditional right of bearing arms—formed the background of the political views of the framers of our own Constitution.

The American experience with citizen armament had been more extensive even than that of Britain. The early colonists brought their own arms and secured additional ones from the government. As early as September 1622, they were being armed not only with muskets but with "three hundred short pistols with firelocks".[60] Virginia in 1623 ordered that no one was to "go or send abroad with a sufficient party well armed" and each plantation was to insure that there was "sufficient of powder and ammunition within the plantation".[61] In 1631 it ordered that no one work their fields unarmed and required militia musters on a weekly basis following church services: "All men that are fittinge to bear armes, shall bring their peeces to church ..."[62] By 1673 the colony provided that persons unable to purchase firearms from their own finances would be supplied guns by the government and required to pay a reasonable price when able to do so. Similar legislation was imposed in the other colonies. The first session of the legislature of the New Plymouth Colony required "that every free man or other inhabitant of this Colony provide for himself and each under him able to beare armes, a sufficient musket and other serviceable peece for war" with other equipment.[63] Similar measures were enacted in Connecticut in 1650.

When the colonies began drifting toward revolution following the elections of 1760, the colonists were thus well equipped for their role. The British government began extensive troop movements into Boston in 1768 to reduce opposition, and the town government responded by urging its citizens to arm themselves and be prepared to defend themselves against the deprivations of the soldiers. When Tories responded that this order was illegal, the colonial newspapers responded that the right of personal armament was guaranteed to every Englishman. The Boston Evening Post asserted that (pg.54) "It is certainly beyond human art and sophistry, to prove that the British subjects, to whom the privilege of possessing arms is expressly recognized by the Bill of Rights, and to live in a province where the law requires them to be equipped with arms, are guilty of an illegal act, in calling upon one another to be provided with them, as the law directs."[64] The New York Journal Supplement argued that the proposal "was a measure as prudent as it was legal" and that "it is a natural right which the people have reserved to themselves, confirmed by the Bill of Rights, to keep arms for their own defense...."[65] There can be little doubt from these passages that the American colonists viewed the English 1688 Declaration of Rights as recognizing an individual right to own private firearms for self defense—even defense against government agents.

Years passed before these proposals were actually put into effect, but the warning signs were present long before the revolution itself broke out, and some British heeded them. Pitt, the great Whig minister and friend of the Colonies, had warned that "three millions of Whigs, with arms in their hands, are a very formidable body."[66] Rather than the conciliation he called for, the result was an attempt to disarm the Americans—an attempt which brought on the Revolution. In December, 1774, for instance, export of guns and powder to the colonies was prohibited.[67] When a group of British regulars quietly emptied a militia powder magazine in September, 1774, the reaction was dramatic. To some "it seemed part of a well designed plan to disarm the people";[68] others were inflamed by incorrect rumors that six colonists had been killed during the raid. Over 60,000 armed citizens turned out, heading toward Boston, prepared for war.[69] This was more men under arms than would be boasted by the entire British military establishment at the time. Fortunately for that establishment, the colonists were convinced that their actions were premature and returned to their homes. By September, a Massachusetts town had instituted "the Minutemen", a group of select militia.[70] Others formed special companies of militia—one of which in Virginia included George Washington and George Mason, who would later draft the Virginia Declaration of Rights.[71] In December the Maryland Convention called upon the colonies to form a "well regulated militia" and illustrated what it meant by instructing all citizens between the ages of 16 and 50 to arm themselves and form into companies.[72] The following month the Fairfax Committee of Public Safety, chaired by George Washington, joined in this resolution, further defining its intent with the comment that "A well regulated militia, composed of gentlemen, freeholders, and other freemen, is the natural strength and only security of a free government", and recommending all persons between 16 and 50 to "provide themselves with good firelocks".[73] When Patrick Henry shortly thereafter gave his famed "give me liberty or give me death" speech, the resolution which he moved by his oration began "Resolved, that a well regulated militia, composed of gentlemen and freemen, is the natural strength and only security of a free government".[74]

The Colonials did not have long to wait. General Gage, military governor of Boston, was already writing to London with regard to   the "idea of disarming certain counties."[75] In April, 1775, Gage made the mistake of repeating his earlier raid upon a militia arsenal. This time there was firing and a number of colonists were killed. The regulars were compelled to fight their way back to Boston, swamped under the harassing fire of militia who swarmed in on their flanks; without a last minute relief attack from Boston the entire column might have been forced to surrender by ammunition exhaustion. The British lost nearly 300 men in killed, wounded, and missing. Within a few days 16,000 militia descended upon Boston and besieged the area. During a British attack on Breeds Hill, colonial sharpshooters (one of whom commented that he fired "taking deliberate aim, as at a squirrel, and saw a number of men fall")[76] inflicted disastrous losses on British troops. Over 1,000 regulars fell, 40 percent of the attacking force and over a tenth of the entire British army in the Colonies. Officers suffered especially serious losses; one rifleman was said to have shot down twenty officers in ten minutes; every single member of Gage's staff was shot down.[77]

In the meantime the militia throughout the rest of the Colonies seized political control at the grass roots. Tories were quickly put down; British foraging parties cut off; the mechanisms of government and administration lay solidly in the hands of revolutionaries. While the British during the French and Indian War were supplied primarily from the Colonies, throughout the revolution they would have to draw primarily from their homeland. The constant damage to British foraging parties ultimately led to a shipping problem which, one historian judges, would have ended the war by 1782 in any event.[78]

The militia played no minor role in the fighting: "Seldom has an armed force done so much with so little—providing a vast reservoir of manpower for a multiplicity of military needs, fighting (often unaided by Continentals) in the great majority of the 1,331 land engagements of the war."[79]

Following the war the colonies were temporarily governed under the Articles of Confederation, which permitted a federal force necessary to garrison forts and prohibited states from maintaining any standing forces. During these years a number of militia proposals were put forward by George Washington, Alexander Hamilton, Baron Steuben and Henry Knox.[80] All involved a general militia—in which essentially every free citizen would serve—and a "select militia". Steuben's proposal gave the greatest emphasis to the select militia; he would have had a small force of 21,000 select militiamen, chosen by volunteering, who would train one month out of each year. None of these proposals became law.

By 1787 the difficulties with the Articles of Confederation were becoming insurmountable, and work began on a new Constitution. As adopted, the Constitution gave Congress the power to provide "for organizing, arming and disciplining the militia" but it could "govern" only those in federal service, while the states would have the power of appointing officers and actually training the militia according to the uniform system of discipline. Militiamen would be subject to federal martial law only when called into active service.

In the state conventions called to ratify the Constitution, the proposal faced serious opposition. A major part of the opposition,   later termed anti-Federalist, focused on the fact that the Constitution lacked a Bill of Rights. The British Bill of Rights was called into attention as a precedent for such a measure. In the conflicts in the states three themes relating to citizen armament soon became apparent. The first was the acceptance by both Federalist and anti-Federalist of the critical role of the armed citizen, the second was a distrust both of standing armies and of select militia, like the modern National Guard; the third was pressure for a Bill of Rights which would include provisions guaranteeing rights of individual armament.

These thoughts began to take form in Connecticut, the fourth state to ratify. An anti-Federalist article in the Connecticut Journal objected strongly to the failure to outlaw a standing army and went on to criticize the Constitution's militia provisions as permitting the formation of a select militia: "This looks too much like Baron Steuben's militia, by which a standing army was meant and intended."[81] In Pennsylvania the opposition became even stiffer as the sentiment for a Bill of Rights grew. In a pamphlet hurriedly written to support adoption of the Constitution without the Bill of Rights, Noah Webster argued that the existing universal citizen armament made a standing army of little danger. He claimed that a standing army is oppressive only when it is "superior to any force that exists among the people" since otherwise it "would be annihilated on the first exercise of acts of oppression." He advised that the general armament of Americans rendered any constitutional limitations on a standing army unnecessary:

> Before a standing army can rule, the people must be disarmed; as they are in almost every kingdom of Europe. The supreme power in America cannot enforce unjust laws by the sword; because the whole body of the people are armed and constitute a force superior to any band of regular troops that can be, on any pretense, raised in the United States."[82]

In the convention the fighting was heavy. Delegate John Smiley argued that "Congress may give us a select militia which will, in fact, be a standing army.... When a select militia is formed, the people in general may be disarmed."[83] (The universal hostility to a select militia forms a most convincing refutation to the current argument that the "militia" referred to in the Second Amendment is the National Guard. On the contrary, virtually every citation to such militia during the drafting and ratification period views them as an evil comparable to a standing army and stresses that only a militia composed of the entire body of the populace armed and trained will protect freedom). Ultimately, Delegate Robert Whitehill moved a series of fifteen proposed amendments which would have established a bill of rights protecting freedom of conscience, speech, press, and virtually every other right ultimately incorporated into the Bill of Rights. This proposal was not adopted in Pennsylvania but was widely read in the Colonies and formed the inspiration for later proposals.[84] Its provision of keeping and bearing arms made it very clear that the right protected was to be an individual right:

> That the people have a right to bear arms for the defense of themselves and their own state, or the United States, or for the purpose of killing game; and no law shall be passed for disarming the people or any of them, unless for crimes committed, or real danger of public injury from individuals....[85]

In the Massachusetts Convention similar thoughts were expressed. Delegate Sedgwick asked whether a standing army "could subdue a nation of freemen, who know how to prize liberty, and who have arms in their hands?"[86] Sam Adams, who had done so much to bring on the revolution, spoke convincingly for the anti-Federalist position. He called for a bill of rights which would have provided "that the said Constitution shall never be construed to authorize Congress to infringe the just liberty of the press or the rights of conscience; or to prevent the people of the United States who are peaceable citizens from keeping their own arms...."[87] Like the Pennsylvania minority, Adams clearly considered the right of armament as a right of individual citizens to own personal arms.

In the following months additional states ratified, bringing the total to eight. A ninth vote was needed before the necessary majority would be obtained and the Constitution would become binding upon the states which had ratified to date. That critical vote was provided by New Hampshire, which added to its ratification a recommendation for a bill of rights including the provision that "Congress shall never disarm any citizen unless such as are or have been in actual rebellion."[88] A clearer statement of an absolute individual right could not have been drafted. The major commercial state—New York—and major intellectual state—Virginia—still remained to be heard from.

The Virginia Convention set the record for legal and intellectual talent. Major participants included Patrick Henry, George Mason, James Madison and John Marshall. The major writings of the period came from Richard Henry Lee, who had in the Continental Congress moved the drafting of the Declaration of Independence. In his "Letters from the Federal Farmer to the Republican" he warned that Congress might suddenly undermine the strength of the "yeomanry of the country" who possessed the lands, "possess arms, and are too strong a body of men to be openly offended."[89] He added "This might be done in a great measure by the Congress, if disposed to do it, by modeling the militia. Should one-fifth or one-eighth of the men capable of bearing arms be made a select militia, as has been proposed ... and all the others put upon a plan that will render them of no importance, the former will answer all the purposes of an army, while the latter will be defenseless."[90] Like others in Connecticut and Pennsylvania, Lee feared a "select militia" similar to the modern National Guard, which he considered a betrayal of the militia tradition and similar to a standing army. In strong terms he advised:

> First, the Constitution ought to secure a genuine, and guard against a select militia, by providing that the militia shall always be kept well organized, armed and disciplined, and include, according to the past and general   usage of the states, all men capable of bearing arms, and that all regulations tending to establish this general useless and defenseless, by establishing select corps of militia or distinct bodies of military men, not having permanent attachments in the community, to be avoided.[91]

He extensively criticized select militia and argued that on the contrary "to preserve liberty, it is essential that the whole body of people always possess arms, and be taught alike, especially when young, how to use them...."[92] In the Convention, Patrick Henry seconded Lee's judgments. Henry joined with Lee—and with Sam Adams and others who defended individual armament—explaining that "The great object is that every man be armed" and that "Everyone who is able may have a gun."[93] While Virginia ratified, it did so with a call for a bill of rights, including a recognition "that the people have the right to keep and bear arms; that a well-regulated militia, composed of the body of the people trained to arms is the proper, natural and safe defense of a free state."[94]

From Virginia, the debate moved to New York. The New York controversy gave ris~ ~ the famed "Federalist Papers." Since these were devoted to justifying adoption of the cons.. u..on without a Bill of Rights, they are at best of marginal utility in interpreting the early amendments to the Constitution. Even so, their authors stressed citizen armament as a bulwark of liberty which made adoption of the Constitution safe. Hamilton, no friend of the militia (and little friend of democracy, for that matter) attacked proposed limits on standing armies in Federalists 25 and 26. In Federalist 29 he suggested that militia could not be expected to tolerate much professional training: "little more can reasonably be aimed at with respect to the people at large than to have them properly armed and equipped." This armed but untrained citizenry, together with a select militia would ensure liberty despite a standing army: "That army can never be formitable to the liberties of the people while there is a large body of citizens, little if at all inferior to them in discipline and use of arms ..."

Madison in Federalist 46 argued the point at greater length, stressing citizen armament and state governments as bulwarks of freedom:

> Besides the advantage of being armed, which the Americans possess over the people, the existence of subordinate governments, to which the people are attached and by which the militia officers are appointed, forms a barrier against the enterprises of ambition ... notwithstanding the military establishments in the several kingdoms of Europe, which are carried as far as the public resources will bear, the governments are afraid to trust the people with arms.

If those people were armed and formed into militia units by subordinate governments, Madison asserted, "It may be affirmed with the greatest assurance that the throne of every tyranny in Europe would be speedily overturned in spite of the legions which surround it." To him citizen armament was not merely a matter of   military service or collective defense, but a guarantee of all other freedoms, to be used if necessary, against the government.

New York joined in ratifying, but by an even closer margin than most states: a shift of two votes out of fifty-seven cast would have rejected the constitution. It proposed amendments, including a recognition "That the people have a right to keep and bear arms; that a well-regulated militia, including the body of the people capable of bearing arms, is the proper, natural, and safe defense of a free state."

Only a few weeks later, word came that North Carolina had joined Rhode Island in rejecting the proposed constitution, citing the lack of a bill of rights. Among the amendments they called for before the delegates would sign was a provision identical to the New York and Virginia "Keep and bear arms" sections.

The constitution thus went into effect with eleven ratifications. But the pressing need for a bill of rights was clear. Not only had two states repudiated the new constitution, but five of the ratifying states had demanded such a bill and influential minorities in two more had striven unsuccessfully for it. (While freedom of speech was designated by only three ratifying states, the right to bear arms was mentioned by all five which called for a bill of rights, as well as by both groups of minority delegates and the dissenting North Carolina convention. This constitutional preference poll would suggest the ratifying conventions considered the right of private armament to be even more important than free speech.)

The Constitution carried in New York and eventually in every other state: but the anti-Federalist sentiment for a bill of rights also triumphed. Ultimately James Madison was put to the task of drafting a bill of rights. From the many proposals by the state conventions, he eventually distilled a limited number of rights deserving specific recognition, protecting the rest with the "catch-all clauses" of the Ninth and Tenth Amendments. The rights given express recognition were primarily procedural. Only the First and Second Amendments created substantive rights and these were a very small number of rights: speech, press, assembly, and keeping and bearing arms. These were viewed as the critical matters upon which the federal government might not infringe, under any conditions (and even by proceeding in accord with the procedural guarantees of the Fourth, Fifth and Sixth Amendments). Madison's initial proposal for what became the Second Amendment was worded: "The right of the people to keep and bear arms shall not be infringed; a well armed and well regulated militia being the best security of a free country; but no person religiously scrupulous of bearing arms shall be compelled to render military service in person."

There is no doubt that Madison saw this as an individual right. His earliest drafts of the Bill of Rights did not separate those proposals into numbered amendments which would follow the constitution. Instead, the amendments would have been inserted into the body of the constitution at specified points. Madison did not place the right to keep and bear arms as a limitation on Congress's power over the militia, set out in Article I section 8 of the constitution. Instead, he grouped the right to arms with rights of freedom of religion, speech and press, to be inserted "in article first, section nine, between clauses 3 and 4."[95] This would have put these provisions immediately following the general limitations of congressional power over citizens—outlawing suspension of habeas corpus, bills of attainder and ex post facto laws. Madison viewed his right to keep and bear arms proposal as a civil right, not a limit on federalization of the militia. Further, in an outline of a proposed speech on introduction of the Bill of Rights, Madison mentioned these "relate 1st to private rights," and indicated he meant to criticize the 1689 Declaration of Rights as too narrow: "No freedom of the press—conscience—Gl. warrants ... attainders—arms to Protestants."[96] Apparently, he felt the 1689 recognition that "Protestants may have arms for their defense" should be extended to all, that the second amendment would broaden, not narrow, this.

Like most of his draft, the wording was both lengthy and convoluted. In the House of Representatives his proposals were edited extensively; since "the right of the people" was already contained in the provision, the comment that the militia would consist "of the body of the people" was deleted. The religious exemption was removed in view of objections that the Congress might exempt too many people on these grounds and thus destroy the concept of the militia. When the proposal was submitted to the Senate, it was proposed that the right be limited to keeping and bearing arms "for the common defense", but the Senate refused the amendment, retaining it in its broadest form.[97]

Contemporaries of the first Congress clearly viewed the Second Amendment as creating an individual right. When St. George Tucker, then a professor at William and Mary School of Law and later a Justice of the Virginia Supreme Court, published a five-volume edition of Blackstone's Commentaries in 1803, he commented that "whenever standing armies are kept up, and the right of the people to keep and bear arms is, under any color or pretext whatsoever, prohibited, liberty, if not already annihilated, is on the brink of destruction. In England, the people have been disarmed, generally under the specious pretext of preserving the game."[98] He criticized the British Bill of Rights for limiting its guarantee of arms ownership to Protestants, whereas the American right was "without any qualification as to their condition or degree, as is the case in the British government."[99] William Rawle in his 1825 "View of the Constitution" suggested that:

> The prohibition is general. No clause in the Constitution could by any rule of construction be conceived to give to Congress a power to disarm the people.[100]

Tucker and Rawle had unique advantages in interpreting the Bill of Rights. Tucker had fought in the Revolutionary militia and was twice wounded in action. He was a close friend of Jefferson, an associate of Madison, and had a brother in the first Senate. Rawle was a friend of Washington and was offered the post of first Attorney General.

The Congress itself made its intent clear when the second Congress adopted the Militia Act of 1792. This required every "free able bodied white male citizen.... who is or shall be of the age of 18 years, and under the age of 45 years" to be enrolled in the   militia and "within six months thereafter, provide himself with a good musket or firelock," plus ammunition and equipment.[101] The bill remained on the books until 1903. Thus, from the subsequent enactments of Congress, as well as the contemporaneous statements of the drafters and their associates, there can be little doubt that the drafters of the Second Amendment viewed that amendment as creating an individual right to keep and carry arms for purposes ranging from self protection to hunting to acquisition of military skills.

The right of individual citizens to keep and bear arms found early recognition by the courts, in a solid chain of precedent stretching forward for nearly two centuries. In 1813, Kentucky adopted the first general concealed weapon ban and nine years later the act was struck down as an invasion of the right to keep and bear arms.[102] Similar statutes were later upheld in other States—upon the grounds that only one form of carrying, not all forms, were restricted.[103] The Alabama Supreme Court, for instance, added:

> We do not desire to be understood as maintaining, that in regulating the manner of wearing arms, the legislature has no limit other than its own discretion. A statute which, under the pretence of regulating, amounts to a destruction of the right, or which requires arms to be so borne as to render them wholly useless for the purpose of defense would be clearly unconstitutional.[104]

Likewise, when Georgia in 1837 enacted the first ban on pistol ownership, its supreme court promptly struck it down, holding in the process that the second amendment applied to the states. It explained the amendment's meaning: "The right of the whole people, old and young, men, women, and boys, and not militia only, to keep and bear arms of every description, and not merely such as are used by the militia, shall not be infringed ... and this for the important end to be achieved, the rearing up and qualifying of a well-regulated militia, so vitally necessary to the security of a free state."[105]

Second amendment issues rarely came before the federal courts at this time, simply because there were no federal controls on arms ownership. But the position of the United States Supreme Court was indicated in the famed *Dred Scott* case, where it held that the free black Americans were not citizens. The majority indicated that if blacks were regarded as citizens, "entitled to the privileges and immunities of citizens," they would have freedom of speech and assembly, "and to keep and carry arms wherever they went."[106]

Post civil war arms enactments encountered judicial limitations arising at the individual right to keep and bear arms. Tennessee, for instance, had to amend its constitution to expressly grant legislative power to "regulate the wearing of arms." Even so, its 1870 ban on carrying small ("pocket") pistols barely passed constitutional muster, the court warning that the legislature might not prohibit the carrying of "all manner of arms" since the power to regulate "does not fairly mean the power to prohibit."[107] Arkansas upheld a ban on pistol carrying only by construing it to apply only to pocket pistols and not to rifles, shotguns, or larger handguns. "To prohibit a citizen from wearing or carrying a war arm ... is an unwarranted restriction upon the constitutional right to keep and bear arms. If cowardly and dishonest men sometimes shoot unarmed men with army pistols or guns, the evil must be prevented by the penitentiary and the gallows, and not by a general deprivation of a constitutional privilege."[108] A similar technique was used to construe Missouri's 1875 carrying ban to apply only to concealed carry, the court citing with approval the concept that legislatures might not limit carrying so as to make the arms useless for defense.[109]

Nor has recognition of the right to keep and bear arms been lacking in our century. City bans on handgun carrying have been struck down in North Carolina ("the right to bear arms is a most essential one to every free people and should not be whittled down by technical constructions")[110]

Tennessee,[111] and New Mexico.[112] The Michigan Supreme Court has stricken a ban on gun ownership by non-citizens with the comment that "the guarantee of the right of every person to bear arms in defense of himself means the right to possess arms for legitimate use in defense of himself (and) his property."[113] A similar statute was stricken in Colorado, its Supreme Court expressly rejecting the "collective rights" approach.[114] The U.S. Supreme Court, in *United States v. Miller*,[115] held that a court cannot merely take judicial notice that an arm is within the second amendment's protections, but explained:

> The Constitution as originally adopted granted to the Congress power "to provide for calling forth the Militia (etc.) ..." With obvious purpose to assure the continuation and render possible the effectiveness of such forces the declaration and guarantee of the second amendment were made. It must be interpreted and applied with that end in view.
>
> The signification attributed to the term "militia" appears from the debates in the Convention, the history and legislation of the colonies and states, and the writings of approved commentators. These show plainly enough that the militia comprised all males physically capable of acting in concert for the common defense ... and further, that ordinarily when called for service these men were expected to appear bearing arms supplied by themselves and of the kind in common use at the time.

The right to keep and bear arms has found its most recent recognition in two 1980 decisions in Oregon[116] and Indiana,[117] the first striking down a very narrow arms possession ban, the second strictly limiting power to refuse carrying licenses.

In summary, the right to keep and bear arms is, in all probability, the oldest right memorialized in the Bill of Rights. Its common law right extends beyond our written records forward to the 1689 Declaration of Rights—so largely a response to individual disarmament under laws of the 1660's—and to our own Revolution, brought on primarily by British attempts at disarmament of the colonists. The recognition of the right in our own Bill of Rights is a natural outgrowth of that experience and of demands for preservation   of a clearly individual right to own and carry arms. It is a right reserved to "the people"—the same "people" who possess the right to assemble, and security from unreasonable searches and seizures, the "people" whom the tenth amendment distinguishes from "the states." It is clearly not a right relating solely to the National Guard, which had no legal recognition prior to 1903, and whose 18th century predecessors were criticized by Richard Henry Lee and other constitutional figures as equal in danger to standing armies. Rather, it is a right reserved to individual citizens, to possess ("keep") and carry ("bear") arms for personal and political defense of themselves and their rights.

REFERENCES

*.   David T. Hardy received his Bachelor of Arts degree from the University of Arizona where he graduated cum laude in 1972. He received his Juris Doctorate from the University of Arizona College of Law in 1975. He graduated magna cum laude and served as Associate Editor of the Arizona Law Review from 1974 to 1975. Mr. Hardy is a member of the Bar of the Supreme Court of the United States, the Fourth and Ninth Circuit U.S. Courts of Appeals, and the Arizona Supreme Court, and is a partner in the law firm of Sando and Hardy, Tucson, Arizona. He serves on the Legal Advisory Board of the Second Amendment Foundation, is a member of the American Civil Liberties Union and the National Rifle Association.

Mr. Hardy has written extensively in the area of law and firearms regulation. He is the co-author of a lengthy article titled: "Of Arms and the Law," 51 Chicago-Kent Law Review 62 (1974), author of "Firearms Ownership and Regulation," 20 Wm. & Mary L. Rev. 235 (1978) and "Gun Laws and Gun Collectors," 85 Case & Comment 3 (Jan.-Feb. 1978). He would like to acknowledge, with gratitude, the assistance of Bob Dowlut, Frances Averly, and Barbara Goldman in preparation of this report.

1.   3 W. Churchill, A History of the English Speaking Peoples 168 (1957). E. W. Williams, The Eighteenth Century Constitution 399-401 (Cambridge University 1960). Despite existence of this censorship, freedom of press was completely omitted from the 1688 "Declaration of Rights."

2.   1 John Tebbel, A History of Book Publishing in the United States 45 (1972).

3.   In 1763, to be precise, when John Wilkes won substantial civil awards against ministers who issued general warrants for search and arrest of those responsible for an alleged seditious libel. G. Rude, Wilkes and Liberty 27-29 (1962); Churchill, *supra*, at 165-67. "From the "Glorious Revolution onwards, Secretaries of State had, for nearly a hundred years, been issuing similar warrants ... and, until April 1763, their validity had never been challenged in a Court of law." Rude, *supra*, at 29.

4.   Charles Hollister, Anglo-Saxon Military Institutions 27 (Oxford University 1962). Hollister's excellent study is matched only by Brooks, "The Development of Military Obligations in Eighth and Ninth Century England," in England before the Conquest 69 (Clemoes and Hughes, ed. Cambridge University 1971).

5.   William Blackstone, Commentaries on the Common Law of England, Book 1 Ch.XIII; 1 J. Bagley & P. Rowley, a Documentary History of England 1066-1540, at p.152.

6.   H. W. C. Davis, England Under the Normans and Angevins 75 (1957).

7.   1 Francis Grose, Military Antiquities Respecting a History of the British Army 9-11 (London, 1812). "Assize" was a term which had several meanings in medieval law. In this sense it signified a proclamation or piece of legislation which was intended to modify or expand traditional law, rather than simply construe it—the earliest form of what we today would consider true legislation. W. L. Warren, Henry II, at 281 (1973).

8.   Bagley & Rowley, *supra*, at 155-56.

9.   E. G. Heath, The Grey Goose Wing 109 (1971).

10.   Robert Hardy, The Longbow: A Social and Military History of 129 (1977).

11.   *Id.*

12.   *Id.* at 128. These price limitations would be repeated through to the reign of Henry VIII, along with requirements for import of longbows and quotas on less expensive longbows.

13.   7 Edward I c.2 (1279).

14.   1 Statutes of the Realm 151, 230 (London, 1810).

15.   2 Edw.III c.3 (1328).

16.   1 W. Hawkins, Pleas of the Crown 267 (6th ed. 1788). *See also* Rex V. Knight, 87 Eng. Rep. 75 (King's Bench 1686); Rex V. Dewhurst, 1 State Trails (New Series) 529 (1820).

17.   L. Kennet & J. Anderson, The Gun in America 12, 15 (1975); N. Perrin, Giving Up the Gun 58 (1975).

18.   19 Henry VI c.4 (1503).

19.   3 Henry VIII c.3, 13 (1511).

20.   6 Hen.VIII c.13 (1514).

21.   14 & 15 Hen. VIII c.7 (1523).

22.   33 Hen. VII c.6 (1541).

23.   Perrin, *supra*, at 59-60.

24.   "Thai gon crokyd, and ben feble, not able to fight, nor to defend ye realm; nor thai have wepen, nor money to bie thaim wepen withall." Sir John Fortescue, The Governance of England 114 (C. Plummer, ed., Oxford, 1885). The Venetian ambassador to France confirmed this in a 1537 report of peasants taken into military service: "They were brought up in slavery, with no experience of handling weapons, and since they have suddenly passed from total servitude to freedom, sometimes they no longer want to obey their master." 1 R. Laffont, The Ancient Art of Warfare 485 (1966).

25.   Jim Hill, The Minutemen in War and Peace 26-27 (1968). "Militia" was apparently derived from the French word "milice" which in turn can be related to the Latin term "miles", or soldier.

26.   The foremost study of the militia system under Elizabeth is Lindsay Boynton, The Elizabethan Militia (1967).

27.   C. G. Cruickshank, Elizabeth's Army 24-25 (2d ed. 1968).

28.   Richard Ollard, This War Without an Enemy 53 (1976).

29.   *See generally* Correlli Barnett, Britain's Army 89-90 (1970); Charles Firth, Cromwell's Army (1962).

30.   Michael Gruber, The English Revolution 125 (1967); Barnett, *supra*, at 107.

31.   John Childs, The Army of Charles II at 9 (1976).

32.   Joyce Malcolm, Disarmed: The Loss of the Right to Bear Arms in Restoration England, 11 (Mary Ingraham Bunting Institute, Radcliffe College, 1980).

33.   8 Calendar of State Papers (Domestic), Charles II, No. 188, p. 150 (July, 1660).

34.   J. R. Western, The English Militia in the Eighteenth Century 11-13 (1965).

35.   14 Car.II c.3 (1662). The political background of the passage of this enactment is discussed in Western, *supra*, at 11.

36.   A few examples: "Think Fauntleroy an untoward fellow; arms for thirty or forty were found in his house last year" (68 Calendar of State Papers (Domestic) Charles II, No. 35, p. 44 (February, 1662); [Jacob Knowles, arrested for] "dangerous designs, he having been taken on the guard with a pistol upon him," (70 Calendar of State Papers (Domestic), Charles II, No. 13, p. 83 (March, 1662); "Hearing of a nonconformist meeting, issued warrant for the search of arms; the officers being denied entrance broke open the doors, and found 200 or 300 persons." (88 Calendar of State Papers (Domestic), Charles II, No. 56, p. 332).

37.   22 & 23 Car. II, c.25 (1671).

38.   Andrew Browning, English Historical Documents 1660-1714, at 81 (1953).

39.   2 Calendar of State Papers (Domestic), James II, No. 1212 at p. 314 (December, 1686).

40.   3 Thomas Macaulay, The History of England in the Accession of Charles II, 136-37 (London, 1856).

41.   1 Gul. & Mar., sess. 2, c.2 (1689).

42.   James Jones, The Revolution of 1688 in England 316-317 (London, 1972).

43.   L. Brevold & R. Ross, The Philosophy of Edmund Burke 192 (1970).

44.   1 Gul. & Mar., sess. 2, c.2 (1689).

45.   Joyce Malcolm, Disarmed: The Loss of the Right to Bear Arms in Restoration England 16 (Mary Ingraham Bunting Institute, Radcliffe College, 1980).

46.   *See* Rohner, "The Right to Bear Arms: A phenomenon of Constitutional History," 16 Cath. U. L.Rev. 53, 59 (1966).

47.   2 Philip, Earl of Hardwicke, Miscellaneous State Papers From 1501-1726, at 407-417 (London, 1778).

48.   Journal of the House of Commons From December 26, 1688 to October 26, 1693, at 5, 6, 21-22 (London 1742).

49.   Western, *supra*, at 339.

50.   Journal of the House of Commons, *supra*, at 25.

51.   Western, *supra*, at 339.

52.   Algernon Sidney, Discourses Concerning Government 156 (3d ed., London 1751) (Library of Congress, Rare Books Collection).

53.   Robert Molesworth, An account of Denmark as it Was in The Year 1692, at 123 (London, 1692; reprinted, Copenhagen, 1976).

54.   Francis Hotoman, Franco-Gallia XXVIII (Tr. by Robert Molesworth, 1721) (Library of Congress, Rare Books Collection).

55.   But a few examples: in 1773, Harvard's library contained Harrington and Molesworth; Sidney was added by 1790. The College of New Jersey (today Princeton) boasted Sidney by 1760, as did the New York Society Library. John Adams' private library contained a two volume edition of Sidney and Molesworth; Jefferson at various times bought several different editions of both authors. H. Colbourn, The Lamp of Experience 200-18 (1965).

56.   Clinton Rossiter, The Political Thought of The American Revolution 55 (1963).

57.   Barnett, *supra*, at 174.

58.   30 Geo. II c.2 (1757). This power was invoked during the waves of rioting which spread across the English nation in 1766. Tony Hayter, The Army and The Crowd in Mid-Georgian England 158 (1978).

59.   The North British Intelligencer, Vol. 1 at p.20 (Edinburgh, 1776). (Library of Congress Rare Books Collection).

60.   Harold Gill, The Gunsmith in Colonial Virginia 3 (1974).

61.   1 William Hening, The Statutes at Large: Being a Collection of All The Laws of Virginia From The First Session of The Legislature in The Year 1619, at 127 (New York 1823).

62.   *Id.* at 173-74.

63.   William Brigham, The Compact With The Charter and Laws of The Colony of New Plymouth 31 (Boston, 1836).

64.   Oliver Dickerson, ed. Boston Under Military Rule 61 (1936).

65.   *Id.* at 79.

66.   1 William Gordon, The History of The Rise, Progress and Establishment of The Independence of The United States 442-43 (London, 1788). (Library of Congress Rare Books Collection).

67.   John Alden, General Gage in America 224 (1948).

68.   Stephen Patterson, Political Parties in Revolutionary Massachusetts 103 (1973).

69.   *Id.*

70.   *Id.* at 104-05; Gavin, *supra*, at 64.

71.   1 Kate Rowland, The Life of George Mason 181, 430-32 (1892).

72.   *Id.* at 182-83; Donald Higginbotham, "The American Militia: A Traditional Institution With Revolutionary Responsibilities," *in* Reconsideration on The Revolutionary War 92 (1978).

73.   Rowland, *supra*, at 183, 427-28.

74.   Hezekiah Miles, Republication of The Principles and Acts of The Revolution in America 278 (New York, 1876).

75.	1 The Political Writings of Thomas Paine at 111 (Boston, 1856).

76.	Charles Flood, Rise and Fight Again 61 (1976).

77.	Willard Wallace, Appeal to Arms 43 (1951); Joe Huddleston, Colonial Riflemen in The American Revolution 25 (1978).

78.	I. Christie, Crisis of Empire 106 (1966).

79.	Higginbotham, *supra*, at 103.

80.	The best study of these proposals is John McAuley Palmer's Washington, Lincoln, Wilson: Three War Statesmen (1930). Palmer was responsible for locating Washington's militia plan, which had been missing from Congressional archives for over a century.

81.	3 Merrill Jensen, ed., The Documentary History of The Ratification of The Constitution 378 (1976).

82.	Noah Webster, An Examination Into The Leading Principles of The Federal Constitution Proposed by The Late Convention, *reprinted in* Paul Ford, ed., Pamphlets on The Constitution of The United States 56 (New York, 1888).

83.	2 Jensen, *supra*, at 508.

84.	E. Dumbauld, The Bill of Rights and What It Means Today 11 (1959).

85.	2 Jensen, *supra*, at 597-98.

86.	2 Jonathan Elliot, ed., Debates in The Several State Conventions on The Adoption of The Federal Constitution 97 (2d ed. 1888).

87.	Paul Lewis, The Grand Incendiary 359-60 (1973).

88.	Joseph Walker, Birth of The Federal Constitution: A History of The New Hampshire Convention 51 (Boston, 1888); Documents Illustrative of The Formation of The Union of The American States 1026 (House of Representatives Document 398: Government Printing Office 1927).

89.	Walter Bennett, ed., Letters From The Federal Farmer to The Republican 21 (1978).

90.	*Id.* at 21-22.

91.	*Id.* at 124.

92.	*Id.*

93.	Debates and Other Proceedings of The Convention of Virginia ... taken in shorthand by David Robertson of Petersburg, 275 (2nd ed., Richmond, 1805).

94.	Documents Illustrative of The Formation of The Union, *supra*, at 1030.

95.	[Ed. footnote missing in original]

96.	[Ed. footnote missing in original]

97.	*See generally,* 1 J. Goebel, History of the Supreme Court of the United States 456 ( ).

98.	1 S. Tucker, ed., Blackstone's Commentaries 300 (Philadelphia, 1803).

99.	*Id.* at 143.

100.	W. Rawle, A View of the Constitution 125-6 (2d ed. 1829).

101.	Act of May 8, 1792. *See generally* J. Mahony, The American Militia: Decade of Decision (1960).

102.	*Bliss v. Commonwealth*, 12 Ky. 90 (1822).

103.	*State v. Mitchell*, 3 Ind. (Blackf.) 229 (1839). State v. Reid, 1 Ala. 612 (1840); State v. Buzzard, 4 Ark. 18 (1842).

104.	*State v. Reid, supra.*

105.	*Nunn v. State*, 1 Ga. 243, 251(1846).

106.	*Dred Scott v. Sanford*, 60 U.S. 393, 417 (1857).

107.	*Andrew v. State*, 50 Tenn. 165, 8 Am. Rep. 8 (1971). The Andrews Court went on to note that "this right was intended ... to be exercised and enjoyed by the citizen as such, and not by him as a soldier ..." 8 Am. Rep. at 17.

108.	*Wilson v. State*, 33 Ark. 557, 34 Am. Rep. 52 (1878).

109.	*State v. Wilforth*, 85 Mo. 528, 530 (1882).

110.	*State v. Kerner*, 181 N.C. 574, 107 S.E. 222 (1921).

111.	*Glasscock v. City of Chattanooga*, 157 Tenn. 518, 11 S.W. 2d. 678 (1928).

112.	*City of Las Vegas v. Moberg*, 82 N.M. 626, 485 P. ad 737 (1971) ("an ordinance may not deny the people the constitutionally guaranteed right to bear arms.")

113.	*People v. Zerillo*, 219 Mich. 635, 189 N.W. 927 (1923).

114.	*People v. Nakamura*, 99 Colo. 262, 62, P. 2d 246 (1936).

115.	*United States v. Miller*, 307 U.S. 175, 178-79 (1939).

116.	*State v. Kessler*, 289 Ore. 359, 614 p. 2d 94 (1980).

117.	*Schubert v. DeBard*, _____ Ind. App. _____, 398 NE2d 1139 (1980).

[Originally published as Report of the Subcommittee on the Constitution of the Committee on the Judiciary, United States Senate, 97th Cong., 2d Sess., The Right to Keep and Bear Arms, 68-82 (1982) ("Other Views"). Reproduced in the 1982 Senate Report, pg. 68-82. Dr. Halbrook is the author of FREEDMEN, THE FOURTEENTH AMENDMENT, AND THE RIGHT TO BEAR ARMS, 1866-1876 which may be obtained from amazon.com]

THE FOURTEENTH AMENDMENT AND THE RIGHT TO KEEP AND BEAR ARMS: THE INTENT OF THE FRAMERS

By Stephen P. Halbrook[*]

A well regulated militia being necessary to the security of a free state, the right of the people to keep and bear arms shall not be infringed. —U.S. Const. amend. II.

... No state shall make or enforce any law which shall abridge the privileges or immunities of citizens of the United States; nor shall any state deprive any person of life, liberty, or property, without due process of law; nor deny to any person within its jurisdiction the equal protection of the laws. —U.S. Const. amend. XIV, § 1.

If African Americans were citizens, observed Chief Justice Taney in *Dred Scott v. Sandford*,[1] "it would give to persons of the negro race ... the full liberty of speech ...; to hold public meetings upon political affairs, *and to keep and carry arms wherever they went*."[2] If this interpretation ignores that Articles I and II of the Bill of Rights designate the respective freedoms guaranteed therein to "the people" and not simply the citizens (much less a select group of orators or militia), contrariwise *Dred Scott* followed antebellum judicial thought in recognizing keeping and bearing arms as an individual right[3] protected from both federal and state infringement.[4] The exception to this interpretation were cases holding that the Second Amendment only protected citizens[5] from federal, not state,[6] infringement of the right to keep and bear arms, to provide judicial approval of laws disarming black freemen and slaves.

Since the Fourteenth Amendment was meant to overrule *Dred Scott* by extending individual constitutional rights to black Americans and by providing protection thereof against state infringement,[7] the question arises whether the framers of Amendment XIV and related enforcement legislation recognized keeping and bearing arms as an individual right on which no state could infringe. The congressional intent in respect to the Fourteenth Amendment is revealed in the debates over both Amendments XIII and XIV as well as the Civil Rights Act of 1866, the Anti-KKK Act of 1871, and the Civil Rights Act of 1875. Given the unanimity of opinion concerning state regulation of privately held arms by the legislators who framed the Fourteenth Amendment and its enforcement legislation, it is surprising that judicial opinions and scholarly articles fail to analyze the Reconstruction debates.[8]

A. ARMS AND SLAVERY

---

[*] J.D. 1978 Georgetown University; Ph.D. 1972 Florida State University, Member, Virginia State Bar, various federal court bars. The Author has taught legal and political philosophy at George Mason University, Howard University and Tuskegee Institute.

This is a revision of a portion of the author's The Jurisprudence of the Second and Fourteenth Amendments, IV GEORGE MASON L. REV. (1981)

Having won their national independence from England through armed struggle, post-Revolutionary War Americans were acutely   aware that the sword and sovereignty go hand in hand, and that the firearms technology ushered in a new epoch in the human struggle for freedom. Furthermore, both proponents and opponents of slavery were cognizant that an armed black population meant the abolition of slavery, although plantation slaves were often trusted with arms for hunting.[9] This sociological fact explained not only the legal disarming of blacks but also the advocacy of a weapons culture by abolitionists. Having employed the instruments for self-defense against his pro-slavery attackers, abolitionist and Republican Party founder Cassius Marcellus Clay wrote that "`the pistol and the Bowie knife' are to us as sacred as the gown and the pulpit."[10] And it was John Brown who argued that "the practice of carrying arms would be a good one for the colored people to adopt, as it would give them a sense of their manhood."[11]

The practical necessities of the long, bloody Civil War, demanding every human resource, led to the arming of blacks as soldiers. While originally they considered it a "white man's war," Northern authorities by 1863 were organizing black regiments on a wide scale. At the same time, black civilians were forced to arm themselves privately against mob violence. During the anti-draft riots in New York, according to a Negro newspaper of the time, "The colored men who had manhood in them armed themselves, and threw out their pickets every day and night, determined to die defending their homes.... Most of the colored men in Brooklyn who remained in the city were armed daily for self-defense."[12]

Toward the end of the war Southerners began to support the arming and freeing of slaves willing to fight the invaders, and the Virginia legislature, on passing a bill providing for the use of black soldiers, repealed its laws against the bearing of arms by blacks.[13] One opponent of these measures declared: "What would be the character of the returned negro soldiers, made familiar with the use of fire-arms, and taught by us, that freedom was worth fighting for?"[14] Being evident that slaves plus guns equaled abolition, the rebels were divided between those who valued nationhood to slavery and those who preferred a restored union which might not destroy the servile condition of black labor.

As the movement began before the end of the war for the complete abolition of slavery via the Thirteenth Amendment, members of the U.S. Congress recognized the key role that the bearing of arms was already playing in the freeing of the slaves. In debate over the proposed Amendment, Rep. George A. Yeaman (Unionist, Ky.) contended that whoever won the war, the abolition of slavery was inevitable due to the arming of blacks:

> Let proclamations be withdrawn, let statutes be repealed, let our armies be defeated, let the South achieve its independence, yet come out of the war ... with an army of slaves made freemen for their service, who have been contracted with, been armed and drilled, and have seen the force of combination. Their personal status is enhanced.... They will not be returned to slavery.[15]

At the same time, members of the slavocracy were planning to disarm the freedmen. Arguing for speedy adoption of the Thirteenth Amendment, Rep. William D. Kelley (R., Penn.) expressed shock at the words of an anti-secessionist planter in Mississippi who expected the union to restore slavery. Kelly cited a letter from a U.S. brigadier general who wrote: "`What,' said I, `these men who have had arms in their hands?' `Yes,' he said, `we should take the arms away from them, of course.'"[16]

The northern government won the war only because of the arming of the slaves, according to Sen. Charles Sumner (R., Mass.), who argued that necessity demanded "first, that the slaves should be declared free; and secondly, that muskets should be put into their hands for the common defense.... Without emancipation, followed by the arming of the slaves, rebel slavery would not have been overcome."[17]

B. THE CIVIL RIGHTS ACT OF 1866

After the war was concluded, the slave codes, which limited access of blacks to land, to arms, and to the courts, began to reappear in the form of the black codes,[18] and United States legislators turned their attention to the protection of the freedmen. In support of Senate Bill No. 9, which declared as void all laws in the rebel states which recognized inequality of rights based on race, Sen. Henry Wilson (R., Mass.) explained in part: "In Mississippi rebel State forces, men who were in the rebel armies, are traversing the State, visiting the freedmen, disarming them, perpetrating murders and outrages on them...."[19]

When Congress took up Senate Bill No. 61, which became the Civil Rights Act of 1866,[20] Sen. Lyman Trumbull (R., Ill.), Chairman of the Senate Judiciary Committee, indicated that the bill was intended to prohibit inequalities embodied in the black codes, including those provisions which "prohibit any negro or mulatto from having fire-arms."[21] In abolishing the badges of slavery, the bill would enforce fundamental rights against racial discrimination in respect to civil rights, the rights to contract, sue and engage in commerce, and equal criminal penalties. Sen. William Saulsbury (D., Del.) added: "In my State for many years, and I presume there are similar laws in most of the southern States, there has existed a law of the State based upon and founded in its police power, which declares that free negroes shall not have the possession of firearms or ammunition. This bill proposes to take away from the States this police power...." The Delaware Democrat opposed the bill on this basis, anticipating a time when "a numerous body of dangerous persons belonging to any distinct race" endangered the state, for "the State shall not have the power to disarm them without disarming the whole population."[22] Thus, the bill would have prohibited legislative schemes which in effect disarmed blacks but not whites. Still, supporters of the bill were soon to contend that arms bearing was a basic right of citizenship or personhood.

In the meantime, the legislators turned their attention to the Freedmen's Bureau Bill. Rep. Thomas D. Eliot (R., Mass.) attacked an Opelousas, Louisiana ordinance which deprived blacks of various civil rights, including the following provision: "No freedman who is not in the military service shall be allowed to carry firearms, or any kind of weapons, within the limits of the town of Opelousas without the special permission of his employer ... and   approved by the mayor or president of the board of police."[23] And Rep. Josiah B. Grinnell (R., Iowa) complained: "A white man in Kentucky may keep a gun; if a black man buys a gun he forfeits it and pays a fine of five dollars, if presuming to keep in his possession a musket which he has carried through the war."[24] Yet the right of blacks to have arms existed partly as self-defense against the state militia itself, which implied that militia needs were not the only constitutional basis for the right to bear arms. Sen. Trumbull cited a report from Vicksburg, Mississippi which stated: "Nearly all the dissatisfaction that now exists among the freedmen is caused by the abusive conduct of this militia."[25] Rather than restore order, the militia would typically "hand some freedman or search negro houses for arms."[26] As debate returned to the Civil Rights Bill, Rep. Henry J. Raymond (R., N.Y.) explained of the rights of citizenship: "Make the colored man a citizen of the United States and he has every right which you or I have as citizens of the United States under the laws and Constitution of the United

States.... He has a defined status; he has a country and a home; a right to defend himself and his wife and children; a right to bear arms...."[27] Rep. Roswell Hart (R., N.Y.) further states: "The Constitution clearly describes that to be a republican form of government for which it was expressly framed. A government ... where 'no law shall be made prohibiting a free exercise of religion;' where 'the right of the people to keep and bear arms shall not be infringed;'...."[28] He concluded that it was the duty of the United States to guarantee that the states have such a form of government.[29]

Rep. Sidney Clarke (R., Kansas) referred to an 1866 Alabama law providing: "That it shall not be lawful for any freedman, mulatto, or free person of color in this State, to own firearms, or carry about his person a pistol or other deadly weapon."[30] This same statute made it unlawful "to sell, give, or lend fire-arms or ammunition of any description whatever, to any freedman, free negro, or mulatto...."[31] Clarke also attacked Mississippi, "whose rebel militia, upon the seizure of the arms of black Union Soldiers, appropriated the same to their own use."[32]

> Sir, I find in the Constitution of the United States an article which declares that "the right of the people to keep and bear arms shall not be infringed." For myself, I shall insist that the reconstructed rebels of Mississippi respect the Constitution in their local laws....[33]

Emotionally referring to the disarming of black soldiers, Clarke added:

> Nearly every white man in that State that could bear arms was in the rebel ranks. Nearly all of their able-bodied colored men who could reach our lines enlisted under the old flag. Many of these brave defenders of the nation paid for the arms with which they went to battle.... The "reconstructed" State authorities of Mississippi were allowed to rob and disarm our veteran soldiers....[34]

In sum, Clarke presupposed a constitutional right to keep privately held arms for protection against oppressive state militia.

C. THE FOURTEENTH AMENDMENT

The need for a more solid foundation for the protection of freedmen as well as white citizens was recognized, and the result was a significant new proposal—the Fourteenth Amendment. A chief exponent of the amendment, Sen. Jacob M. Howard (R., Mich.), referred to "the personal rights guaranteed and secured by the first eight amendments of the Constitution; such as freedom of speech and of the press; ... the right to keep and bear arms...."[35] Adoption of the Fourteenth Amendment was necessary because presently these rights were not guaranteed against state legislation. "The great object of the first section of this amendment is, therefore, to restrain the power of the States and compel them at all times to respect these great fundamental guarantees."[36]

The Fourteenth Amendment was viewed as necessary to buttress the objectives of the Civil Rights Act of 1866. Rep. George W. Julian (R., Ind.) noted that the act

> Is pronounced void by the jurists and courts of the South. Florida makes it a misdemeanor for colored men to carry weapons without a license to do so from a probate judge, and the punishment of the offense is whipping and the pillory. South Carolina has the same enactments... Cunning legislative devices are being invented in most of the States to restore slavery in fact.[37]

It is hardly surprising that the arms question was viewed as part of a partisan struggle. "As you once needed the muskets of the colored persons, so now you need their votes," Sen. Sumner explained to his fellow Republicans in support of black suffrage in the District of Columbia.[38] At the opposite extreme, Rep. Michael C. Kerr (D., Ind.) an opponent of black suffrage and of the Fourteenth Amendment, attacked a military ordinance in Alabama that set up a volunteer militia of all males between ages 18 and 45 "without regard to race or color" on these grounds:

> Of whom will that militia consist? Mr. Speaker, it will consist only of the black men of Alabama. The white men will not degrade themselves by going into the ranks and becoming a part of the militia of the State with negroes.... Are the civil laws of Alabama to be enforced by this negro militia? Are white men to be disarmed by them?[39]

Kerr predicted that the disfranchisement of white voters and the above military measures would result in a "war of races."[40]

D. THE ANTI-KKK ACT

Although the Fourteenth Amendment became law in 1868, within three years the Congress was considering enforcement legislation to suppress the Ku Klux Klan. The famous report by Rep. Benjamin F. Butler (R., Mass.) on violence in the South assumed that the right to keep arms was necessary for protection against the militia but also against local law enforcement agencies. Noting instances of "armed confederates" terrorizing the negro, the report stated that "in many counties they have preceded their outrages upon him by disarming him, in violation of his right as a citizen to `keep and bear arms,' which the Constitution expressly says shall never be infringed."[41] The congressional power based on the Fourteenth Amendment to legislate to prevent states from depriving any U.S. citizen of life, liberty, or property justified the following provision of the committee's anti-KKK bill:

> That whoever shall, without due process of law, by violence, intimidation, or threats, take away or deprive any citizen of the United States of any arms or weapons he may have in his house or possession for the defense of his person, family, or property, shall be deemed guilty of a larceny thereof, and be punished as provided in this act for a felony.[42]

Rep. Butler explained the purpose of this provision in these words:

> Section eight is intended to enforce the well-known constitutional provision guaranteeing the right in the citizen to "keep and bear arms," and provides that whoever shall take away, by force or violence, or by threats and intimidation, the arms and weapons which any person may have for his defense, shall be deemed guilty of larceny of the same. This provision seemed to your committee to be necessary, because they had observed that, before these midnight marauders made attacks upon peaceful citizens, there were very many instances in the South where the sheriff of the county had preceded them and taken away the arms of their victims. This was specially noticeable in Union County, where all the negro population were disarmed by the sheriff only a few months ago under the order of the judge...; and then, the sheriff having disarmed the citizens, the five hundred masked men rode at night and murdered and otherwise maltreated the ten persons who were in jail in that county.[43]

The bill was referred to the Judiciary Committee, and when later reported as H.R. No. 320 the above section was deleted—probably because its proscription extended to simple individual larceny over which Congress had no constitutional authority, and because state or conspiratorial action involving the disarming of blacks would be covered by more general provisions of the bill. Supporters of the rewritten anti-KKK bill continued to show the same concern over the disarming of freedmen. Sen. John Sherman (R., Ohio) stated the Republican position: "Wherever the negro population preponderates, there they [the KKK] hold their sway, for a few determined men ... can carry terror among ignorant negroes ... without arms, equipment, or discipline."[44]

Further comments clarified that the right to arms was a necessary condition for the right of free speech. Sen. Adelbert Ames (R., Miss.) averred: "In some counties it was impossible to advocate Republican principles, those attempting it being hunted like wild beasts; in other, the speakers had to be armed and supported by   not a few friends."[45] Rep. William L. Stoughton (R., Mich.) exclaimed: "If political opponents can be marked for slaughter by secret bands of cowardly assassins who ride forth with impunity to execute the decrees upon the unarmed and defenseless, it will be fatal alike to the Republican party and civil liberty."[46]

Section 1 of the bill, which was taken partly from Section 2 of the Civil Rights Act of 1866 and survives today as 42 U.S.C. § 1983, was meant to enforce Section 1 of the Fourteenth Amendment by establishing a remedy for deprivation under color of state law of federal constitutional rights of all people, not only former slaves. This portion of the bill provided:

> That any person who, under color of any law, statute, ordinance, regulation, custom, or usage of any State, shall subject, or cause to be subjected, any person within the jurisdiction of the United States to the deprivation of any rights, privileges, or immunities to which ... he is entitled under the Constitution or laws of the United States, shall ... be liable to the party injured in an action at law, suit in equity, or other proper proceeding for redress...."[47]

Rep. Washington C. Whitthorne (D., Tenn.), who complained that "in having organized a negro militia, in having disarmed the white man," the Republicans had "plundered and robbed" the whites of South Carolina through "unequal laws," objected to Section 1 of the anti-KKK bill on these grounds:

> It will be noted that by the first section suits may be instituted without regard to amount or character of claim by any person within the limits of the United States who conceives that he has been deprived of any right, privilege, or immunity secured him by the Constitution of the United States, under color of any law, statute, ordinance, regulation, custom, or usage of any State. This is to say, that if a police officer of the city of Richmond or New York should find a drunken negro or white man upon the streets with a loaded pistol flourishing it, &c., and by virtue of any ordinance, law, or usage, either of city or State, he takes it away, the officer may be sued, because the right to bear arms is secured by the Constitution, and such suit brought in distant and expensive tribunals.[48]

The Tennessee Democrat assumed that the right to bear arms was absolute, deprivation of which created a cause of action against state agents under Section 1 of the anti-KKK bill. In the minds of the bill's supporters, however, the Second Amendment as incorporated in the Fourteenth Amendment recognized a right to keep and bear arms safe from state infringement, not a right to commit assault or otherwise engage in criminal conduct with arms by pointing them at people or wantonly brandishing them about so as to endanger others. Contrary to the congressman's exaggerations, the proponents of the bill had the justified fear that the opposite development would occur, i.e., that a black or white man of the wrong political party would legitimately have or possess arms and a police officer of the city of Richmond or New York who was   drunken with racial prejudice or partisan politics would take it away, perhaps to ensure the success of an extremist group's attack. Significantly, none of the representative's colleagues disputed his assumption that state agents could be sued under the predecessor to § 1983 for deprivation of the right to keep arms.

Rep. William D. Kelly (R., Penn.), speaking after and in reply to Rep. Whitthorne, did not deny the argument that Section 1 allowed suit for deprivation of the right to possess arms, but emphasized the arming of the KKK. He referred to "great numbers of Winchester rifles, and a particular species of revolving pistol" coming into Charleston's ports. "Poor men, without visible means of support, whose clothes are ragged and whose lives are almost or absolutely those of vagrants, are thus armed with new and costly rifles, and wear in their belts a brace of expensive pistols."[49] These weapons were used against Southern Republicans, whose constitutional rights must thereby be guaranteed by law and arms.

However, like Congressman Whitthorne, Rep. Barbour Lewis (R., Tenn.) also decried the loss of state agent's immunity should the bill pass: "By the first section, in certain cases, the judge of a State court, through acting under oath of office, is made liable to a suit in the Federal Court and subject to damages for his decision against a suitor, however honest and conscientious that decision may be; and a ministerial officer is subject to the same pains and penalties...."[50]Tennessee Republicans and Democrats alike thus agreed that what is today § 1983 provided an action for damages against state agents in general for deprivation of constitutional rights.

Debate over the anti-KKK bill naturally required exposition of Section 1 of the Fourteenth Amendment, and none was better qualified to explain that section than its draftsman, Rep. John A. Bingham (R., Ohio):

> Mr. Speaker, that the scope and meaning of the limitations imposed by the first section, fourteenth amendment of the Constitution may be more fully understood, permit me to say that the privileges and immunities of citizens of a State, are chiefly defined in the first eight amendments to the constitution of the United States. Those eight amendments are as follows:

> ARTICLE I

> Congress shall make no law respecting an establishment of religion, or prohibiting the free exercise thereof, or abridging the freedom of speech, or of the press, or the right of the people peaceably to assemble, and to petition the Government for a redress of grievances.

> ARTICLE II

> A well-regulated militia being necessary to the security of a free State, the right of the people to keep and bear arms shall not be infringed.... [Amendments III-VIII, also listed by Bingham, are here omitted.]

These eight articles I have shown never were limitations upon the power of the States, until made so by the Fourteenth Amendment. The words of that amendment, "no State shall make or enforce any law which shall abridge the privileges or immunities of citizens of the United States," are an express prohibition upon every State of the Union....[51]

This is a most explicit statement of the incorporation thesis by the architect of the Fourteenth Amendment. Although he based the incorporation on the privileges and immunities clause and not the due process clause as did subsequent courts of selective incorporation, Rep. Bingham could hardly have anticipated the judicial metaphysics of the twentieth century in this respect. In any case, whether based on the due process clause or on the privileges and immunities clause, the legislative history supports the view that the incorporation of Amendments I-VII was clear and unmistakable in the minds of the framers of Amendment XIV.

In contrast with the above legal analysis, some comments on the enforcement of the Fourteenth Amendment returned to discussion of power struggle between Republicans and unreconstructed Confederates. While Republicans deplored the armed condition of white Southerners and the unarmed state of black Southerners, Democrats argued that the South's whites were disarmed and endangered by armed carpetbaggers and negro militia. Thus, Rep. Ellis H. Roberts (R., N.Y.) lamented the partisan character of KKK violence: "The victims whose property is destroyed, whose persons are mutilated, whose lives are sacrificed, are always Republicans. They may be black or white...." Of the still rebellious whites: "Their weapons are often new and of improved patterns; and however poor may be the individual member he never lacks for arms or ammunition.... In many respects the Ku Klux Klan is an army, organized and officered, and armed for deadly strife."[52]

Rep. Boyd Winchester (D., Ky.) set forth the contrary position, favorably citing a letter from an ex-governor of South Carolina to the reconstruction governor regretting the latter's "Winchester rifle speech" which "fiendishly proclaimed that this instrument of death, in the hands of the negroes of South Carolina, was the most effective means of maintaining order and quiet in the State."[53] Calling on the governor to "disarm your militia," the letter referred to the disaster which resulted "when you organized colored troops throughout the State, and put arms into their hands, with powder and ball, and denied the same to the white people."[54] The letter proceeded to cite numerous instances where the "colored militia" murdered white people. According to Rep. Winchester, it was the arming of blacks and disarming of whites which resulted in white resistance. "It would seem that wherever military and carpetbagger domination in the South has been marked by the greatest contempt for law and right, and practiced the greatest cruelty toward the people, Ku Klux operations have multiplied."[55]

An instance of black Republican armed resistance to agents of the state who were in the Klan was recounted in a letter cited by Rep. Benjamin F. Butler:

> Then the Ku Klux fired on them through the window, one of the bullets striking a colored woman ... and wounding her through the knee badly. The colored men then fired on the Ku Klux, and killed their leader or captain right there on the steps of the colored men's house.... There he remained until morning when he was identified, and proved to be "Pat Inman," a constable and deputy sheriff....[56]

By contrast, Rep. Samuel S. Cox (D., Ohio) assailed those who "arm negro militia and create a situation of terror," exclaimed that South Carolinians actually clamored for United States troops to save them from the rapacity and murder of the negro bands and their white allies," and saw the Klan as their only defense: "Is not repression the father of revolution?" The congressman compared the Klan with the French Jacobians, Italian Carbonari, and Irish Fenians.[57] Rep. John Coburn (R., Ind.) saw the situation in an opposite empirical light, deploring both state and private disarming of blacks. "How much more oppressive is the passage of a law that they shall not bear arms than the practical seizure of all arms from the hands of the colored men?"[58]

The next day Rep. Henry L. Dawes (R., Mass.) returned to a legal analysis which again asserted the incorporation thesis. Of the anti-Klan bill he argued:

> The rights, privileges, and immunities of the American citizen, secured to him under the Constitution of the United States, are the subject-matter of this bill....
>
> ... In addition to the original rights secured to him in the first article of amendments he had secured the free exercise of his religious belief, and freedom of speech and of the press. Then again he has secured to him the right to keep and bear arms in his defense. [Dawes then summarizes the remainder of the first eight amendments.] ...
>
> ... And still later, sir, after the bloody sacrifice of our four years' war, we gave the most grand of all these rights, privileges, and immunities, by one single amendment to the Constitution, to four millions of American citizens....
>
> ... [I]t is to protect and secure to him in these rights, privileges, and immunities this bill is before the House.[59]

Rep. Horatio C. Burchard (R., Ill.), while generally favoring the bill insofar as it provided against oppressive state action, rejected the interpretation by Dawes and Bingham regarding the definition of "privileges and immunities," which Burchard felt were contained only in Articles IV, V, and VI rather than I-VIII. However, Burchard still spoke in terms of "the application of their eight amendments to the States,"[60] and in any case Dawes had used the terms "*rights,* privileges and immunities." The anti-Klan bill finally was passed along partisan lines as An Act to Enforce the Provisions of the Fourteenth Amendment.[61]

E. THE CIVIL RIGHTS ACT OF 1875

After passage of the anti-Klan bill, discussion concerning arms persisted as interest developed toward what became the Civil Rights Act of 1875, now 42 U.S.C. § 1984. A report on affairs in the South by Sen. John Scott (R., Penn.) indicated the need for further enforcement legislation: "negroes who were whipped testified that those who beat them told them they did so because they had voted the radical ticket, and in many cases made them promise that they would not do so again, and wherever they had guns took them from them."[62]

Following the introduction of the civil rights bill the debate over the meaning of the privileges and immunities clause returned. Sen. Matthew H. Carpenter (R., Wis.) cited *Cummings v. Missouri,*[63] a case contrasting the French legal system, which allowed deprivation of civil rights, "and among these of the right of voting, ... of bearing arms," with the American legal system, averring that the Fourteenth Amendment prevented states from taking away the privileges of the American citizen.[64]

Sen. Allen G. Thurman (D., Ohio) argued that the "rights, privileges, and immunities of a citizen of the United States" were included in Amendments I-VIII. Reading and commenting on each of these amendments, he said of the Second: "Here is another right of a citizen of the United States, expressly declared to be his right—the right to bear arms; and this right, says the Constitution, shall not be infringed." After prodding from John A. Sherman (R., Ohio), Thurman added the Ninth Amendment to the list.[65]

The incorporationist thesis was stated succinctly by Senator Thomas M. Norwood (D., Ga.) in one of the final debates over the civil rights bill. Referring to a U.S. citizen residing in a Territory, Senator Norwood stated:

> His right to bear arms, to freedom of religious opinion, freedom of speech, and all others enumerated in the Constitution would still remain indefeasibly his, whether he remained in the Territory or removed to a State.
>
> And those and certain others are the privileges and immunities which belong to him in common with every citizen of the United States, and which no State can take away or abridge, and they are given and protected by the Constitution ...
>
> The following are most, if not all, the privileges and immunities of a citizen of the *United States:*
>
> The right to writ of *habeas corpus*; of peaceable assembly and of petition; ... to *keep and bear arms*; ... from being deprived of the right to vote on account of race, color or previous condition of servitude.[66]

Arguing that the Fourteenth Amendment created no new rights but declared that "certain existing rights should not be abridged by States," the Georgia Democrat explained:

> Before its [Fourteenth Amendment] adoption any State might have established a particular religion, or restricted freedom of speech and of the press, or *the right to bear arms* ... A State could have deprived its citizens of any of the privileges and immunities contained in those eight articles, but the Federal Government could not ....
>
> ... And the instant the Fourteenth amendment became a part of the Constitution, every State was at that moment disabled from making or enforcing any law which would deprive any citizen of a State of the benefits enjoyed by citizens of the United States under the first eight amendments to the Federal Constitution.[67]

In sum, in the understanding of Southern Democrats and Radical Republicans alike, the right to keep and bear arms, like other Bill of Rights freedoms, was made applicable to the states by the Fourteenth Amendment.

The framers of the Fourteenth Amendment and of the civil rights acts of Reconstruction, rather than predicating the right to keep and bear arms on the needs of an organized state militia, based it on the right of the people individually to possess arms for protection against any oppressive force—including racist or political violence by the militia itself or by other state agents such as sheriffs. At the same time, the militia was understood to be the whole body of the people, including blacks. In discussion concerning the Civil Rights Act of 1875, Sen. James A. Alcorn (R., Miss.) defined the militia in these terms: "The citizens of the United States, the Posse comitatus, or the militia if you please, and the colored man composes part of these."[68] Every citizen, in short, was a militiaman. With the passage of the Fourteenth Amendment, the right and privilege individually to keep and bear arms was protected from both state and federal infringement.[69]

REFERENCES

1.   Dred Scott v. Sanford, 60 U.S. (19 How.) 393 15 L. Ed. 691 (1857).

2.   15 L. Ed. at 705 [Emphasis added]. *And see id.* at 719.

3.   Protection of the "absolute rights of individuals" to personal security, liberty, and private property is secured in part by "the right of bearing arms—which with us is ... practically enjoyed by every citizen, and is among his most valuable privileges, since it furnishes the means of resisting as a freeman ought, the inroads of usurpation." 1 Henry St. Geo. Tucker, Commentaries on the Laws of Virginia 43 (1831) (reference to U.S. Constitution). And see St. Geo. Tucker, 1 Blackstone, Commentaries *144 n.40 (1st ed. 1803); W. Rawle, A View of the Constitution 125-26 (1829); 3 J. Story, Commentaries on the Constitution 746 (1833); Bliss vs. Commonwealth, 2 Litt. (Ky.) 90, 13 Am. Dec. 251 (1822); Simpson vs. State, 13 Tenn. Reports (5 Yerg.) 356 (1833); Nunn v. State, 1 Ga. 243 (1846). Cf. State v. Buzzard, 4 Ark, 18 (1843).

4.   W. Rawle, supra note 3, at 125-26, stated: "The prohibition is general. No clause in the Constitution could by any rule of construction be conceived to give to congress a power to disarm the people. Such a flagitious attempt could only be made under some general pretence by a state legislature. But if in any blind pursuit of inordinate power, either should attempt it, this amendment may be appealed to as a restraint on both."
        Similarly, it was stated in Nunn v. State, 1 Ga. 243, 250-51 (1846):
        "The language of the second amendment is broad enough to embrace both Federal and state governments—nor is there anything in its terms which restricts its meaning.... Is it not an unalienable right, which lies at the bottom of every free government?"
And see cases cited at 68 C.J. Weapons § 4 n.60 (1934).
        According to II J. Bishop, Criminal Law § 124 (3rd ed. 1865): "Though most of the amendments are restrictions on the general government alone, not on the States, this one seems to be of a nature to bind both the State and National legislatures." Approved in English v. State, 35 Tex. 473 (1872). For an analysis of U.S. Supreme Court cases related to whether the Second and/or Fourteenth Amendments prohibit state action which infringes on keeping and bearing arms, see S. Halbrook, The Jurisprudence of the Second and Fourteenth Amendments, IV George Mason L. Rev. (1981).

5.   State v. Newson, 27 N.C. 203, 204 (1844), Cooper v. Savannah, 4 Ga. 72 (1848).

6.   State v. Newson, 27 N.C. 203, 207 (1844). Cf. cases cited at 68 C.J. Weapons § 5, n.19,21,22; § 8, n.37,40 (1934).

7.   "What was the fourteenth article designed to secure? ... [T]hat the privileges and immunities of citizens of the United States shall not be abridged or denied by the United States or by any State; defining also, what it was possible was open to some question after the Dred Scott decision, who were citizens of the United States." Sen. George F. Edmunds (R., Vt.), CONG. GLOBE, 40th Cong., 3rd Sess., pt. 1, 1000 (Feb. 8, 1869).

8.   While it "cannot turn the clock back to 1868 when the Amendment was adopted," *Brown v. Board of Education of Topeka,* 347 U.S. 483, 492 (1954), the Supreme Court is compelled to interpret Amendment XIV and Reconstruction legislation in accord with the Congressional intent. *Lynch v. Household Finance Corp.,* 405 U.S. 538, 549 (1972); *Monell v. Dep't. of Social Servies of City of New York,* 436 U.S. 658 (1978) ("fresh analysis of debate on the Civil Rights Act of 1871," *id.* 665, justified overruling *Monroe v. Pape,* 365 U.S. 167 [1961]). *Cf.* Fairman, Does the Fourteenth Amendment Incorporate the Bill of Rights? The Original Understanding, 2 Stanford L. Rev. 5, 44-45, 57-58, 119-20 (1949) (while contending that the Bill of Rights in general was not intended to apply to the states, cited references to the Second Amendment in congressional debates support incorporation).
        Though beyond the scope of this study, the history of the prohibition of arms possession by native Americans or Indians presents a parallel example of the use of gun control to suppress or exterminate non-white ethnic groups. While legal discrimination against blacks in respect to arms was abolished during Reconstruction, the sale of arms and ammunition to "hostile" Indians remained a prohibition. E.g., 17 stat., 457, 42nd Cong., 3rd Sess., ch. 138 (1873). *See also Sioux Nation of Indians v. United States,* 601 F.2d 1571, 1166 (Ct. Cl. 1979): "Since the Army has taken from the Sioux their weapons and horses, the alternative to capitulation to the government's demands was starvation ..." The federal government's special restrictions on selling firearms to native Americans were abolished finally in 1979. Washington Post, Jan. 6, 1979, § A, at 11, col. 1.

9.   See *State v. Hannibal,* 51 N.C. 57 (1859); *State v. Harris,* 51 N.C. 448 (1859); D. Hundley, Social Relations in our Southern States 361 (1860). Blacks were experienced enough in the use of arms to play a significant, though unofficial, role as Confederate Soldiers, some even as sharpshooters. H. Blackerby, Blacks in Blue and Gray 1-40 (Tusculoosa, Ala. 1979); J. Obatala, Black Confederates, Players 13 ff. (April, 1979). In Louisiana, the only state in the Union to include blacks in the militia, substantial numbers of blacks joined the rebellion furnishing their own arms. M. Berry, *Negro Troops in Blue and Gray,* 8 LOUISIANA HISTORY 165-66 (1867).

10.   The Writings of Cassius Marcellus Clay 257 (H. Greeley ed. 1848).

11.   DuBois, John Brown 106 (1909).

12.   J. McPherson, The Negro's Civil War 72-73 (1965). While all may be fair in love and war, experiences during the conflict suggest that deprivation of one right is coupled with deprivation of others. When the secession movement began, Lincoln suspended habeas corpus and enstated the disarming of citizens and military arrests in Maryland and Missouri. In the latter state, the death penalty was enstated by union officers for those caught with arms, and after an order was issued to arm the militia by random seizures of arms, the searches provided the occasion for general looting. See 3 War of the Rebellion 466-67 (Series 1) and 13 id. at 506; R.

Brownlee, Gray Ghosts of the Confederacy 37, 85, & 170 (L.S.U. 1958). The situation became so harsh for Northerners themselves that the Northern Democratic Platform of 1864 declared in its fourth resolution against the suppression of free speech and press and the denial of the right of the people to bear arms in their defense. E. Pollard, The Lost Cause 574 (1867).

13.   61 The War of the Rebellion, ser. 1, pt. 2, 1068 & 1315 (1880-1901); R. Durden, The Gray & The Black 250 (1972).

14.   R. Durden, supra note 13, at 169.

15.   Cong. Globe, 38th Cong., 2nd Sess., pt. 1, 171 (Jan. 9, 1865).

16.   Id. 289 (Jan. 18, 1865).

17.   Id., 39th Cong., 1st Sess., pt. 1, 674 (Feb. 6, 1866). But see id. at pt. 4, 3215 (June 16, 1866) (allegation by Rep. William E. Niblack (D., Ind.) that the majority of Southern blacks "either adhered from first to last to the rebellion or aided and assisted by their labor or otherwise those who did so adhere.").

18.   DuBois, Black Reconstruction In America 167, 172, & 223 (New York 1962).

19.   Cong. Globe, 39th Cong., 1st Sess., pt. 1, 40 (Dec. 13, 1865).

20.   Civil Rights Act, 14 Stat. 27 (1866). A portion of this act survives as 42 U.S.C. § 1982: "All citizens of the United States shall have the same right in every State and Territory as is enjoyed by white citizens thereof to inherit, purchase, lease, sell, hold, and convey real and personal property."

21.   Cong. Globe, 39th Cong., 1st Sess., pt. 1, 474 (Jan. 29, 1866).

22.   Id. 478.

23.   Id. 517 (Jan. 30, 1866).

24.   Id. 651 (Feb. 5, 1866).

25.   Id. 941 (Feb. 20, 1866).

26.   Id.

27.   Id., pt. 2, 1266 (Mar. 8, 1866).

28.   Id. 1629 (Mar. 24, 1866).

29.   Id. 3.

30.   Id. 1838 (Apr. 7, 1866).

31.   Id.

32.   Id.

33.   Id.

34.   Id. 1839. Ironically, Clarke's home state, Kansas, adopted measures to prohibit former Confederates from possessing arms. Kennett & Anderson at 154.

35.   Cong. Globe, 39th Cong., 1st Sess., pt. 3, 2765 (May 23, 1866).

36.   Id. 2766. Italics added.

37.   Id., pt. 4, 3210 (June 16, 1866).

38.   Id., 2nd Sess., pt. 1, 107 (Dec. 13, 1866).

39.   Id., 40th Cong., 2nd Sess. pt. 3, 2198 (Mar. 28, 1868).

40.   Id.

41.   1464 H.R. REP. No. 37, 41st Cong., 3rd Sess. 3 (Feb. 20, 1871).

42.   Cong. Globe, 42nd Cong., 1st Sess., pt. 1, 174 (Mar. 20, 1871). Introduced as "an act to protect loyal and peaceable citizens in the south ...", H.R. No. 189.

43.   H.R. Rep. No. 37, supra note 26, at 7-8.

44.   Cong. Globe, 42nd Cong., 1st Sess., pt. 1, 154 (Mar. 18, 1871).

45.   Id. 196 (Mar. 21, 1871).

46.   Id. 321 (Mar. 28, 1871).

47.   Id., pt. 2, Appendix, 68. Passed as the Enforcement Act, 17 Stat. 13 (1871), § 1 survives as 42 U.S.C. § 1983: "Every person who, under color of any statute, ordinance, regulation, custom, or usage, of any State or Territory, subjects, or causes to be subjected, any citizen of the United States or other person within the jurisdiction thereof to the deprivation of any rights, privileges, or immunities secured by the Constitution and laws, shall be liable to the party injured in an action at law, suit in equity, or other proper proceedings for redress." The action for conspiracy to deprive persons of rights or privileges under 42 U.S.C. § 1985 derives from the same act.

48.   Cong. Globe, 42nd Cong., 1st Sess., pt. 1, 337 (Mar. 29, 1871).

49.   Id. 339.

50.   Id. 385 (Apr. 1, 1871).

51.   Id., pt. 2, Appendix, 84 (Mar. 31, 1871).

52.   Id., pt. 1, 413 (Apr. 3, 1871).

53.   Id. 442 (Apr. 3, 1871).

54.   Id.

55.   Id. Nathan Bedford Forrest told Congressional investigators in 1871 that the Klan originated in Tennessee for self defense against the militia of Governor William G. Brownlow. N. Burger and J. Bettersworth, South of Appomattox 129, 132, and 137 (1959). Still, two years before, Forrest denounced Klan lawlessness because "the order was being used ... to disarm harmless negroes having no thought of insurrectionary movements, and to whip both whites and blacks." C. Bowers, THE TRAGIC ERA 311 (1929). The outrages in turn allegedly furnished "a plausible pretext for the organization of State militias to serve the purposes of Radical politics." C. Bowers at 311. Carpetbagger controlled militias were deeply involved in political violence to influence elections, and were blamed for infringing on their opponents' constitutional rights to free speech and to keep and bear arms, among numerous other abuses. E.g., C. Bowers at 439 and passim; O. Singletary, Negro Militia and Reconstruction 35-41, 74-75 (1963).

56.   Cong. Globe, 42nd Cong., 1st Sess., pt. 1, 445 (Apr. 4, 1871).

57.   Id. 453.

58.   Id. 459.

59.   *Id.* 475-76 (Apr. 5, 1871). [Emphasis added].

60.   Id., 2, Appendix, 314.

61.   17 Stat. 13, 42nd Cong., 1st Sess., ch. 22 (1871).

62.   1484 S. Rep. No. 41, 42nd Cong., 2nd Sess., pt. 1, 35 (Feb. 19, 1872).

63.   *Cummings v. Missouri*, 71 U.S. 277, 321 (1866).

64.   Cong. Globe, 42nd Cong., 2nd Sess., pt. 1, 762 (Feb. 1, 1872).

65.   *Id.*, pt. 6, Appendix, 25-26 (Feb. 6, 1872). On Amendment IX as a source of an individual right to keep and bear arms, *see* Caplan, *Restoring the Balance: The Second Amendment Revisited*, 5 Fordham Urban L.J. 31, 49-50 (1976). See also 2 Cong. Rec. 43rd Cong., 1st Sess., pt. 1, 384-385 (Jan. 5, 1874) (statement by Rep. Robert Q. Mills (D., Tex.) that Amendment XIV adopts Bill of Rights privileges).

66.   Cong. Rec., 43rd Cong., 1st Sess., pt. 6, Appendix, 241-242 (May 4, 1874). Emphasis added.

67.   *Id.* 242. Italic added.

68.   *Id.* (May 22, 1874). The antebellum exclusion of blacks from the armed people as militia was commented on by Sen. George Vickers (D., Md.), who recalled a 1792 law passed by Congress: "That every free able-bodied white male citizen shall be enrolled in the militia." Vickers added that as late as 1855 New Hampshire "confined the enrollment of militia to free white citizens." Cong. Globe, 41st Cong., 2nd Sess., pt. 2, 1558-59 (Feb. 25, 1870). Exclusion of a right to bear arms by blacks was further evidence of their lack of status as citizens. See 1464 H.R. Rep. No. 22, 41st Cong., 3rd Sess. 7 (Feb. 1, 1871), citing Cooper v. Savannah, 4 Ga. 72 (1848) (not entitled to bear arms or vote).

69.   While unrelated to the debates over the Fourteenth Amendment, congressional deliberation over whether the federal government could abolish militias in the Southern states also gave rise to exposition of the Second Amendment. In support of repeal of a statute prohibiting the Southern militias, Sen. Charles R. Backalew (D., Penn.) pointed out that the U.S. President favored repeal of the statute because at all times, both when it was placed upon the statute-book and every moment since, it was and is in his judgement a violation of the Constitution of the United States. One of the amendments to our fundamental law expressly provides that "the right of the people to keep and bear arms shall not be infringed"—of course by this Government; and it gives the reason that a well-regulated militia in the several divisions of the country is necessary for the protection and for the interests of the people. Cong. Globe, 40th Cong., 3rd Sess., pt. 1, 83-84.

     George F. Edmunds (R., Vt.) worried that repeal of the statute "will authorize anybody and everybody in the State of Texas, under what they call its ancient militia laws ... to organize a militia hostile to the Government," id. at 81, and thus advocated "a selected militia" chosen by State and federal governments. Id. In contrast, Garrett Davis (D. Ky.) stated: "Wherever a State organizes a government it has of its own inherent right and power authority to organize a militia for it. Congress ... has no right to prohibit that State from the organization of its militia." *Id.* at 84. Willard Warner (R., Ala.) stressed the first clause of the Second Amendment to form militias independent of federal control: we have the right now, being restored to our full relations to the Federal Government, to organize a militia of our own, and that we could have done so at any time in the past, this law to the contrary notwithstanding. Article two of the amendments of the Constitution provides that—

> "A well regulated militia being necessary to the security of a free State, the right of the people to keep and bear arms shall not be infringed." *Id.* at 85.

The prohibitionary statute was repealed, *id.* at 86. *Cf.* Houston v. Moore, 18 U.S. 1, 16-17 (1820).

     Thus, while debates over the militia question suggested that the Second Amendment precluded federal legislation which prohibited the states or the people from forming militias, debates over the Fourteenth Amendment demonstrate the intent of Congress to preclude state militias or other state action from infringing on the individual right to keep and bear arms.

[Originally published as Report of the Subcommittee on the Constitution of the Committee on the Judiciary, United States Senate, 97th Cong., 2d Sess., The Right to Keep and Bear Arms, 83-109 (1982) ("Other Views"). Reproduced in the 1982 Senate Report, pg. 83-109.]

THE SECOND AMENDMENT TO THE UNITED STATES CONSTITUTION GUARANTEES AN INDIVIDUAL RIGHT TO KEEP AND BEAR ARMS

(By James J. Featherstone, Esquire, General Counsel, National Rifle Association of America and Richard E. Gardiner, Esquire, Robert Dowlut, Esquire, Office of the General Counsel)

A well regulated Militia, being necessary to the security of a free State, the right of the people to keep and bear Arms, shall not be infringed.

The values of the Framers of the Constitution must be applied in any case construing the Constitution. Inferences from the text and history of the Constitution should be given great weight in discerning the original understanding and in determining the intentions of those who ratified the Constitution. The precedential value of cases and commentators tends to increase, therefore, in proportion to their proximity to the adoption of the Constitution, the Bill of Rights or any other amendments. *Powell v. McCormack*, 395 U.S. 486, 547 (1969).

A. COMMON LAW DEVELOPMENT OF THE RIGHT TO KEEP AND BEAR ARMS

The right to keep and bear arms was not created by the Second Amendment; rather, this basic individual right, developed in England before this continent was colonized, pre-dated the constitution and was part of the common law heritage of the thirteen original colonies.

Sir William Blackstone, an authoritative source of the common law for colonists and, therefore, a dominant influence on the drafters of the original Constitution and its Bill of Rights, set forth in his Commentaries the absolute rights of individuals as: personal security, personal liberty, and possession of private property, I *Blackstone Commentaries* 129, these absolute rights being protected by the individual's right to have and use arms for self-preservation and defense. As Blackstone observed, individual citizens were therefore entitled to exercise their "natural right of resistance and self-preservation, when the sanctions of society and laws are found insufficient to restrain the violence of oppression." *Id.* at 144.[1] Clearly evident in this statement is Blackstone's recognition that the exercise of an individual's absolute rights could be imperiled by a standing army as well as by private individuals, a view supported by his observation that "Nothing ... ought to be more guarded against in a free state than making the military power ... a body too distinct from the people." *Id.* at 414. To prevent such an occurrence, Blackstone not only believed in the individual's right to have and use arms, but further believed that for its defense a nation should rely not on a standing army, but the citizen soldier. Plainly, for such a concept to be a reality, it was necessary that all able-bodied males possess and be capable of using arms.

Blackstone was not alone in his view that the common law recognized the individual's right to possess arms: in his Pleas of the   Crown, Hawkins noted that "every private person seems to be authorized by the Law to arm himself for [various] purposes." 1 William Hawkins, *Pleas of the Crown*, ch. 28, Section 14, p. 171 (7th ed. 1795). In agreement with Blackstone was Sir Edward Coke who wrote that "the laws permit the taking up of arms against armed persons," 2 E. Coke Institutes of the Laws of England, 574 (Johnson & Warner, ed. 1812).

It was within this legal tradition of the individual's right to have and use arms for his own defense and self-preservation as well as to enable him to contribute to the common defense, that the spark which ignited the American Revolution was struck. The British, by attempting to seize large stores of powder and shot, sought to deny the Massachusetts colonists the ability to protect their absolute rights. The colonists retaliated by exercising their common law right to keep and bear arms, using the very arms which the British wished to render ineffective.[2] It is beyond question that prior to the Second amendment the common law recognized a fundamental individual right to keep and bear arms, subject only to a certain limited police power to regulate the bearing of arms so as not to terrify the good people of the land. 4 Blackstone Commentaries 149.

B. THE HISTORY OF THE SECOND AMENDMENT

The Second amendment to the United States Constitution provides:

> A well regulated Militia, being necessary to the security of a free State, the right of the people to keep and bear Arms shall not be infringed.

The history of the Second Amendment indicates that its purposes were to secure to each individual the right to keep and bear arms so that he could protect his absolute individual rights as well as carry out his obligation to assist in the common defense. It is evident that the framers of the Constitution did not intend to limit the right to keep and bear arms to a formal military body or organized militia, but intended to provide for an "unorganized" armed citizenry prepared to assist in the common defense against a foreign invader or a domestic tyrant. This concept of an unorganized, armed citizenry clearly recognized the right, and moreover the duty, to keep and bear arms in an individual capacity.

One of the gravest decisions faced by the Framers of the Constitution was whether the federal government should be permitted to maintain a standing army. Because of their personal experiences in and prior to the Revolution, the Framers of the Constitution realized that although useful for national defense, a standing army was particularly inimical to the continued safe existence of those absolute rights recognized by Blackstone and generally inimical to personal freedom and liberty.

Unwilling, however, to forego completely the national defense benefits of a standing army, the Framers developed a compromise position. The federal government was granted the authority to "raise and support" an army, subject to the restrictions that no appropriation of money for the army would be for more than two years and civilian control over the army would be maintained. U.S. Constitution. Article I, Section 8, Clause 12. Furthermore, knowing that the militiaman or citizen soldier had made possible the success of the American Revolution for Independence,[3] the Framers recognized that a militia would provide the final bulwark against both domestic tyranny and foreign invasion. Congress, however, was given only limited authority over the militia; it could "govern ... [only] such part of the [the militia] as may be employed in the Service of the United States ...," leaving to the states "the Appointment of the Officers, and the Authority of training the Militia ..." (emphasis added) U.S. Constitution, Article I, Section 8, Clause 16.

It is evident from the underscored language of Clause 16 that, in addition to that part of the militia over which the Constitution granted Congress authority, there exists a residual, unorganized militia that is not subject to congressional control. The United States Code, in Title 10, Section 311, continues to recognize the distinction between the organized and unorganized militia:

(a) The militia of the United States consists of all able-bodied males at least 17 years of age and, except as provided in section 313 of title 32, under 45 years of age who are, or who have made a declaration of intention to become, citizens of the United States and of female citizens of the United States who are commissioned officers of the National Guard.

(b) The classes of the militia are: (1) The organized militia, which consists of the National Guard and the Naval Militia; and (2) The unorganized militia which consists of the members of the militia who are not members of the National Guard or the Naval Militia.

This distinction, recognized by the Framers in the Constitution, was first codified in the Militia Act of 1792, which defined both an "organized" militia, and an "enrolled" militia.[4] The unorganized or enrolled militia were not actually in service, but were nonetheless available to assist in the common defense should conditions necessitate either support of the organized militia or possibly defense against internal oppression. As fully explained later, the members of the unorganized militia were expected to be familiar with the use of firearms and to appear bearing their own arms. Obviously, they could be so prepared only if all individuals were guaranteed the right to keep and bear arms.

In his comments on the rights protected by the Constitution, a leading constitutional commentator, in discussing the right protected by the Second Amendment, wrote:

The Right is General. It may be supposed from the phraseology of this provision that the right to keep and bear arms was only guaranteed to the militia; but this would be an interpretation not warranted by the intent. The militia, as has been elsewhere explained, consists of those persons who, under the law, are liable to the performance of military duty, and are officered and enrolled for service when called upon. But the law may make provision for the enrollment of all who are fit to perform military duty, or of a small number only, or it may wholly omit to make any provision at all; and if the right were limited to those enrolled, the purpose of this guarantee might be defeated altogether by the action or neglect to act of the government it was meant to hold in check. *The meaning of the provision undoubtedly is, that the people, from whom the militia must be taken, shall have the right to keep and bear arms, and they need no permission or regulation of law for the purpose.* But this enables the government to have a well regulated militia; for to bear arms implies something more than the mere keeping; it implies the learning to handle and use them in a way that makes those who keep them ready for their efficient use; in other words, it implies a right to meet for voluntary discipline in arms, observing in doing so the laws of public order. (Emphasis added.) Thomas M. Cooley, LL.D., General Principles of Constitutional Law in the United States of America, 298-299 (3rd ed. 1898).

When the Constitution was sent to the states for ratification, several states, chief among them Virginia, were concerned that in spite of the restrictions written into the main body of the Constitution, a federal standing army might still threaten the hard-won liberties of the people. In Federalist No. 46, written prior to the ratification of the Constitution, James Madison discussed how a federal standing army, which he estimated in 1788 would consist of "one twenty-fifth part of the number able to bear arms," might be checked or controlled:

> To these [the standing army troops] would be opposed a militia amounting to near half a million of citizens with arms in their hands, officered by men chosen from among themselves, fighting for their common liberties, and united and conducted by [state] governments possessing their affections and confidence. It may well be doubted whether a militia thus circumstanced could ever be conquered by such a proportion of regular troops. Those who are best acquainted with the late successful resistance of this country against the British Arms will be most inclined to deny the possibility of it. *Besides the advantage of being armed, which the Americans possess over the people of almost every other nation.* The existence of subordinate governments to which the people are attached, and by which the militia officers are appointed, forms a barrier against the enterprises of ambition, more insurmountable than any which a simple government of any form can admit of. Notwithstanding the military establishments in the several kingdoms of Europe, ... the governments [of Europe] are afraid to trust the people with arms. (Emphasis added.)

Alexander Hamilton, too, although more favorably inclined toward a strong central government, feared the detrimental effects on individual liberty that might result from the existence of a federal standing army. He explained in Federalist No. 29 how, under the proposed constitution, a federal standing army could be avoided or at least restrained:

> The attention of the government ought particularly to be directed to the formation of a select corps of moderate size upon such principles as will really fit it for service in case of need. By thus circumscribing the plan it will be possible to have an excellent body of well trained militia ready to take the field whenever the defense of the State shall require it. This will not only lessen the call for military establishments; but if circumstances should at any time oblige the government to form an army of any magnitude, that army can never be formidable to the liberties of the people, while there is a large body of citizens little if at all inferior to them in discipline and the use of arms, who stand ready to defend their rights and those of their fellow citizens. This appears to me the only substitute that can be devised for a standing army; the best possible security against it if it should exist.

Hamilton evidently felt that the militia composed of the body of the people would provide a deterrent to a federal standing army or the organized militia, only because the people had the right to keep and bear arms. The states, however, wanted this right to be guaranteed explicitly. A number of them, therefore, proposed amending the Constitution to guarantee an individual right to keep and bear arms.

Consonant with the request of the states, the Congress proposed twelve amendments to the Constitution, one of which concerned the right to keep and bear arms.[5] In its original form, as proposed by James Madison of Virginia, the Second Amendment (the fourth proposed amendment) read:

The right of the people to keep and bear arms shall not be infringed; a well-armed and well-regulated militia being the best security of a free country; but no person religiously scrupulous of bearing arms shall be compelled to render military service in person.

Congressman Elbridge Gerry of Massachusetts opposed the amendment in this form because the provision exempting persons with religious scruples from bearing arms might be used by the federal government arbitrarily to declare an individual religiously scrupulous, thereby denying him the right to bear arms. Gerry offered an amendment modifying the religious exemption to apply only to religious sects and not to individuals. In the course of the floor debate, Gerry discussed the Second Amendment and the purpose of the militia:

> This declaration of rights, I take it, is intended to secure the people against the maladministration of the Government, if we could suppose that, in all cases, the rights of the people would be attended to, the occasion for guards of this kind would be removed. Now, I am apprehensive, sir, that this clause would give an opportunity to the people in power to destroy the Constitution itself. They can declare who are those religiously scrupulous, and prevent them from bearing arms.
>
> What, sir, is the use of a militia? It is to prevent the establishment of a standing army, the bane of liberty. Now, it must be evident that, under this provision, together with their other powers, Congress could take such measures with respect to a militia, as to make a standing army necessary. Whenever Governments mean to invade the rights and liberties of the people, they always attempt to destroy the militia, in order to raise an army upon their ruins. This was done actually by Great Britain at the commencement of the late Revolution. They used every means in their power to prevent the establishment of an effective militia to the Eastward. The Assembly of Massachusetts, seeing the rapid progress that administration were making to devest them of their inherent privileges, endeavored to counteract them by the organization of a militia; but they were always defeated by the influence of the Crown. [Interruption.]
>
> No attempts they made were successful, until they engaged in the struggle which emancipated them at once from their thraldom. Now, if we give a discretionary power to exclude those from militia duty who have religious scruples, we may as well make no provision on this head. For this reason, [I wish] the words to be altered so as to be confined to persons belonging to a religious sect scrupulous of bearing arms. 1 Annals of Congress 749-750 (August 17, 1789).

Gerry plainly understood in making his proposal that one purpose of the amendment was to ensure the existence of the militia composed of the body of the people since the organized militia was subject to federal service; therefore it was necessary to protect the right of all people, that is, each individual, to keep and bear arms.[6] Gerry recognized that only if all individuals, those whose liberties were to be protected, were capable of using arms, could the militia truly serve as the final bulwark against a foreign invader or domestic tyrant. Following Gerry's discussion, the proposed amendment was revised to eliminate any reference to a religious exemption from keeping and bearing arms.

Supporting Gerry's view that the Second Amendment protected an individual right is that the Senate, while also considering the proposed amendments, soundly rejected a proposal to insert the phrase "for the common defense" after the words "bear arms," (1 History of the Supreme Court of the United States, 450 (J. Goebel, Jr. ed. 1971), 2 B. Schwartz, The Bill of Rights: A Documentary History 1153-54 (1971)), thereby emphasizing that the purpose of the Second Amendment was not merely to provide for the common defense, but also to protect the individual's right to keep and bear arms for his own defense and self-preservation.

Not removed from the originally proposed version, however, was the term "well-regulated." Contrary to modern usage, wherein "regulated" is generally understood to mean "controlled" or "governed by rule", in its obsolete form pertaining to troops, "regulated" is defined as "properly disciplined." II Compact Edition, Oxford English Dictionary 2473 (1971). In the Oxford English Dictionary, moreover, the verb "discipline," in its earlier usage, is defined as   "to instruct, educate, train." I Compact Edition, Oxford English Dictionary 741 (1971). Furthermore, as a noun, "discipline," which is etymologically "concerned ... with practice or exercises," refers to a field of "learning or knowledge" or the "training effect of experience" that, in relation to arms, is defined as "training in the practice of arms ..." Ibid. Plainly then, by using the term "well-regulated," the Framers had in mind not only the individual ownership and possession of firearms but also the voluntary undertaking of practice and training with such firearms so that each person could become experienced with and competent in the use of firearms and thereby be prepared, should the need arise, to carry out his militia obligation. This conclusion is in complete accord with the comment of Thomas M. Cooley, supra, p. 7.

Consistent with this view is a plan drafted by George Mason, the Framer of the Virginia Declaration of Rights and one of the Framers of the Constitution for the inhabitants of Fairfax County, Virginia, in February, 1775, whereby "all the able-bodied Freemen from eighteen to fifty Years of Age" were to "embody [them]selves into a Militia for th[e] County." I Papers of George Mason 215 (U. of N.C. Press, 1970). They did so because they were "thoroughly convinced that a well-regulated militia, composed of the Gentlemen, Freeholders, and other Freemen, is the natural Strength and only safe & stable security of a free Government, & that such Militia will relieve our Mother Country from any Expense in our Protection and Defense, will obviate the Pretence of a necessity for taxing us on that account, and render it unnecessary to keep any standing Army (ever dangerous to liberty) in this Colony ..." Ibid.

Thus, each subscriber agreed, "... we do Each of us, for ourselves respectively, promise and engage to *keep* a good Firelock in proper Order, & to furnish Ourselves as soon as possible with, & *always keep by us*, one Pound of Gunpowder, four Pounds of Lead, one Dozen Gun-Flints, & a pair of Bullet-Moulds, with a Cartouch Box, or powder-horn, and Bag for Balls. That we will use our best Endeavours to perfect ourselves in the Military Exercise & Discipine ..." (Emphasis added.) Id. at 216.

Finally, the state ratifying conventions provide an excellent insight into the perception of the Framers that the Second Amendment guaranteed to each individual the right to keep and bear arms.

In New Hampshire the ratifying convention advanced a proposal which provided that "Congress shall never disarm *any citizen* unless such as are or have been in Actual Rebellion." (Emphasis added.) Debates in the Federal Convention of 1787 as Reported by James Madison, 658 (Hunt & Scott ed. 1920).

Pennsylvania proposed a provision stating that "the people have the right to bear arms for the defense of themselves, their state, or the United States, and for killing game, and no law shall be enacted for disarming the people except for crimes committed or in a case of real danger of public injury from *individuals* ... " (Emphasis added.) E. Dumbauld, *The Bill of Rights and What It Means Today* 12 (1957).

And in Massachusetts, Samuel Adams proposed an amendment requiring that the "Constitution be never construed to authorize Congress to ... prevent the people of the United States, who are   peaceable *citizens* from keeping their *own* arms." (Emphasis added.) Pierce & Hale, Debates of the Massachusetts Convention of 1788 86-87.

The significance of the foregoing history is that the joining of "a well regulated militia" with "the right to keep and bear arms" was a natural and logical result of the experience of the men who had led the Revolution. Only if individuals had the right to keep and bear arms could the people provide for their own defense and self-preservation as well as in their capacity as members of the militia, provide for the common defense from a foreign invader or as a check against the internal usurpation of liberty by a standing army of the central government.

The Bill of Rights must be read in conjunction with the Constitution as an integrated whole. The seven articles comprising the main body of the Constitution establish a form of government and grant that government certain powers to effectuate governance of the United States. The first ten amendments, however, recognize the possibility of abuses against individuals by the government the Constitution established; thus, certain individual rights are guaranteed and protected. The fact that one of those protected and guaranteed rights, the right to keep and bear arms, is joined with language expressing one of its purposes or goals, in no way permits a construction which limits or confines the exercise of that right. To hold otherwise is to violate the principle that the guarantees and protections of the Bill of Rights must be interpreted to give liberty the broadest possible scope and further to turn a blind eye toward the common law and history of the adoption of the Second Amendment. The Supreme Court of Oregon recently recognized this principle by stating:

> We are not unmindful that there is current controversy over the wisdom of a right to bear arms, and that the original motivations for such provision might not seem compelling if debated as a new issue. Our task, however, in construing a constitutional provision, is to respect the principles given the status of constitutional guarantees and limitations by the drafters; it is not to abandon these principles when this fits the needs of the moment.

State v. Kessler, 289 Or. 359, 614 P.2d 94, 95 (1980).

C. JUDICIAL INTERPRETATION

A conclusion that the Second Amendment does not guarantee an individual right is not supported by *United States v. Miller*, 307 U.S. 174 (1939), or other cases which the Supreme Court and other courts have considered.

In *United States v. Cruikshank*, 92 U.S. 542 (1876), the first case in which the Supreme Court had the opportunity to interpret the Second Amendment, the court recognized that the right of the people to keep and bear arms existed prior to the Constitution by stating that such a right "is not a right granted by the Constitution ... [n]either is it in any manner dependent upon that instrument for its existence." 92 U.S. at 552. The indictment charged, inter alia, a conspiracy by Klansmen to prevent and hinder blacks from exercising their civil rights, including the bearing of arms for lawful purposes. The Court held, however, that the Second Amendment guaranteed that the right to keep and bear arms shall not be infringed by Congress and hence did not apply to the instant case since the violation alleged was by fellow-citizens, not the federal government.

In *Presser v. State of Illinois*, 116 U.S. 252 (1886), although the Supreme Court affirmed the holding in *Cruikshank*, i.e. that the Second Amendment applied only to action by the federal government, it apparently found the states without power to infringe upon the right to keep and bear arms, stating at 265:

> It is undoubtedly true that all citizens capable of bearing arms constitute the reserved military force or reserve militia of the United States as well as of the States, and in view of this prerogative of the general government, as well as of its general powers, *the States cannot, even laying the constitutional provision in question out of view, prohibit the people from keeping and bearing arms, so as to deprive the United States of their rightful resource for maintaining the public security and disable the people from performing their duty to the general government.* (Emphasis added.)

The idea of the armed people maintaining "public security" mentioned in this passage from *Presser*, was based on the common law concept that loyal individuals had the right and duty to resist malefactors and the disloyal, such as robbers and burglars, and to use deadly force, if necessary, to do so. The Second Amendment thus also contemplates the right of the people to keep and bear arms so as to be continuously able to maintain the "security of a free State" by aiding in the enforcement of criminal laws such as by making citizens' arrests and aiding peace officers in arresting malefactors. Joyce Lee Malcolm, Disarmed: The Loss of the Right to Bear Arms in Restoration England, p. 5 (Cambridge: The Mary Ingraham Bunting Institute of Radcliffe College, 1980). *Rex v. Compton*, 22 Liber Assisarum (Book of Assizes 1347) placitum 55, trans. in J.H. Beale, Jr., A Selection of Cases and other Authorities Upon Criminal Law, p. 501 (2d ed. 1907). E. Coke Institutes of the Laws of England at 56 (1648). Bohlen and Shulman, Arrest With and Without A Warrant, 75 U.Pa.L.Rev. 485, 497 (1927).

In *United States v. Miller*, supra, decided in 1939, the only case in which the Supreme Court has had the opportunity to apply the Second Amendment to a federal firearms statute, the Court carefully avoided making an unconditional finding of the statute's constitutionality; it instead devised a standard by which federal statutes relating to firearms are to be judged. The holding of the Court in *Miller*, however, should be viewed as only a partial guide to the meaning of the Second Amendment[7] primarily because neither defense counsel nor defendants appeared before the Supreme Court, nor was any brief filed on their behalf giving the Court the benefit of argument supporting the trial court's holding that Section 11 of the National Firearms Act was unconstitutional. As a result of the absence of the normal adversarial process, the Court was presented with only the prosecution's view of the Second Amendment, a view which, needless to say, was in favor of the constitutionality of Section 11 of the National Firearms Act. In   spite of this severe and critical limitation on its decision-making process, the Court's decision in some degree took account of the common law view of the right to keep and bear arms as well as the historical background of the Second Amendment.

The heart of the Court's ruling is found at the beginning of the opinion; it states:

> *In the absence of any evidence* tending to show that possession or use of a "shotgun having a barrell of less than eighteen inches in length" at this time has some reasonable relationship to the preservation or efficiency of a well regulated militia, we cannot say that the Second Amendment guarantees the right to keep and bear such

an instrument. Certainly it is not within judicial notice that this weapon is any part of the ordinary military equipment or that its use could contribute to the common defense. (Emphasis added.) 307 U.S. at 178.

Two independent thoughts are expressed here: one, that for the keeping and bearing of a firearm to be constitutionally protected, that firearm's possession or use must have some reasonable relationship to the preservation of a well regulated militia; and two, that in this case, the Court would not take judicial notice that a short-barrelled shotgun met such a test. It remanded the case to the trial court for the taking of evidence on that question.[8] The Court's first point, that the right to keep and bear an arm is dependent on the firearm's military value, is faulty, however, because the Court failed to consider fully the common law (see section B above), and misinterpreted cited authorities. Rather, the Court only briefly discussed the common law and, moreover, did not consider the history of the adoption of the Second Amendment, both of which support the proposition that the Second Amendment guarantees and protects a fundamental individual right. As to the misinterpretation of cited authorities, a result undoubtedly of the one-sided argument, one important example should suffice.

In support of its position that the Second Amendment's protection and guarantee was limited to "ordinary military equipment" or weapons whose use "could contribute to the common defense," the Court cited one case, *Aymette v. State*, 21 Tenn. 154 2 Humph. 154 (1840). In *Aymette*, however, the Tennessee Supreme Court was construing not the Second Amendment but the provision of Tennessee's constitution guaranteeing the right to keep and bear arms, a provision which, unlike the Second Amendment, spoke of each citizen's right to keep and bear arms only as it related to the common defense. The Tennessee court thus reasoned that not all objects which could conceivably be used as weapons were protected by the Tennessee Constitution, but only those weapons "such as usually employed in civilized warfare." Id. at 158. This limitation is not, however, applicable to the Second Amendment since the First Congress, while debating what ultimately became the Second Amendment, emphatically rejected the "common defense" language upon which the *Aymette* decision turned. It is plain, therefore, that the interpretation of the Second Amendment in *Miller* is more limited than it should be and that the Second Amendment protects the keeping and bearing of all types of arms which could   be carried by individuals. Moreover, the rejection of the "common defense" limitation signified the Framers' intention that the constitutional guarantee of the right to keep and bear arms was not inextricably tied to a militia nexus, but existed independently of it. Even accepting, however, that a militia or common defense nexus was necessary, *Aymette* went on to say that, "The citizens have an unqualified right to keep the weapon." Id. at 160.

One other comment should be made about *Aymette*. What Judge Green was discussing when he said that the legislature could pass laws concerning arms was that laws could be enacted which would punish the misuse of such arms. As an example, Judge Green noted that the legislature could punish a set of ruffians for entering a theatre or a church with drawn swords, guns, and fixed bayonets to the terror of the audience; he went on to observe, moreover, that "the citizens have an unqualified right to keep the weapon" and to bear it except to "terrify the people, or for purposes of private assassination." Id. at 160.

One of the chief values of the *Miller* opinion is its discussion of the development and structure of the militia which, the Court pointed out, consisted of "all males physically capable of acting in concert for the common defense" and that "when called for service these men were expected to appear bearing arms *supplied by themselves* and of the kind in common use at the time." (Emphasis added.) 307 U.S. at 179. The other significant value of *Miller* is its implicit rejection of the view that the Second Amendment guarantees the right to keep and bear arms only to those individuals who are members of the militia. Had the Court reviewed the Second Amendment as guaranteeing the right to keep and bear arms only to "all males physically capable of acting in concert for the common defense" it would certainly have discussed whether Miller met the qualifications for inclusion in the militia as it did with regard to the military value of a short-barrelled shotgun. That it did not signifies the Court's acceptance of the fact that the right to keep and bear arms is guaranteed to each individual without regard to his relationship with the militia.

The *Miller* Court examined in detail, at pages 179-182, not only the duty to assist in the common defense but indeed the legal obligation each individual then had to possess the arms necessary to undertake that common defense. For example, in Massachusetts there were laws which levied fines and penalties against adult males who failed to possess arms and ammunition. In Virginia and New York all males of certain ages were required to own and possess their own firearms at their own expense, and to appear bearing said arms when so notified.

It is clear that *Miller*, for all its shortcomings and limitations, supports the view that the Second Amendment protects and guarantees a fundamental individual right to keep and bear arms, subject to the restriction that only a certain category or categories of arms may, of right, be individually owned and possessed, i.e. those arms whose possession or use are reasonably related to the preservation or efficiency of the militia. As aptly put by Mr. Justice Black, in discussing *Miller* and the Second Amendment, "although the Supreme Court has held this amendment to include only arms necessary to a well-regulated militia, as so construed its   prohibition is absolute." Black, The Bill of Rights, 35 N.Y.U.L. Rev. 865, 873 (1960).[9]

In *United States v. Tot*, 131 F.2d 261 (3rd Cir. 1942), the Third Circuit cited *Miller* in upholding the conviction under the Federal Firearms Act of a felon for possessing a pistol which had traveled in interstate commerce.[10]

The Third Circuit did not deny that individuals have the right to keep and bear arms; it merely stated, in dicta, its view that the Second Amendment was adopted as a protection for the states in the maintenance of their militia organizations against possible encroachments by the federal power. The heart of the Third Circuit's holding is that it was entirely reasonable for Congress to prohibit the receipt of weapons from interstate transactions by persons who have previously by due process of law been shown to be aggressors against society and that this classification did not infringe upon the preservation of the well-regulated militia protected by the Second Amendment.

The Court could have gone on to point out that the maintenance of the militias of the states is dependent upon the right of individuals, who may be called upon to serve in the militias, to keep and bear arms.

In *Cases v. United States*, 131 F.2d 916 (1st Cir. 1942), the First Circuit upheld the constitutionality of the Federal Firearms Act of 1938. In so doing it observed that apparently under *Miller* although the federal government could *limit* the keeping and bearing of arms by a certain type of individual, it could not

> ... *prohibit* the possession or use of any weapon which has any reasonable relationship to the preservation or efficiency of a well regulated militia. (emphasis added) 131 F.2d at 922,

a distinction arising from *Miller*'s holding that the protections of the Second Amendment are limited to those firearms with a militia nexus. The Court indicated its unwillingness to accept the broad reach of *Miller* when it reasoned that it was already outdated because in "commando units" some sort of military use seems to have been found for almost any modern, lethal weapon. If this were true, concluded the court, the protection of the Second Amendment as set forth in *Miller* would be absolute except for antique weapons which have no modern military use since, as the court accurately observed, "... almost any other [weapon] might bear some reasonable relationship to the preservation or efficiency of a well regulated militia unit of the present day ..." Id. at 922.

The First Circuit failed to consider the unambiguous wording of the Second Amendment in reaching its conclusion. The Second Amendment speaks not only of the right to keep arms, but to bear them as well, implying that the category of arms, the possession of which is protected, is limited to those arms that an ordinary individual can bear and does not extend to weapons such as cannons, trench mortars, and antitank guns, which cannot be carried by an ordinary individual. Also not protected are instrumentalities such as bombs which, although conceivably they could be carried by a single individual, are not arms in the sense used in the Second Amendment; rather, the historically and constitutionally protected   arms are those such as muskets, shotguns, rifles and pistols, which are ordinarily possessed by private individuals. To argue, ad absurdum, as the *Cases* court did, that all weapons are protected by the Second Amendment overlooks the fact that the Framers of the Bill of Rights were fully aware of the existence of heavier, horse-drawn and crew served arms which the individual was physically incapable of bearing. Had framers of the Bill of Rights intended to protect all weapons, they would not have linked the right to bear arms with the right to keep arms.[11]

Since, however, the Supreme Court did not review the *Cases* decision, *Miller* persists as that Court's guidance to the interpretation of the Second Amendment.

It is clear, therefore, based on analysis of the decided cases, the common law, and the history of the Second Amendment that the Second Amendment guarantees an individual's right to keep and bear arms.

D. THE RIGHT TO SELF-DEFENSE

The right to keep and bear arms is inextricably connected to the individual's absolute and inalienable right of self-defense which is, of course, derived from the Natural Law.

As referred to earlier, Blackstone clearly recognized as a natural right that of keeping and using arms for "resistance and self-preservation." I *Blackstone Commentaries* 144. The basic right to defend one's person with deadly force has, moreover, been recognized by the Supreme Court, *Beard v. United States*, 158 U.S. 550 (1895) and every state in the union. For example, in *State v. Dawson*, 272 N.C. 535, 159 S.2d, 1, 9 and 11 (1968), the Supreme Court of North Carolina, in interpreting a provision of that state's constitution which tracked the language of the Second Amendment, held that the individual right of self-defense was assumed by the Framers, and that any statute or construction of a common law rule which would amount to a destruction of the right to bear arms would be unconstitutional. Also, the *State v. Kessler*, supra, the court noted that "the necessity of self protection in a frontier society also was a factor" in guaranteeing the right to keep and bear arms.

The right to defend one's person is so fundamental that it was not set forth in the constitution but certainly exists as one of those rights included in the penumbra of unwritten rights surrounding the First, Second, Third, Fourth, Fifth, and Ninth Amendments. It is manifestly an inalienable right, incapable of surrender to the central government and encompassed by the Ninth Amendment as retained by the people.

II. *Antebellum judicial construction*

In the period from the adoption of the constitution to the War Between the States, keeping and bearing arms was treated as a virtually unquestioned right of each individual. The fundamental right to have arms was based in part on the political lessons of the Revolutionary experience. "None but an armed nation can dispense with a standing army," Jefferson wrote in 1803. "To keep ours armed and disciplined, is therefore at all times important." The   Jefferson Cyclopedia 553 (1900). In 1814, Jefferson further observed that "we cannot be defended but by making every citizen a soldier, as the Greeks and Romans who had no standing armies." Id. at 551. In addition to the prevention of aggression from domestic tyranny or foreign invasion, individual possession of arms functioned to provide a basic means of self-defense, as well as of subsistence for hunters.

That the Second Amendment secured an individual right to keep and bear arms was not an issue for partisan politics, and the courts fairly consistently so held. The major exception to this rule appeared in the context of slavery. Specifically, to disarm slaves as well as black freemen, certain courts originated the views that the guarantee was limited to citizens rather than to all people and that the Second Amendment did not restrain the states. The exceptions were aberrations to prevent black freedom, as most courts which analyzed the Second Amendment regarded all individuals as having the right and construed it as a restraint on state infringement.

A. JUDICIAL COMMENTARIES

Although Federalist and Republican differences in interpretation of the Constitution appeared early in judicial thought on subjects as diverse as the general welfare clause and the right of free speech, these points of divergence did not arise with respect to the Second Amendment. William Rawle, one of the first commentators on the Second Amendment, analyzed its two basic clauses in some detail:

> In the second article, it is declared, that a *well regulated militia is necessary to the security of a free state;* a proposition from which few will dissent. Although in actual war, the services of regular troops are confessedly more valuable; yet, while peace prevails, and in the commencement of a war before a regular force can be raised, the militia form the palladium of the country. They are ready to repel invasion, to suppress insurrection, and preserve the good order and peace of government....
>
> The corollary, from the first position, is, that the right of the people to keep and bear arms shall not be infringed.
>
> The prohibition is general. No clause in the Constitution could by any rule of construction be conceived to give to congress a power to disarm the people. Such a flagitious attempt could only be made under some general pretense by a state legislature. But if in any blind pursuit of inordinate power, either should attempt it, this amendment may be appealed to as a restraint on both.

W. Rawle, A view of the Constitution, 125-56 (1829).

Rawle's analysis stresses the significance of the first clause of the Second Amendment as an imperative for a militia system as opposed to a standing army. Clause two is then treated both in its linkage to clause one in that the individual right to keep and bear arms encourages a militia system, and independently as recognition of a fundamental right to have arms unrestrained by state no less than federal legislation. In negative remarks on English policy,   Rawle also clarified that the right to have arms is deemed more absolute in America than Britian, and that the Second Amendment protects individual use of arms for non-militia purposes such as hunting.

St. George Tucker, a veteran of the Revolutionary War and an early Justice of the Supreme Court of Virginia, followed Blackstone closely in regard to the common law right to have arms, at the same time stressing the more absolute character of the right under American law:

> The right of bearing arms—which with us is not limited and restrained by an arbitrary system of game laws as in England; but, is practically enjoyed by every citizen, and is among his most valuable privileges, since it furnishes the means of resisting as a freeman ought, the inroads of usurpation.... I St. Geo. Tucker, Commentaries on the Laws of Virginia, 43 (1831).

In addition to his explicit characterization of keeping and bearing arms as an individual right, elsewhere Justice Tucker distinguished the language of the English Bill of Rights that subjects may have arms for their defense, "suitable to their condition and degree, and such as are allowed by law," from the Second Amendment, wherein the right to have arms exists "without any qualification as to their condition or degree, as in the case of the British government." I *Blackstone Commentaries* *144 n. 40 (St. Geo. Tucker, ed. 1803).

B. STATE CASES

A provision of the Kentucky Constitution, "The right of the citizens to bear arms in defense of themselves and the state, shall not be questioned," provided the occasion for perhaps the first state judicial opinion on the nature and source of the right to bear arms. *Bliss v. Commonwealth*, 2 Litt. (Ky.) 90, 13 Am. Dec. 251 (1822). Defendant appealed his conviction for having worn a sword cane by asserting the unconstitutionality of an act prohibiting concealed weapons. The court held, "Whatever restrains the full and complete exercise of that right, though not an entire destruction of it, is forbidden by the explicit language of the constitution." Id. at 91-92. Observing that wearing concealed weapons was considered a legitimate practice when the constitutional provision was adopted, the court reasoned:

> The right existed at the adoption of the constitution; it had then no limits short of the moral power of the citizens to exercise it, and in fact consisted in nothing else but in the liberty of the citizens to bear arms. Diminish that liberty, therefore, and you necessarily restrain the right, and such is the diminution and restraint, which the act in question most indisputably imports, by prohibiting the citizens wearing weapons in a manner which was lawful to wear when the constitution was adopted. Id. at 92.[12]

Whether carrying and wearing dangerous weapons constituted an affray at common law was the issue in the Tennessee case of *Simpson v. State*, 13 Tenn. Reports (5 Yerg.) 56 (1833). The Court answered in the negative, citing Blackstone for the proposition that violence which terrifies the people must also be present. The government cited Serjeant Hawkins, Pleas of the Crown, Bk. 1, ch. 28, sec. 4, regarding the Statute of Northampton, 2 Edw. 3, c.3(1328), that an affray could exist where one is armed with unusual weapons which naturally cause terror to the people, but the court rejected those "ancient English statutes, enacted in favour of the king, his ministers, and other servants" which provided that "no man ... except the king's servants, & c. shall go or ride armed by night or by day." 13 Tenn. Reports (5 Yerg.) 358 (1833). The court seemed resentful of royal privilege in noting that the same source adds "persons of quality are in no danger of offending against this statute by wearing their common weapons" and, while rejecting the existence of a common law abridgement of the right to bear arms (*Id.* at 359), argued in the alternative that any such abridgement would be abrogated by the state constitution, which provided "that the freemen of this State have a right to keep and bear arms for their common defense."

> By this clause of the constitution, an express power is given and secured to all the free citizens of the State to keep and bear arms for their defense, without any qualification whatever as to their kind or nature.... *Id.* at 360.

The classic antebellum opinion which held that the Second Amendment protects an individual right from both state and federal infringement, but that the manner in which arms could be borne was a proper subject for regulation, was *Nunn v. State*, 1 Ga. 243 (1846). An ambiguous Georgia statute proscribed breast pistols, but not horseman's pistols, which were not worn openly. While upholding the proscription of concealed weapons, the court said that the state constitutions "confer no *new rights* on the people which did not belong to them before," that no legislative body in the Union could deny citizens the privilege of being armed to defend self and country, and that the colonial ancestors had this right which "is one of the fundamental principles, upon which rests the great fabric of civil liberty...." Id. at 249.

Anticipating twentieth century selective incorporation by referring to the First, Fourth, Fifth, and Sixth Amendments as binding on both state and federal governments, the court reasoned:

> The language of the second amendment is broad enough to embrace both Federal and state government--nor is there anything in its terms which restricts its meaning.... Is this a right reserved to the States or to themselves? Is it not an unalienable right, which lies at the bottom of every free government? We do not believe that, because the people withheld this arbitrary power of disfranchisement from Congress, they ever intended to confer it on the local legislatures. This right is too dear to be confided to a republican legislature. Id. at 250.

The Georgia court explained the relation between individual arms possession and the militia by reference to the fact that "in order to train properly that militia, the unlimited right of the people to keep and bear arms shall not be impaired," (*Id.* at 251), and added that both constitutional and natural rights were at stake. Contending that the state governments were prohibited from violating the rights to assembly and petition, against unreasonable searches and seizures, to an impartial jury in criminal prosecutions, and to assistance of counsel, the court continued:

> Nor is the right involved in this discussion less comprehensive or valuable: "The right of the people to bear arms shall not be infringed." The right of the whole people, old and young, men, women and boys, and not militia only, to keep and bear arms of every description, and not such merely as are used by the militia, shall not be infringed, curtailed or broken in upon, in the smallest degree; and all this for the

important end to be attained: the rearing up and qualifying a well-regulated militia, so vitally necessary to the security of a free State. Our opinion is that any law, State or Federal, is repugnant to the Constitution, and void, which contravenes this right.... Id. at 251.

In the Texas case of *Cockrum v. State*, 24 Tex. 394 (1859), the Court explained that the object of the Second Amendment was that "the people cannot be effectually oppressed and enslaved, who are not first disarmed." Id. at 401, and added:

The right of a citizen to bear arms, in lawful defense of himself or the State, is absolute. He does not derive it from the State government. It is one of the "high powers" delegated directly to the citizen, and "is excepted out of the general powers of government." A law cannot be passed to infringe upon or impair it, because it is above the law, and independent of the lawmaking power. Id. at 401-402.

C. SLAVERY AND THE DRED SCOTT DILEMMA

Despite the general rule in the antebellum courts that the Second Amendment guaranteed an individual right to keep and bear arms free from both federal and state infringement, to disarm blacks a few courts took the view that only citizens could have arms and that the Second Amendment did not apply to the states. In some states, free and slave blacks were disarmed by law to maintain their servile condition. State legislation which prohibited arms bearing by blacks was held to be constitutional owing to the lack of status of African Americans as citizens, despite the fact that the United States Constitution and most state constitutions referred to arms bearing as a right of "the people" rather than "the citizen."

In *State v. Newsom*, 27 N.C. 203 (1844), the Supreme Court of North Carolina upheld "an act to prevent free persons of color from carrying fire arms" on the ground that "the free people of color cannot be considered as citizens." Id. at 204. The court also stated: "in the second article of the amended Constitution, the States are neither mentioned nor referred to. It is therefore only restrictive of the powers of the Federal Government." Id. at 207. In *Cooper v. Savannah*, 4 Ga. 72 (1848), Georgia found its similar provision constitutional on the following logic: "Free persons of color have never been recognized here as citizens, they are not entitled to bear arms, vote for members of the legislature, or to hold any civil office." Id. at 72.

The practical hardships suffered by individual blacks due to restrictive legislation is exemplified in State v. Hannibal, 51 N.C. (6 Jones) 57 (1859), which indicates that in the eighteenth century it was not illegal for a black to carry guns, but he was required to obtain a court certificate to hunt. An enactment in 1854 provided that "no slave shall go armed with a gun, or shall keep such weapons," with a penalty of up to 39 lashes. Id. at 57. In this instance, a master had given two slaves guns to guard his store at night, and the slaves were sentenced to twenty lashes each. Id. at 57.

Just as virtually the only antebellum state cases which limited the right to have arms functioned to disarm blacks, the ruling of the U.S. Supreme Court in Dred Scott v. Sandford, 60 U.S. (19 How.) 393, 15 L.Ed. 691 (1857), conceded that if members of the African race were "citizens," they would be "entitled to the privileges and immunities of citizens" and would be exempt from special "police regulations" applicable to them.

It would give to persons of the negro race, who were recognized as citizens in any one State of the Union, the right to enter every other State whenever they pleased, singly or in companies ...; and it would give them full liberty of speech ...; to hold public meetings upon political affairs, and *to keep and carry arms wherever they went.* (emphasis added) 60 U.S. at 417.

It is clear, therefore, that the Supreme Court included among the rights of every citizen the right to have arms wherever he goes; it is equally evident that in granting citizenship to African Americans by Amendments XIII and XIV, blacks were later guaranteed the fundamental rights of citizens. The Court's language also suggests that the right to have and carry arms anywhere is a right of national citizenship which the states cannot infringe any more than can the federal government—that the Second Amendment applies to the states.

Explaining further the rights of citizens, Chief Justice Taney observed that:

The Federal Government can exercise no power over his person or property, beyond what that instrument confers, nor lawfully, deny any right which it has reserved.... Nor can Congress deny the people the right to keep and bear arms, nor the right to trial by jury, nor compel anyone to be a witness against himself in a criminal proceeding. 60 U.S. at 450.

III. *The Framers of the fourteenth amendment intended that the guarantees of the second amendment would be applied to the States*

After the War Between the States, judicial commentators continued to interpret the Second Amendment as protecting an individual right from both state and federal infringement. The right to keep and bear arms and other Bill of Rights freedoms were viewed   as common law rights explicitly protected by the Constitution. T. Farrar, Manual of the Constitution, 59, 145 (1867). Joel P. Bishop wrote in 1865:

The constitution of the United States provides, that, "a well-regulated militia being necessary to the security of a free State, the right of the people to keep and bear arms shall not be infringed." This provision is found among the amendments; and; though most of the amendments are restrictions on the General Government alone, not on the States, this one seems to be of a nature to bind both the State and National legislatures. II J. Bishop, Commentaries on the Criminal Law, Section 124 (1865).

Yet Bishop's references to "statutes relating to the carrying of arms by negroes and slaves" (II J. Bishop, supra, n. 2, at 120, n. 6), and to an "act to prevent free people of color from carrying firearms" (*Id.* at 125, n. 2) exemplified the need for further constitutional guarantees to clarify and protect the rights of all individuals.

A. FIREARMS AND THE ABOLITION OF SLAVERY

Having won their national independence from England through armed struggle, post-Revolutionary War Americans were acutely aware that the sword and sovereignty go hand-in-hand, and that distribution of firearms among the oppressed ushered in a new epoch in the human struggle for freedom. Furthermore, both proponents and opponents of slavery were cognizant that an armed black population meant the abolition of slavery, although some blacks were trusted with arms to guard property, for self defense, and for hunting. This sociological fact explained not only the legal disarming of blacks, but also the advocacy of a weapons culture by abolitionists. Having employed the instruments for self-defense against his pro-slavery attackers, abolitionist and Republican Party founder Cassius Marcellus Clay wrote that "'the pistol and the Bowie knife' are to us as sacred as the gown and the pulpit." 7 The Writings of Cassius Marcellus Clay, 257 (H. Greeley ed. 1848).

B. THE CIVIL RIGHTS ACT OF 1866

After the Civil War, the slave codes, which limited access of blacks to land, to arms, and to the courts, began to reappear in the form of black codes, (W. DuBois, Black Reconstruction in America, 167, 172, and 223 (1962); E. Coulter, The South During Reconstruction 40 (1947)) and United States legislators turned their attention to the protection of the freedmen. In support of Senate Bill No. 9, which declared as void all laws in the rebel states which recognized inequality of rights based on race, Sen. Henry Wilson (R., Mass.) explained in part: "In Mississippi rebel State forces, men who were in the rebel armies, are traversing the State, visiting the freedmen, disarming them, perpetrating murders and outrages on them...." Cong. Globe, 39th Cong., 1st Sess., pt. 1, 40 (Dec. 13, 1865).

When Congress took up Senate Bill No. 61, which became the Civil Rights Act of 1866, (14 Stat. 27 (1866)) Sen. Lyman Trumbull (R., Ill.), Chairman of the Senate Judiciary Committee, indicated   that the bill was intended to prohibit inequalities embodied in the black codes, including those provisions which "prohibit any negro or mulatto from having fire-arms." Cong. Globe, 39th Cong., 1st Sess., pt. 1, 474 (Jan. 29, 1866). In abolishing the badges of slavery, the bill would enforce fundamental rights against racial discrimination in respect to civil rights, the rights to contract, sue and engage in commerce, and equal criminal penalties. Sen. William Saulsbury (D., Delaware) added:

> In my State for many years, and I presume there are similar laws in most of the southern states, there has existed a law of the State based upon and founded in its police power, which declares that free negroes shall not have the possession of firearms or ammunition. This bill proposes to take away from the States this police power...." Id. at 474.

The Delaware Democrat opposed the bill on this basis, anticipating a time when "a numerous body of dangerous persons belonging to any distinct race" endangered the state, for "the State shall not have the power to disarm them without disarming the whole population." Id. at 478. Thus, the bill would have prohibited legislative schemes which in effect disarmed blacks, but not whites. Still, supporters of the bill were soon to contend that arms bearing was a basic right of citizenship or personhood.

In the meantime, the legislators turned their attention to the Freedman's Bureau Bill. Rep. Thomas D. Eloit (R., Mass.) attacked an Opelousas, Louisiana ordinance which deprived blacks of various civil rights, including the following provision: "No freedman who is not in the military service shall be allowed to carry firearms, or any kind of weapons, within the limits of the town of Opelousas without the special permission of his employer ... and approved by the mayor or president of the board of police." Id. at 517 (Jan. 30, 1866). And Rep. Josiah B. Grinnell (R., Iowa) complained: "A white man in Kentucky may keep a gun; if a black man buys a gun he forfeits it and pays a fine of five dollars, if presuming to keep in his possession a musket which he has carried through the war." Id. at 651 (Feb. 5, 1866).

As debate returned to the Civil Rights Bill, Rep. Henry J. Raymond (R., N.Y.) explained of the rights of citizenship: "Make the colored man a citizen of the United States and he has every right which you or I have as citizens of the United States under the laws and Constitution of the United States.... He has a defined status; he has a country and a home; a right to defend himself and his wife and children; a right to bear arms...." Id., pt. 2, 1266 (Mar. 8, 1866). Rep. Roswell Hart (R., N.Y.) concluded that it was the duty of the United States to guarantee that the states have a republican form of government, "A government ... where 'no law shall be made prohibiting a free exercise of religion;' where 'the right of the people to keep and bear arms shall not be infringed;' ..." Id. at 1629 (Mar. 24, 1866).

Rep. Sidney Clarke (R., Kansas) objected to an 1866 Alabama law providing: "That it shall not be lawful for any freedman, mulatto, or free person of color in this State to own firearms, or carry about his person a pistol or other deadly weapon." Id. at 1838 (April 7,   1866). Clarke also attacked Mississippi, "whose rebel militia, upon the seizure of the arms of black Union soldiers, appropriated the same to their own use." Id. at 1838.

> Sir, I find in the Constitution of the United States an article which declares that "the right of the people to keep and bear arms shall not be infringed." For myself, I shall insist that the reconstructed rebels of Mississippi respect the Constitution in their local laws.... Id. at 1838.

C. THE FOURTEENTH AMENDMENT

The need for a more solid foundation for the protection of freedmen as well as white citizens was recognized, and the result was a significant new proposal—the Fourteenth Amendment. A chief exponent of the amendment, Sen. Jacob M. Howard (R., Mich.), referred to the "personal rights guaranteed and secured by the first eight amendments of the Constitution; such as freedom of speech and of the press; ....*the right to keep and to bear arms*...." [*emphasis added*] Cong. Globe, 39th Cong. 1st Sess. pt. 3, 2765 (May 23, 1866). Adoption of the Fourteenth Amendment was necessary because these rights were not then effectively guaranteed against state legislation. "The great object of the first section of this amendment is, therefore, to restrain the power of the States and compel them at all times to respect these great fundamental guarantees." Id. at 2766.

The Fourteenth Amendment was viewed as necessary to buttress the objectives of the Civil Rights Act of 1866. Rep. George W. Julian (R., Ind.) noted that the act

> Is pronounced void by the jurists and courts of the South. Florida makes it a misdemeanor for colored men to carry weapons without a license to do so from a probate judge, and the punishment of the offense is whipping and the pillory. South Carolina has the same enactments.... Cunning legislative devices are being invented in most of the States to restore slavery in fact. Id. at pt. 4, 3210 (June 15, 1866.)

D. THE ANTI-KKK ACT

Within three years of the adoption of the Fourteenth Amendment in 1868, Congress was considering enforcement legislation to suppress the Ku Klux Klan. The famous report by Rep. Benjamin F. Bulter (R., Mass.) on violence in the South assumed that the right to keep arms was necessary for protection not only against the militia, but also against local law enforcement agencies. Noting instances of "armed confederates" terrorizing the negro, the report stated that "in many counties they have preceded their outrages upon him by disarming him, in violation of his right as a citizen to 'keep and bear arms,' which the Constitution expressly says shall never by infringed," 1464 H.R. Rep. No. 37, 41st Cong., 3rd Sess. 3 (Feb. 20, 1871). The congressional power based on the Fourteenth Amendment to legislate to prevent states from depriving any U.S. citizen of life, liberty, or property accounted for the following provision of the committee's anti-KKK bill.

That whoever shall, without due process of law, by violence, intimidation, or threats, take away or deprive any citizen of the United States of any arms or weapons he may have in his house or possession for the defense of his person, family, or property, shall be deemed guilty of a larceny thereof, and be punished as provided in this act for a felony. Cong. Globe, 42nd Cong., 1st Sess., pt. 1, 174 (Mar. 20, 1871).

Rep. Butler explained the purpose of this provision in these words:

Section eight is intended to enforce the well-known constitutional provision guaranteeing the right in the citizen to 'keep and bear arms,' and provides that whoever shall take away, by force or violence, or by threats and intimidation, the arms and weapons which any person may have for his defense, shall be deemed guilty of larceny of the same. This provision seemed to your committee to be necessary, because they had observed that, before these midnight marauders made attacks upon peaceful citizens there were very many instances in the South where the sheriff of the county had preceded them and taken away the arms of their victims. This was specially noticeable in Union County, where all the negro population were disarmed by the sheriff only a few months ago under the order of the judge....; and then, the sheriff having disarmed the citizens, the five hundred masked men rode at night and murdered and otherwise maltreated the ten persons who were in jail in that county. H.R. Rep. No. 37, supra, note 38, at 7-8.

The bill was referred to the Judiciary Committee, and when later reported as H.R. No. 320 the above section was deleted—undoubtedly because its proscription extended to simple individual larceny over which Congress had no constitutional authority, and because state or conspiratorial action involving the disarming of blacks would be covered by more general provisions of the bill. Supporters of the rewritten anti-KKK bill continued to show the same concern over the disarming of freedmen as they had prior to the adoption of the Fourteenth Amendment. Sen. John Sherman (R., Ohio) stated the Republican position: "Wherever the negro population preponderates, there they [the KKK] hold their sway, for a few determined men ... can carry terror among ignorant negroes ... without arms, equipment, or discipline." Cong. Globe, 42nd Cong. 1st Sess., pt. 1, 154 (Mar. 18, 1871).

Further comments clarified that the right to arms was a necessary condition for the right of free speech. Sen. Adelbert Ames (R., Miss.) averred: "In some counties it was impossible to advocate Republican principles, those attempting it being hunted like wild beasts; in others, the speakers had to be armed and supported by not a few friends." Id. at 196. (Mar. 21, 1871). Rep. William L. Stoughton (R., Mich.) added: "If political opponents can be marked for slaughter by secret bands of cowardly assassins who ride forth with impunity to execute the decrees upon *the unarmed and defenseless*, it will be fatal alike to the Republican party and civil liberty." [Emphasis added] Id. at 321 (Mar. 28, 1871).

Section 1 of the bill, which was taken partly from Section 2 of the Civil Rights Act of 1866, and survives today as 42 U.S.C. 1983 was meant to enforce Section 1 of the Fourteenth Amendment by establishing a remedy for deprivation under color of state law of federal constitutional rights of all people, not only former slaves. This portion of the bill provided:

> That any person who, under color of any law, statute, ordinance, regulation, custom or usage of any State shall subject, or cause to be subjected, any person within the jurisdiction of the United States to the deprivation of any rights, privileges, or immunities to which ... he is entitled under the Constitution or laws of the United States, shall ... be liable to the party injured in an action at law, suit in equity, or other propoer proceeding for redress ... Id. pt. 2. Appendix, 68. 17 Stat. 13 (1871).

Rep. Washington C. Whitthorne (D., Tenn.), who complained that "in having organized a negro militia in having disarmed the white man," the Republicans had "plundered and robbed" the whites of South Carolina through "unequal laws," objected to Section 1 of the anti-KKK bill on these grounds.

> It will be noted that by the first section suits may be instituted without regard to amount or character of claim by any person within the limits of the United States who conceives that he has been deprived of any right, privilege, or immunity secured him by the Constitution of the United States, under color of any law, statute, ordinance, regulation, custom, or usage of any State. This is to say, that if a police officer of the city of Richmond or New York should find a drunken negro or white man upon the streets with a loaded pistol flourishing it, &c., and by virtue of any ordinance, law or usage, either of city or State, he takes it right away, the officer may be sued, *because the right to bear arms is secured by the Constitution*, and such suit brought in distant and expensive tribunals. [Emphasis added] Cong. Globe, 42nd Cong., 1st Sess., pt. 1, 337 (Mar. 29, 1871).

The Tennessee Democrat assumed that the right to bear arms was absolute, deprivation of which created a cause of action against state agents under Section 1 of the anti-KKK bill. In the minds of the bill's supporters, however, the Second Amendment as incorporated in the Fourteenth Amendment recognized a right to keep and bear arms safe from state infringement, not a right to commit assault or otherwise engage in criminal conduct with arms by pointing them at people or brandishing them so as to endanger others. Contrary to the congressman's exaggerations, the proponents of the bill had the justified fear that the opposite development would occur, i.e. that a black or white man for political reasons would be unconstitutionally deprived of his right to possess arms by state action. Significantly, none of the representative's colleagues disputed his statement that state agents could be sued   under the predecessor to Section 1983 for deprivation of the right to keep arms.

Debate over the anti-KKK bill naturally required exposition of Section 1 of the Fourteenth Amendment, and none was better qualified to explain that section than its draftsman, Rep. John A. Bingham (R., Ohio):

> Mr. Speaker, that the scope and meaning of the limitations imposed by the first section, fourteenth amendment of the Constitution may be more fully understood, permit me to say that the privileges and immunities of citizens of a State, are chiefly defined in the first eight amendments to the Constitution of the United States ....
>
> These eight articles ... never were limitations upon the power of the States, until made so by the fourteenth amendment. The words of that amendment, "no State shall make or enforce any law which shall abridge the privileges or immunities of citizens of the United States" are an express prohibition upon every State of the Union .... Id. at pt. 2, Appendix 84 (Mar. 31, 1871).

This is a most explicit statement of the incorporation thesis by the architect of the Fourteenth Amendment. Although he based the incorporation on the Privileges and Immunities Clause and not the Due Process Clause as have subsequent courts of selective incorporation, Rep. Bingham could hardly have anticipated the judicial metaphysics of the twentieth century in this respect. In any case, whether based on the Due Process Clause or on the Privileges and Immunities Clause, the legislative history supports the view that the incorporation of Amendments I-VIII was clear and unmistakable in the minds of the legislators attempting to effectuate the provision of the Fourteenth Amendment.

Rep. Henry L. Dawes (R. Mass.) also asserted the incorporation thesis when he argued:

> The rights, privileges and immunities of the American citizen, secured to him under the Constitution of the United States, are the subject-matter of this bill...
>
> In addition to the original rights secured to him in the first article of amendments he had secured the free exercise of his religious belief, and freedom of speech and of the press. Then again he has secured to him the *right to keep and bear arms in his defense*.... [Dawes then summarizes the remainder of the first eight amendments.]
>
> And still later, sir, after the bloody sacrifice of our four years' war, we gave the most grand of all these rights, privileges, and immunities, by one single amendment to the Constitution, to four millions of American citizens.
>
> [I]t is to protect and secure to him in these rights, privileges, and immunities this bill is before the House. [emphasis added] *Cong Globe*, 42nd Cong., 1st. Sess., pt. 1, 475-476 (April 5, 1871).

E. THE CIVIL RIGHTS ACT OF 1875

After passage of the anti-KKK bill, discussion concerning arms persisted as interest developed toward what became the Civil Rights Act of 1875, now 42 U.S.C. 1984. A report on affairs in the South by Sen. John Scott (R., Penn.) indicated the need for further enforcement legislation: "negroes who were whipped testified that those who beat them told them they did so because they had voted the radical ticket, and in many cases made them promise that they would not do so again, and wherever they had guns took them from them." 1484 S. Rep. No. 41, 42nd Cong., 2nd Sess., pt. 1, 35 (Feb. 19, 1872).

Following the introduction of the Civil Rights Bill the debate over the meaning of the Privileges and Immunities Clause returned. Sen. Matthew H. Carpenter (R., Wisc.) cited *Cummings v. Missouri*, 71 U.S. 277, 321 (1866) a case contrasting the French legal system, which allowed deprivation of civil rights, "and among these of the right of voting, ... of bearing arms," with the American legal system, stating that the Fourteenth Amendment prevented states from taking away the privileges of the American citizen. *Cong. Globe*, 2nd Sess., pt. 1, 762 (Feb. 1, 1872).

Sen. Allen G. Thurman (D., Ohio) argued that the "rights, privileges, and immunities of a citizen of the United States" were included in Amendments I-VIII. Reading and commenting on each of these amendments, he said of the Second: "Here is another right of a citizen of the United States, expressly declared to be his right—the right to bear arms; and this right, says the Constitution, shall not be infringed." *Id.* at pt. 6, Appendix, 25-26 (Feb. 6, 1872).

The incorporationist thesis was stated succinctly by Senator Thomas M. Norwood (D., Ga.) in one of the final debates over the Civil Rights Bill. Referring to a U.S. citizen residing in a Territory, Senator Norwood stated:

> His right to bear arms, to freedom of religious opinion, freedom of speech, and all others enumerated in the Constitution would still remain indefeasibly his, whether he remained in the Territory or removed to a State.
>
> And those and certain others are the privileges and immunities which belong to him in common with every citizen of the United States, and which no State can take away or abridge, and they are given and protected by the Constitution.
>
> The following are most, if not all, the privileges and immunities of a citizen of the *United States:*
>
> The right to the writ of *habeas corpus;* of peaceable assembly and of petition; ... *to keep and bear arms;* ... from being deprived of the right to vote on account of race, color or previous condition of servitude. [emphasis added] *Cong. Rec.*, 43rd Cong., 1st Sess., pt. 6, Appendix 241-242 (May 4, 1874).

Arguing that the Fourteenth Amendment created no new rights but declared that "certain existing rights should not be abridged by States," the Georgia Democrat explained:

> Before its [Fourteenth Amendment] adoption any State might have established a particular religion, or restricted freedom of speech and of the press, or *the right to bear arms....* A State could have deprived its citizens of any of the privileges and immunities contained in those eight articles, but the *Federal Government* could not...
>
> ...And the instant the fourteenth amendment became a part of the Constitution, every State was at that moment disabled from making or enforcing any law which would deprive any citizen of a State of the benefits enjoyed by citizens of the United States under the first eight amendments to the Federal Constitution. (emphasis added) *Id.* at 242.

In sum, in the understanding of Southern Democrats and Radical Republicans alike, the right to keep and bear arms, like other Bill of Rights freedoms, was made applicable to the states by the Fourteenth Amendment.

REFERENCES

1.   Although the common law in effect in the colonies did not develop any limitation on the absolute right of individuals to keep arms, it did recognize certain restrictions on the manner in which individuals could *use* arms.

2.   Individual colonists, of course, kept their own firearms, with powder and shot, in their residences.

3.   Justice Story wrote in 1833: "The militia is the natural defense of a free country against sudden foreign invasions, domestic insurrections, and domestic usurpations of power by rulers. It is against sound policy for a free people to keep up large military establishments and standing armies in time of peace, both from the enormous expenses, with which they are attended, and the facile means, which they afford to ambitious and unprincipled rulers, to subvert the government, or trample on the rights of the people. *The right of the citizen to keep and bear arms has justly been considered, as the palladium of the liberties of a republic;* since it offers a strong moral check against the usurpation and arbitrary power of rulers; and will generally, even if these are successful in the first instance, enable the people to resist and triumph over them." (emphasis added.) 3 *Commentaries on the Constitution of the United States*, Section 1890, pp. 746-747 (1833).

4.   Actually, the militia embraces a larger class of persons than today's statutory unorganized militia since it consists of at least all persons "physically capable of acting in concert for the common defense." *U.S. v. Miller*, 307 U.S. 174, 179 (1939). The Virginia Constitution, upon which the Bill of Rights was modeled, provides that the militia is "composed of the body of the people." Article I, Section 13.

5.   Of the twelve proposed amendments, all but the first two dealt with the protection of the rights of individuals; all but the first two were ratified. Since, of the ten remaining, Amendments 1 and 3 through 10 have repeatedly been held to secure fundamental individual rights, it is logical that the Second Amendment also secures a fundamental individual right.

6.   The word "people" as used in the First, Fourth, Ninth, and Tenth Amendments has consistently been construed to mean individual.

7.   This view is supported by the Congressional Research Office of the Library of Congress which has observed, "At what point regulation or prohibition of what classes of firearms would conflict with the [Second] Amendment, whether there would be a conflict, the *Miller* case does little more than cast a faint degree of illumination toward answering." *The Constitution of the United States of America, Analysis and Interpretation*, Senate Document No. 92-82.

8.   Applying this test, the defendant would have little difficulty today in demonstrating that possession of such a shotgun is protected by the Second Amendment, since shotguns were military issue in both World Wars, Korea, and Vietnam.

9.   Numerous cases have held that a handgun is an arm for constitutional purposes, for example, in *State v. Kerner*, 181 N.C. 574, 107 S.E. 222, 224 (1921), the Court observed that the "historical use of pistols as 'arms' of offense and defense is beyond controversy...." Similar holdings are found in *In re Brickey*, 8 Ida. 597, 70 P. 609 (1902) and *State v. Rosenthal*, 75 Vt. 295, 55 A. 610 (1903). Moreover, in colonial times pistols saw considerable service as a personal weapon. As a noted historian observed,

    It was considered normal for civilians to carry pocket pistols for protection while traveling ... Among eighteenth century civilians who traveled or lived in large cities, pistols were common weapons. Usually they were made to fit into pockets, and many of these small arms were also carried by military officers. George C. Neumann, The History of Weapons of the American Revolution, pp. 150-151 (Bonanza Books, N.Y. 1967).

10.   Although *Tot* was appealed to the Supreme court, the Second Amendment issue was not addressed by that Court.

11.   This view, moreover, is consistent with the common law which prohibited the bearing of arms when carried in such a manner as would terrify the people. 4 Blackstone Commentaries 149. Furthermore it is consistent with the concept of the militia as a body of persons who maintained firearms in their homes for self-defense and to be ready to contribute to the common defense.

12.   But see *State v. Reid*, 1 Ala. Reports 612, 616-7 (1840), while holding that a statute prohibiting the carrying of concealed weapons was not incompatible with the right to keep and bear arms in defense of self and state, added: "A statute which, under the pretense of regulating, amounts to a destruction of the right, or which requires arms to be so borne as to render them wholly useless for the purpose of defence, would be clearly unconstitutional."

THE RIGHT TO BEAR ARMS:
THE DEVELOPMENT OF THE AMERICAN EXPERIENCE

JOHN LEVIN[*]

I. INTRODUCTION

As THE crime rate in the United States grows and pressures mount for laws restricting the use of firearms, the need for an understanding of the development of the "right to bear arms" has increased. Perhaps more than any other "right" enumerated in the federal and state constitutions, the "right" to bear arms was directed to maintaining a balance of power within our society. The "right to bear arms" developed at a time when a well-armed population was necessary for defense, and when the social and political structure was kept in balance by a balance of armed power.

While the American "right to bear arms" developed at the time of the Revolution, it grew out of the duty imposed on the early colonists to keep arms for the defense of their isolated and endangered communities. The definition of "bearing arms" as the phrase was used in legal instruments up to revolutionary times was "serving in an organized armed force."[1] It did not imply any personal right to possess weapons. For example, when Parliament in drafting the English Bill of Rights[2] or Blackstone in his *Commentaries on the Laws of England*[3] intended to convey the meaning of a personal right to possess arms, they spoke of the right to *have* arms, not of the right to *bear* arms.

II. EARLY HISTORY

A. *The Colonial Period*

The earliest colonial statutes requiring that the colonists arm themselves were Virginia statutes of 1623 stating that "no man go or send abroad without a sufficient party will [sic] armed," and that "men go not to worke in the ground without their arms (and a centinell upon them)."[4] In 1658 Virginia required that "every man able to beare armes have in his house a fixt gunn."[5] The colony, being unable to afford to arm its militia or troops, required them to arm

---

[*] Assistant Professor, Chicago-Kent College of Law, Illinois Institute of Technology. B.A., 1964, Brandeis University; J.D., 1968, Harvard Law School; M.A., 1971, Washington University, St. Louis, Mo.; Admitted to the Illinois Bar in 1968.

[1] *See* the materials on the colonial statutes and on the United States Constitution discussed below.

[2] 1 W & M. I, St. 2, ch. 2 (1689).

[3] W. Blackstone, Commentaries on the Law of England 143-44 (1766).

[4] Acts of the Grand Assembly 1623-1624, Nos. 24 and 25.

[5] Acts of the Grand Assembly 1658-1659, Act 25.

themselves.[6] If the militia, however, found itself under-armed, the county courts could levy on the population for the provision of arms and distribute them to those not provided—the distributees then paying for the arms at a reasonable rate.[7]

Massachusetts in 1632 required each person to "have ... a sufficient musket or other serviceable peece for war ... for himself and each man servant he keeps able to beare arms."[8] In the Code of 1672 men were to provide their own arms, but arms would be supplied to those unable to obtain them. In New York, each town was to keep a stock of arms, and each man between 16 and 60 was to have arms.[9] Even those not obligated to serve in the militia were required to keep arms and ammunition in their houses.[10] The militia provisions of the Connecticut Code of 1650 said, "All persons ... shall beare arms ...; and every male person ... shall have in continual readiness, a good muskitt or other gunn, fitt for service." South Carolina had similar codes.[11]

This duty to keep and bear arms was limited by the interest of colonial governments in preventing the use of firearms for harmful ends. In order to prevent civil disturbances the colonial governments strove to keep arms from falling into the "wrong hands." To provide against Negro insurrections, Virginia forbade Negroes from carrying arms without their masters' certificate.[12] Pennsylvania had a similar provision by 1700,[13] and South Carolina even required that the master keep all arms not in use safely locked up in his house.[14] Virginia forbade the sale of arms or ammunition to Indians,[15] and Massachusetts required that Indians possess a license to carry a gun within certain areas of the colony.[16]

In times of civil disturbance the colonies controlled arms to protect the security of orderly government. For example, in 1692 the Massachusetts Assembly felt it necessary to arrest "such as shall ride, or go armed offensively before any of their majesties' justices or other of their officers or ministers doing their office or elsewhere by night or by day, in fear or affray of their majesties' people."[17]

In addition to those laws preventing arms from falling into the hands of those groups openly hostile to colonial society, statutes regulated the conditions under which arms could be used. As the settlements grew crowded, shooting was restricted in order to protect people and livestock. By 1678 Massachusetts forbade shooting "so near or into any House, Barn, Garden, Orchards or High-Wayes

6   Acts of the Grand Assembly 1684, Act 4.

7   Acts of the Grand Assembly 1673, Act 2.

8   The Compact with the Charter and General Laws of the Colony of New Plymouth 44-45 (1836).

9   Duke of York's Laws (1665-1675).

10   First Gen. Assembly, 2d Sess., ch. 20 (October 1684).

11   S.C. Stat., No. 206 (1703).

12   Acts of the Grand Assembly 1680, Act 10.

13   Penn Stat., ch. 61 § 5 (1700).

14   S.C. Stat., No. 314 (1712).

15   Acts of the Grand Assembly 1633, Act 10.

16   Gen. Ct., Sess. of May 23, 1677.

17   Province Laws 1692-1693, ch. 18, § 6.

in any town or towns of this Jurisdiction, whereby any person or persons shall be or may be killed, wounded or otherwise damaged."[18] In order to prevent fires caused by gunfire, Pennsylvania in 1721 forbade firing a gun within the city of Philadelphia without a special license from the governor.[19] Pennsylvania also forbade hunting by anyone on improved lands without the permission of the owner, and forbade those not qualified to vote from hunting on unimproved lands without the permission of the owner.[20]

Colonial statutes established a duty to keep and bear arms for the defense of the colonies and regulated the use of the arms in circulation. The American Revolution in turn provided fertile ground for the growth of the concept of the right of revolution and the related right to bear arms.

B. The Revolutionary Period

During the revolutionary period the issue of arms and the bearing of arms developed along two distinct lines. One line of development related to the balance of military power between the people and their respective governments. The people feared that if the state or federal government became too powerful, that government would abridge the liberties of the people and impose its will by force. The other line of development related to the balance of military power between the governmental bodies of the union. The state governments feared that if they entrusted too much power in the hands of the central government, that government would destroy the political and military independence of the states. Both lines of development concerned the creation of a military balance within the political structure which would result in the maintenance of liberty of the constituent parts—whether personal liberty under a government or state liberty in a union; and both lines of development resulted in the creation of a "right to bear arms" in order to insure the liberty of those constituent parts.

The colonists, fearful of oppression by governmental power, and being aware of the events of 17th Century England, believed that liberty was guaranteed by giving the rulers as little power as possible and by balancing governmental power with popular power.[21] The foremost factor in this balance of power was the existence of a standing army. Standing armies had been used by the English crown and by continental monarchs to impose their will on their subjects,[22] and royal forces had been used by the English crown to intimidate and control the colonies.[23] In 1774 the Continental Congress declared that keeping a "standing army in these colonies, in time of peace, without the consent of the legislature of that colony, in which such army is kept, is against law."[24] In 1775 the draftsmen of the Declaration of the Causes and Necessity of Taking up Arms[25] gave the presence of royal troops a prominent role in that declaration, and several sections of the Declaration of

---

[18] Council held in Boston, March 28, 1678.

[19] Penn. Stat., ch. 245, § 4 (1721).

[20] Penn. Stat., ch. 246, § 3 (1721).

[21] C.E. Merriam, A History of American Political Theories 83 (1926).

[22] See e.g., G.M. Trevelyan, I-III History of England (1953).

[23] S. Morison, The Oxford History of the American People ch. XII, XIII, and XIV (1965).

[24] R. Perry and J. Cooper, Sources of our Liberties 288 (1959) (hereinafter cited as Sources).

[25] Id. at 295.

Independence were given to the issue.[26] Colonial mistrust of standing armies extended even to colonial troops. In 1776 Sam Adams wrote:

> [A] standing army, however necessary it be at some times, is always dangerous to the liberties of the people. Soldiers are apt to consider themselves as a body distinct from the rest of the citizens. They have their arms always in their hands. Their rules and their discipline is severe. They soon become attached to their officers and disposed to yield implicit obedience to their commands. Such a power should be watched with a jealous eye.[27]

III CONSTITUTIONAL PROVISIONS

The state constitutions framed during the War for Independence reflected the fears of a standing army. The framers felt that such an army would create an overbearing force at the disposal of the state governments. All the states included provisions regarding standing armies and militia in their bills of rights. Several had provisions similar to Virginia's:

> That a well-regulated militia, composed of the body of the people, trained to arms, is the proper, natural, and safe defense of a Free State; that standing armies, in time of peace, should be avoided, as dangerous to liberty; and that in all cases the military should be under strict subordination to, and governed by, the civil power.[28]

Several others were similar to that of Maryland:

XXV.   That a well-regulated militia is the proper and natural defense of a free government.
XXVI.   That standing armies are dangerous to liberty, and ought not to be raised or kept up, without the consent of the Legislature.
XXVII.   That in all cases, and at all times, the military ought to be under strict subordination to and control of the civil power.
XXVIII.   That no soldier ought to be quartered in any house, in time of peace, without the consent of the owner; and in time of war, in such manner only, as the Legislature directs.
XXIX.   That no person, except regular soldiers, mariners, and Marines in the service of this State, or militia when in actual service, ought in any case to be subject to or punishable by martial law.[29]

Some specifically mentioned a "right to bear arms," such as Pennsylvania's:

> That the people have a right to bear arms for the defense of themselves and the State; and as standing armies in the time of peace are dangerous to liberty, they ought not to be kept

---

[26]   *Id.* at 319.

[27]   Letter to James Warren, quoted in M. Jensen, The New Nation—A History of the United States During the Confederation 1781-1789. 29 (1962).

[28]   Sources at 312.

[29]   *Id.* at 348.

up. And that the military should be kept under strict subordination to, and governed by, the civil power.[30]

North Carolina included a "right to bear arms" for the "defense of   the State,"[31] and Massachusetts included such a right for "the common defense."[32] Widespread copying by the draftsmen of state constitutions created, in part, the similarity between provisions.[33] These provisions were to be the basis of the militia provisions in the federal Constitution and Bill of Rights.

When the draftsmen of the majority of the state bills of rights wrote of replacing the standing army with a popular militia, they believed it would remove a source of arbitrary military power from the hands of the state governments and replace it with a military less likely to oppress the people.[34] They attempted to structure the political and military balance in the new states by making the governments less powerful and the citizens more powerful. The "right to bear arms" was a more extreme and revolutionary manifestation of this restructuring. By having a right to "bear arms," *i.e.*, to serve in the armed forces of the state, the people would have far greater military power than if the militia were merely the preferred defense, for the state governments would be unable to maintain a narrowly based standing army against the interests of the people. Rather the people would rely on their "right" to bear arms and demand that the defense force be broadly based.

The "right to *have* arms" was an adjunct to the right of revolution. The right of revolution is the natural right of a people to overthrow their government when that government no longer serves the purpose for which it was formed. By the middle of the 18th century, Blackstone had recognized that the primary rights of Englishmen—"personal security, personal liberty, and private property"—could not be maintained solely by law, for "in vain would these rights be declared, ascertained, and protected by the dead letter of the laws, if the constitution had provided no other method to secure their actual enjoyment."[35] There were auxiliary rights in order to enable the subject to preserve the primary rights, and,

> The fifth and last auxiliary right of the subject ... is that of having arms for their defense, suitable to their condition and degree, and such as are allowed by law. Which ... is indeed a public allowance, under   due restrictions, of the natural right of resistance and self-preservation when the sanctions of society and laws are found insufficient to restrain the violence of oppression.[36]

The provisions in the state constitutions granting a "right to bear arms" were not intended to permit a public allowance of the right of revolution. In the first place, the phrase "to *bear* arms" only

---

[30]   *Id.* at 330.

[31]   *Id.* at 356.

[32]   *Id.* at 376.

[33]   R. Rutland, The Birth of the Bill of Rights 1776-1791 *passim* (1962).

[34]   *See* the material on the discussion of the United States Constitution below.

[35]   *Supra* n.3 at 140.

[36]   *Supra* n.3 at 143-144.

meant serving in an organized armed force.[37] In the second place, the right of revolution, or at least a statement of the principle of that right, was specifically contained in other sections of most state constitutions.[38] In the third place, the guaranty of the "right to bear arms" or similar statements of preference for the militia was contained in that section of the constitutions directly concerned with controlling the military power of the state and not in the section recognizing the right of revolution.

When the Constitutional Convention met on May 14, 1787, it was faced with some issues quite dissimilar to those which had troubled the states. In the years during and immediately following the Revolution, the doctrine of the natural right of revolution was an accepted part of colonial political theory.[39] After the Revolution, however, the need for stable and orderly government grew, and the philosophy of rebellion withered.[40] The fundamental problem facing the convention was not to support and nourish a revolutionary situation, but to create a viable federal government out of the jealous and independent states. One of the major aspects of this problem was the creation of a national army. The delegates to the convention feared that if the new federal government could obtain sufficient military power, it could then impose its will on the states and on the people.

The delegates, however, did not consider the new federal standing army to be a danger to the states or the people since Congress would have strict control over the appropriations for troops, and most delegates assumed that the standing army would be small.[41] The Articles of Confederation had left complete control of land forces in the hands   of the states which raised them,[42] and by 1788 the Army of the Confederation consisted of only 679 officers and men.[43] The question of the balance of military power between the states and the federal government was raised rather on the issue of federal control over the state militia.

On August 18, 1787, a motion was made in the convention to give Congress the power "to make laws for the regulation and discipline of the Militia of the several States reserving to the States the appointments of Officers."[44] Here the military power of the states was at stake. John Dickinson exclaimed that "we are come now to a most important matter, that of the sword .... The states never would or ought to give up all authority over the Militia."[45] Oliver Ellsworth believed that "the whole authority over the Militia ought by no means to be taken away from the States whose consequence would pine away to nothing after such a sacrifice of power."[46] Supporters of the motion recalled how

---

[37] *See* text at n.1, n.2, and n.3.

[38] E. Douglas, Rebels and Democrats *passim* (1965).

[39] C. Becker, The Declaration of Independence 7-8 (1942).

[40] M. Jensen, The New Nation—A History of the United States During the Confederation 1781-1789 (1962).

[41] M. Farrand, II The Records of the Federal Convention of 1787 329-30 (1966).

[42] H. Commager, I Documents of American History 112-13 (7th ed. 1963).

[43] *Supra* n.41 at 365.

[44] *Id.* at 330.

[45] *Id.* at 331.

[46] *Id.*

ineffectual the militia was during the Revolution. They stressed the need for an effective and centralized military.[47]

When the debate continued on August 23rd, Edmund Randolph felt that the militia could be trusted to look after the liberties of the people. He asked, "What dangers there could be that the Militia could be brought into the field and made to commit suicide on themselves. This is a power that cannot from its nature be abused, unless indeed the whole mass should be corrupted."[48] Elbridge Gerry stated, when a motion was made to allow the federal government to appoint the general officers, that "as the States are not to be abolished, he wondered at the attempts that were made to give powers inconsistent with their existence."[49] James Madison replied: "As the greatest danger is that of disunion of the States it is necessary to guard against it by sufficient powers to the Common Government and as the greatest danger to the   liberty is from large standing armies, it is best to prevent them by an effectual provision for a good Militia."[50]

A compromise was reached whereby the federal government would maintain a standing army plus have the authority to regulate and call out the militia, and the states would have authority over the militia except when it was called into federal service. The results of the compromise appear in article I, section 8 of the United States Constitution declaring that Congress shall have power:

> To make Rules for the Government and Regulation of the land and naval Forces;
>
> To raise and support Armies, but no appropriation of Money to that use shall be for a longer term than two Years;
>
> To provide for calling forth the Militia to execute the Laws of the Union, suppress Insurrections and repel Invasions;
>
> To provide for organizing, arming, and disciplining the Militia, and for governing such Parts of them as may be employed in the Service of the United States, reserving to the States respectively, the Appointment of the Officers, and the Authority of training the Militia according to the discipline prescribed by Congress;

Thus, a tentative military balance was achieved between the federal government and the states.

Before the Constitution was ratified, however, its provisions were debated before the state legislatures and in the press. The militia provisions were again argued in terms of the balance of military power between the states and the federal government. Charles Pinckney argued for a federalized militia to give the federal government the power to impose its will on the states:

> The exclusive right of establishing regulations for the Government of the Militia of the United States ought certainly to be vested in the Federal Councils. As standing Armies are contrary to the Constitutions of most of the States, and the nature of our Government, the only immediate aid and support that we can look up to, in case of necessity, is the Militia

---

[47] *Id.*

[48] *Id.* at 387. For a discussion of the relation of the militia to popular uprisings in colonial America, *see* P. Maier, *Popular Uprisings and Civil Authority in Eighteenth-Century America*, 28 Wm. & Mary Q. (3rd Ser. 1970).

[49] *Supra* n.41 at 388.

[50] *Id.*

... Independent of our being obliged to rely on the Militia as a security against Foreign Invasions or Democratic Convulsions, they are in fact the only adequate force the Union possesses, if any should be requisite to coerce a refractory or negligent Member, and to carry the Ordinances and Decrees of Congress into execution. This, as well as the cases I have alluded to, will sometimes make it proper to order the Militia of one State into another. At present the United States possesses no power of directing the Militia, and must depend upon the States to carry their Recommendations upon this subject into execution ... To place therefore a necessary and Constitutional power of defense and coercion in the hands of the Federal authority, and to render our Militia uniform and national, I am decidedly in opinion they should have exclusive right of establishing regulations for their Government and Discipline, which the States should be bound to comply with, as well as with their Regulations for any number of Militia, whose march into another State, the Public safety or benefit should require.[51]

Luther Martin, speaking before the Maryland legislature, argued against the federalized militia as it would give the federal government so great a power that it could destroy the integrity of the states:

[Through] this extraordinary provision, by which the Militia, the only defense and protection which the State can have for the security of their rights against arbitrary encroachments of the general government, is taken entirely out of the power of their respective States, and placed under the power of Congress .... It was argued at the Constitutional convention that, if after having retained to the general government the great powers already granted, and among those, that of raising and keeping up regular troops, without limitations, the power over the Militia should be taken away from the States, and also given to the general government, it ought to be considered as the last *coup de grace* to the State governments; that it must be the most convincing proof, the advocates of this system design the destruction of the State governments, and that no professions to the contrary ought to be trusted: and that every State in the Union ought to reject such a system with indignation, since, if the general government should attempt to oppress and enslave them, they could not have any possible means of self-defense....[52]

Superimposed upon this debate over the balance of power between the states and the federal government was the issue of the balance of power between the people themselves and the new government. To assuage fears that the new federal government would infringe upon the rights of the people, the authors of *The Federalist* raised the factors of militia, arms, and the right of revolution in describing how the new government could be controlled. Federalist Number 28 mentioned the right of revolution:

If the representatives of the people betray their constituents, there is then no recourse left but in the exertion of that original right of self-defense which is paramount to all positive forms of government.[53]

---

[51]   *Id.* III at 118-19.

[52]   *Id.* at 208-09.

[53]   The Federalist, No. 28 (Hamilton).

And the military power of the states:

> When will the time arrive that the federal government can raise and maintain an army capable of erecting a despotism over the great body   of the people of an immense empire, who are in a situation, through the medium of their States governments, to take measure for their own defense, with all the celerity, regularity and system of independent nations?[54]

The 46th Federalist by Madison discussed the armed population and its relationship to the militia and the central government:

> Besides the advantage of being armed, which the Americans possess over the people of almost every other nation, the existence of subordinate governments to which the people are attached, and by which the Militia officers are appointed, forms a barrier against the enterprises of ambition, more insurmountable than any which a simple government of any form can admit. Notwithstanding the military establishments in the several kingdoms of Europe, which are carried as far as the public resources will bear, the governments are afraid to trust the people with arms.[55]

Though the Constitution was ratified, the issue of the federal militia was not resolved until adoption of the second amendment. Several of the states had suggested during their ratifying conventions that a bill of rights be added to the United States Constitution.[56] When such a bill of rights was debated in the First Congress, the militia amendment was first reported out of committee of the House of Representatives reading:

> A well-regulated Militia, composed of the body of the people, being the best security of a free State, the right of the people to keep and bear arms shall not be infringed; but no person religiously scrupulous shall be compelled to bear arms.[57]

Several of the representatives objected to the provision excusing those people "religiously scrupulous" from bearing arms. Elbridge Gerry stated that as the purpose of the militia "is to prevent the establishment of a standing army" it was "evident, that under this provision, together with their own powers, Congress could take such measures with respect to a Militia, as to make a standing army necessary." This could be accomplished by Congress using "a discretionary power to exclude those from the Militia who have religious scruples."[58] In such event, so many citizens would attempt to avoid Militia duty on religious grounds that a standing army would be necessary for national defense.

In any event the religious exemption from the militia was dropped and the amendment in its final form read:

---

[54]   *Id.*

[55]   The Federalist, No. 46 (Madison).

[56]   For a study of the forces at work to create a bill of rights, *supra* n.33.

[57]   1 Annals of Congress 778.

[58]   *Id.* at 778-79.

A well regulated Militia, being necessary to the security of a free State, the right of the people to keep and bear Arms, shall not be infringed.[59]

From the debates it seems clear that the intent of Congress in passing the second amendment was to prevent the federal government from destroying the state militia. Pinckney would keep a defense force uniform and at the disposal of the federal government. Martin was assured that the federal government would not emasculate the states and leave them at the mercy of federal troops. The "right to bear arms" was a corporate right used to insure that a desired balance between liberty and authority within the union would be maintained.

Attempts were made to include a personal right to have arms in the Bill of Rights. Sam Adams introduced a bill in the Massachusetts legislature that the state support an amendment holding that the "Constitution be never construed to authorize Congress to ... prevent the people of the United States, who are peaceable citizens from keeping their own arms."[60] New Hampshire supported a provision that "Congress shall never disarm any citizen unless such as are or have been in Actual Rebellion."[61] Though these provisions were never adopted, they indicate that there has never been any absolute "American" philosophy on the right to bear arms. This confusion arises from America's situation of being a frontier nation created out of revolution and espousing a belief in revolution but which also desires and needs to create an orderly social and political structure.

The result has been the use of the concept of the right to bear arms to support several different, and often contradictory, theories of the relation of armed citizens to the government. The judicial opinions of the courts of the various jurisdictions in the United States best exemplify this situation.

IV. RELEVANT COURT DECISIONS

A. State Courts

The first pronouncement on the right to bear arms was by a Kentucky court in *Bliss v. Commonwealth*.[62] The court held that "the right of   the citizens to bear arms in defense of themselves and the State must be preserved entire," and all legislative acts "which diminish or impair it as it existed when the Constitution was framed are void."[63] Thus an act pronouncing the wearing of concealed arms was declared void. This point of view which considers the right to bear arms as absolute, unabridgeable, and personal is rare. Most cases follow the reasoning of a Texas court which asked "How far personal liberty may be restrained for the prevention of crime."[64]

---

[59] U.S. Const. Amend. II.

[60] Pierce & Hale. Debates of the Massachusetts Convention of 1788 86-87, quoted in Feller and Gotting, *The Second Amendment: A Second Look*, 61 Nw. U. L. Rev. 47 (1966).

[61] Feller and Gotting, *The Second Amendment: A Second Look*, 61 Nw. U. L. Rev. 59 (1966).

[62] 2 Ky. 90 (1822).

[63] *Id.* at 91.

[64] English v. State, 35 Tex. 437, 477 (1872).

A few states adopted the thinking of the early Tennessee case of *Aymette v. State*[65] which held that the right to bear arms was a right of the people to enable them to rise up and defend their rights against an oppressive government. This concept was similar to Blackstone's presentation of the right to bear arms as a public allowance of the right of revolution. Courts holding this theory consider that, as the right is by public allowance, the state can regulate the use of arms to insure the public peace and welfare. This position was well presented by the Arkansas court in *Haile v. State*:[66]

> The constitutional provision sprung from the former tyrannical practice, on the part of governments, of disarming the subjects, so as to render them powerless against oppression. It is not intended to afford citizens the means of prosecuting, more successfully, their private broils in a free government. It would be a perversion of its object, to make it a protection to the citizen, in going, with convenience to himself, and after his own fashion, prepared all time to inflict death upon his fellow citizens, upon the occasion of any real or imaginary wrongs.[67]

While most courts have not attempted to counter the assertion of the right of revolution, an earlier Arkansas court had stated in *State v. Buzzard*[68] that such a right was unnecessary under a free, republican government which could be changed at the will of the people.

The *Aymette* line of cases is perhaps truest to the intention of the draftsmen of the state bills of rights. The right to bear arms was a means of preserving the liberty of the people by balancing the military power in the hands of the state by military power in the hands of the   people. The desire to maintain such a balance has had a long history dating from feudal times, through the English revolution to the present day. Such thinking, however, is rare in judicial opinions. Similarly rare is the unitary concept of society and government expressed by the Kansas court in *City of Salina v. Blakesly*.[69]

> The provision ...that 'the people have the right to bear arms for their defense and security' refers to the people as a collective body. It was the safety and security of society that was being considered when this provision was put into our Constitution .... The provision in question applies only to the right to bear arms as a member of the State Militia, or some other military organization provided for by the law.[70]

Such thinking indicates belief that there is no need to provide for a military balance within the political and social structure when that structure is responsive to the people.

Most state courts have never spoken of the right to bear arms in the sophisticated terms of political balance, but rather treated the right as synonymous with the right of self-defense. In 1950 an Illinois court warned in the construction of an arms control statute "that it is aimed at persons of

---

[65]   2 Tenn. 154 (1840).

[66]   38 Ark. 564 (1882).

[67]   *Id.* at 566.

[68]   4 Ark. 18, 24 (1843).

[69]   70 Kan. 230, 83 P. 619 (1905).

[70]   *Id.* at 231-32, 83 P. at 620.

criminal instincts, and for the prevention of crime, and not against use in the protection of person or property."[71] In *Andrews v. State*,[72] a dissenting judge found that "the right exists only for the purpose of defense: and this is a right which no constitutional or legislative enactment can destroy." The dissent in the Oklahoma case of *Pierce v. State*[73] proclaimed—"From time immemorial, the home, be it ever so humble, has been sacred—the castle of the occupant—with the right to repell [sic] invasion or any trespass."

Answers to such claims vary from the flat declaration in *Buzzard* that individuals have surrendered the right of self-defense to the society as a whole, to the more moderate holding in *Andrews* that "every good citizen is bound to yield his preference as the means to be used, to the demands of the public good."[74] A Michigan court put forth a novel answer saying that the state's power is "subject to the limitation that its exercise be reasonable [and does not result] in the prohibition of   those arms which, by the common opinion and usage of law-abiding people, are [to be kept for] protection of person and property."[75]

These debates over the issue of the right of self-defense, though of primary interest today, have little relation to the intent of the draftsmen of the Bill of Rights. The right of self-defense has had a long history; but its history was parallel to, not connected with, the right to bear arms. The use of the right of self-defense to support a right to bear arms is of modern usage. Nevertheless, its modernity does not affect its relevance. The concept is the supreme law in several states of the union, and is a concept to be considered by any legislature hoping to pass restrictive arms legislation.

The confusion in the state courts over the right to bear arms is partly due to the judicial process itself. A court generally does not base its decision on political theory but considers the facts of the particular case before it. If a court feels a particular restrictive arms statute to be necessary and fair, and if the facts of the case before it are favorable, then the court will uphold the statute using whatever language and doctrine is required to so hold. If the statute appears unfair, if the times are unfavorable, or if the factual situation is difficult, then the court will use the language and doctrine necessary to overturn the statute. For example, a Florida court stated in 1912 that the right to bear arms "was intended to give the people the means of protecting themselves against oppression and public outrage, and was not designed as a shield for the individual man."[76] Fifty years later the court declared that "doubtless the guarantee was intended to secure to the people the right to carry weapons for their protection."[77] Similar situations have occurred in several states.[78] The development of federal doctrine, however, has followed a more constant and evolutionary course.

---

[71] People v. Liss, 406 Ill. 419, 424, 94 N.E. 2d 320, 323 (1950).

[72] 50 Tenn. 165 (1871).

[73] 275 P. 393, 397 (Okla. Crim. Ct. App. 1929).

[74] 50 Tenn. 165, 193 (1871).

[75] People v. Brown, 253 Mich. 537, 541, 235 N.W. 245, 246 (1931).

[76] Carlton v. State, 63 Fla. 1, 9, 50 So. 486, 488 (1912).

[77] Davis v. State, 146 So. 2d 892, 893 (Fla. 1962).

[78] *Cf.* State v. Buzzard, 4 Ark. 18 (1843); Wilson v. State, 33 Ark. 557 (1878); Haile v. State, 38 Ark. 564 (1882); City of Akron v. Williams, 172 N.E. 2d 28 (Mun. Ct. Akron, Ohio 1960); City of Akron v. Williams, 177 N.E. 2d 802 (Ct. App. Ohio 1960), aff'd without opinion, 172 Ohio St. 287, 175 N.E. 2d 174 (1961).

B. Federal Courts

Cases concerning the second amendment arose in the federal courts only after the Civil War. The first of such cases, *U.S. v. Cruickshank*,[79] implied that there was a *personal* right to bear arms upon which Congress could not infringe. The central point of the opinion, however, was to state that the second amendment did not apply to state governments, and such governments could pass whatever legislation they desired without fear of federal sanction.

Cruickshank was not directly concerned with the right to bear arms or the militia, but with civil rights legislation. The first federal case to be directly concerned with arms was *Presser v. Illinois*.[80] Presser was convicted for leading a military parade in violation of an Illinois statute which forbade such parades by any group but the state militia. Presser claimed that the Illinois statute was in violation of the second amendment. The court relied on *Cruickshank* in stating that the "amendment is a limitation only upon the power of Congress and the National Government, and not upon that of the States,"[81] but added a restriction upon the State's power:

> It is undoubtedly true that all citizens capable of bearing arms constitute the reserved military force or reserve Militia of the United States as well as of the States; and, in view of this prerogative of the General Government, as well as of its general powers, the States cannot, even laying the constitutional provision in question out of view, prohibit the people from keeping and bearing arms, so as to deprive the United States of their rightful resource for maintaining the public security, and disable the people from performing their duty to the General Government.[82]

This principle harkens back to the citizen army of Saxon times and had little relevance in 1886. It was understandable, however, that only twenty years after the Civil War, the Supreme Court would be concerned with state attempts to weaken the central government by withholding arms and troops from national service. Nevertheless, the restriction is a complete reversal from the aims of the draftsmen of the Constitution and Bill of Rights which was to restrict the military power of the central government and give the state more leverage.

On one subject *Presser* was quite clear—there was no right to band together in paramilitary organizations:

> Military organization and military drill and parade under arms are subjects especially under the control of the government of every   country. They cannot be claimed as a right independent of law. Under our political system they are subject to the regulation and control of the State and Federal Governments, acting in due regard to their respective prerogatives and powers.[83]

---

[79]   92 U.S. 542 (1874).

[80]   116 U.S. 252 (1886).

[81]   *Id.* at 264.

[82]   *Id.* at 265.

[83]   *Id.* at 266-67.

Thus, whatever right to bear arms was recognized, that right was limited to arms and organizations that did not threaten the security of the government. The court did not approve of an armed population as a balance to governmental power.

For many years after *Presser* the issue of the second amendment appeared in federal courts only in reaffirming the *Cruickshank* holding that the second amendment did not apply to the states.[84] In the 1930's Congress passed two laws, the Federal Firearms Act[85] and the National Firearms Act,[86] to control commerce in certain types of dangerous weapons. Both acts were attacked in court for being in violation of the second amendment. In upholding the National Firearms Act, the district court held in *United States v. Adams*[87] that the second amendment "refers to the Militia, a protective force of government; to the collective body and not individual rights." This language was quoted verbatim by another district court in *United States v. Tot*[88] in upholding the Federal Firearms Act. Neither court went into the problem of the extent to which the collective right could be regulated, but both made clear that no personal right to own arms existed under the federal Constitution.

The issue of regulating the collective right arose in *United States v. Miller*[89] in which the Supreme Court held that as long as the weapon regulated did not have a direct relationship to the arms used in maintaining a well-regulated militia, they could be controlled:

> In the absence of any evidence tending to show that possession or use of a 'shotgun having a barrel of less than eighteen inches in length' at this time has some reasonable relationship to the preservation or efficiency of a well-regulated Militia, we cannot say that the Second Amendment guarantees the right to keep and bear such an instrument.[90]

The difficulty with such an interpretation is that were a weapon to have such a "reasonable relationship" it would be a protected weapon under the second amendment. The circuit court in *Cases v. United States*[91] recognized this problem saying: "But to hold that the Second Amendment limits the federal government to regulations concerning only weapons which can be classed as antiques or curiosities,—almost any other might bear some reasonable relationship to the preservation or efficiency of a well-regulated militia unit of the present day,—is in effect to hold that the limitation of the second amendment is absolute."[92] The court also recognized that such an interpretation would prohibit the federal government from prohibiting private ownership of heavy weapons "even though under the circumstances of such possession or use it would be inconceivable

---

[84]   Miller v. Texas, 153 U.S. 535 (1894).

[85]   15 U.S.C.A. 901-909.

[86]   26 U.S.C.A. 5801-5862.

[87]   11 F. Supp. 216, 219 (S.D. Fla. 1935).

[88]   28 F. Supp. 900, 903 (D. Conn. 1939); rev'd on other grounds, 319 U.S. 403 (1943).

[89]   307 U.S. 174 (1939).

[90]   *Id.* at 178.

[91]   131 F. 2d 916, (1st Cir. 1942); *cert. den. sub. nom.* Cases Velasquez v. United States, 319 U.S. 770 (1943); rehearing denied, 324 U.S. 889 (1945).

[92]   *Id.* at 922.

that a private person could have any legitimate reason for having such a weapon."[93] The court then decided it would be impossible to formulate any general test to determine the limits of the second amendment and each case would have to be decided on its individual merits.

The federal courts have interpreted the right to bear arms contained in the second amendment very narrowly. The right exists only to the extent that the arms are required for a well-regulated militia. Since *Presser*, however, the second amendment has been interpreted as a source of federal power and not as a protection of state power. The need for the old military balance between state and national governments had disappeared, and the federal courts no longer recognized its existence.

Similarly, the federal courts no longer recognized the need for a military balance between the population and its government. Rather, the courts have held that the interests of order and stability must be balanced against the need for revolution, and such interests may outweigh any need for the right of revolution. Thus, there could also be restrictions on other, subsidiary natural rights such as the right to bear arms. As Justice Vinson said in *Dennis v. United States*[94] in upholding the Smith Act:

> That it is within the *power* of the Congress to protect the government of the United States from armed rebellion is a proposition which requires little discussion. Whatever theoretical merit there may be to the argument that there is a "right" to rebellion against dictatorial governments is without force where the existing structure of the government provides for peaceful and orderly change. We reject any principle of governmental helplessness in the face of preparations for revolution, which principle, carried to its logical conclusion, must lead to anarchy.[95]

Even thought the right of revolution has never been recognized by the courts of the United States, armed rebellion has been—and still is—an important part of the American political tradition. From the early Republic to the present day dissident elements who have not been able to achieve their goals within the political structure have resorted to arms as a final resort.[96] In many instances, such elements have been punished as rebellious or treasonable, but in others the use or threat of violence has forced the political structure to compromise with the dissidents. Though not protected by the Constitution, this use of arms is the most important and relevant use of arms today.

V. CONCLUSION

Regardless of the long history of violence and assassination in the United States, the right to bear arms has remained closely and jealously guarded. This right appears to provide the individual with the means of protecting himself against other individuals and of protecting himself against his government. The maintenance of a military balance within the political structure was the genesis of this right, and the desire to continue such a balance will promote its continuation. The right to bear arms supports man in his fear of being defenseless in the face of personal danger or oppression.

---

93   *Id.*

94   341 U.S. 494 (1951).

95   *Id.* at 501.

96   *See* R. Ginger, Age of Excess (1965), and references cited therein.

The possibility, however, of maintaining a military balance within a political structure has become smaller as society has become more complex and warfare more destructive. In the words of Roscoe Pound:

> In the urban industrial society of today a general right to bear efficient arms so as to be enabled to resist oppression by the government would mean that gangs could exercise an extra-legal rule which could defeat the whole Bill of Rights.[97]

Thus, after over three centuries, the right to bear arms is becoming anachronistic. As the policing of society becomes more efficient, the   need for arms for personal self-defense becomes more irrelevant; and as the society itself becomes more complex, the military power in the hands of the government more powerful, and the government itself more responsive, the right to bear arms becomes more futile, meaningless and dangerous.

---

[97]   R. Pound, The Development of Constitutional Guarantees of Liberty 91 (1957).

Standing Armies And Armed Citizens: An Historical Analysis of The Second Amendment

By Roy G. Weatherup[*]

I. Introduction: Guns and the Constitution

As a result of a steadily rising crime rate in recent years, a sharp public debate over the merits of federal firearms regulation has developed. "Crime in the streets" has become a national preoccupation; politicians cry out for "law and order"; and the handgun has become a target of attention. The number of robberies jumped from 138,000 in 1965 to 376,000 in 1972, while murders committed by guns shot up from 5,015 to 10,379 in the same period, and the proportion of cases in which the murder weapon was a firearm rose from 57.2 percent to 65.6 percent.[1] The recent attempt on the life of President Ford in Sacramento by an erstwhile member of the "Manson Gang" serves to heighten the terror of a nation already stunned by the assassinations of John F. Kennedy, Martin Luther King and Robert F. Kennedy, and the maiming of George Wallace. Many people assert that these tragedies could have been prevented by keeping the murder weapons out of the hands that used them. Others vehemently dispute this claim.

The free flow of firearms across state lines has undermined the traditional view of crime and gun control as local problems. In New York City, long noted for strict regulation of all types of weapons, only 19 percent of the 390 homicides of 1960 involved pistols, by 1972, this proportion had jumped to 49 percent of 1,691. In 1973, there were only 28,000 lawfully possessed handguns in the nation's largest city, but police estimated that there were as many as *1.3 million* illegal handguns, mostly imported from southern states with lax laws.[2] These statistics give credence to the arguments of proponents of gun control that federal action is needed, if only to make local laws enforceable.

The great majority of the American people now support registration of both handguns and rifles. When the Gallup Poll asked the   question: "Do you favor or oppose registration of all firearms?" in a recent survey, more than two-thirds (67 percent) favored the concept, while 27 percent opposed it, and 6 percent had no opinion. Even gun-owners endorsed registration by a margin of 55 percent to 39 percent with 6 percent undecided.[3] Yet, although the intensity of belief

---

[*]   J.D., 1972 Stanford University; Member of the California Bar.

[1]   U.S. BUREAU OF THE CENSUS, STATISTICAL ABSTRACT OF THE UNITED STATES: 1974, at 147-51. (95th ed. 1974).

[2]   N.Y. Times, Dec. 2, 1973, § 1, at 1, col. 5 (city ed.).

[3]   L.A. Times, June 5, 1975, § 1, at 29, col. 1.

is undoubtedly far stronger in the minority than in the majority Congress has remained dormant.[4] The zeal of those individuals dedicated to the preservation of the "right to keep and bear arms" in its present form cannot be doubted.

American history has often seen social and political problems transformed into constitutional issues.[5] The gun control issue is no exception to this phenomenon, and particular attention has been focused on the Second Amendment to the United States Constitution, which provides: "A well regulated Militia, being necessary to the security of a free State, the right of the people to keep and bear Arms, shall not be infringed."

Proponents of gun control seize the phrase "a well regulated Militia" and find in it the sole purpose of the constitutional guarantee. They therefore assert that "the right of the people to keep and bear Arms" is a collective right which protects only members of the organized militia, e.g., the National Guard, and only in the performance of their duties. It is their belief that no one else can claim a personal right   to keep and bear arms for any purpose whatsoever, criminal or otherwise.

Opponents maintain that having guns is a constitutionally protected individual right, similar to other guarantees of the Bill of Rights. Some hold this right to be absolute, while others would allow reasonable restrictions, perhaps even licensing and registration. Still others would limit the protection of the Second Amendment to individuals capable of military service and to weapons useful for military purposes. The essential characteristic of the "individualist" interpretation, as opposed to the "collectivist" view, is that the Second Amendment precludes, to some extent at least, congressional interference in the private use of firearms for lawful purposes such as target shooting, hunting and self-defense.

It is one of the ironies of contemporary politics that the many of the most vocal supporters of "law and order" are persistent critics of federal firearms regulation. "Guns don't kill people; people kill people" is their philosophy. Firearms in private hands are viewed as a means of protecting an individual's life and property, as well as a factor in helping to preserve the Republic against foreign and domestic enemies. Whereas strict constructionism is often the preferred doctrine in interpreting the constitutional rights of criminals, such a narrow view of the Second Amendment is unacceptable. Far from being narrowly construed, the Second Amendment is held out to be a bulwark of human freedom and dignity as well as a means of safeguarding the rights of the individual against encroachment by the federal government. It thus becomes a weapon in the arsenal of argument

---

[4]   Congressional lethargy cannot be attributed to a lack of proposed legislation. At every session of the Congress, a number of bills for the control of handguns and other weaponry are introduced, only to be shunted to committee and never heard from again. For example, the following is only a partial listing of proffered statutes for the First Session of the 94th Congress: S. 750 was introduced by Senator Hart (Mich.) to prohibit the importation, manufacture, sale, purchase, transfer, receipt, possession or transportation of handguns unless authorized by federal or state authorities. S. 1477, introduced by Senator Kennedy (Mass.) and known as the Federal Handgun Control Act of 1975 is basically a registration and licensing statute. It would prohibit the private sale or manufacture of handguns under six inches in length. (Both bills are currently pending in the Senate Judiciary Subcommittee on Juvenile Delinquency.)

S. 1880, authored by Senator Bayh (Ind.) was passed by the Senate by a vote of 68 to 25, only to die on the floor of the House of Representatives. Entitled the Violent Crime and Repeat Offender Act of 1975, it would have provided additional penalties for felonies committed with firearms, and required the prompt reporting of theft of firearms by licensees.

In addition, there is a major bill pending in the House of Representative which is not duplicated in the Senate. H.R. 2381 would prohibit the importation and manufacture of hollow-point bullets. This bill is now pending in the House Ways and Means Committee as well as in the House Interstate and Foreign Commerce Committee.

[5]   See, e.g., Roe v. Wade, 410 U.S. 113 (1973) (the question of abortion); Schechter Corp. v. United States, 295 U.S. 495 (1935) (the New Deal's National Recovery Administration); Dred Scott v. Sanford, 60 U.S. (19 How.) 393 (1857) (the spread of slavery controversy).

against gun control, and each new proposal is said to infringe upon the rights of the people to keep and bear arms.

The clash between "collectivist" and "individualist" interpretations of the Second Amendment has not been definitely resolved. Even members of Congress believe that their power to regulate firearms is limited by the existence of an individual right to have, to hold, and to use them. Senator Hugh Scott, Republican of Pennsylvania, writes in *Guns & Ammo* magazine: "As my record shows, I have always defended the right-to-bear-arms provision of the Second Amendment. I have a gun in my own home and I certainly intend to keep it."[6]

There has been very little case law construing the Second Amendment, perhaps because there has been very little federal legislation on the subject of firearms. This may change, and it may become necessary for the Supreme Court to rule upon constitutional challenges to federal statutes based on the Second Amendment. Even before this occurs, it would be helpful to dispel the uncertainties that exist in Congress about the extent of federal legislative power.

In order to determine accurately the intended meaning of the Second Amendment, it is necessary to delve into history. It is necessary to consider the very nature of a constitutional guarantee—whether it is an inherent, fundamental right, derived from abstract human nature and natural law or, alternatively, a restriction on governmental power imposed after experience with abuse of power.

Historically, the right to keep and bear arms has been closely intertwined with questions of political sovereignty, the right of revolution, civil and military power, military organization, crime and personal security. The Second Amendment was written neither by accident nor without purpose; it was the product of centuries of Anglo-American legal and political experience. This development will be examined in order to determine whether the "collectivist" or "individualist" construction of the Second Amendment is correct.[7]

II. The Evolution of British Military Power

Victorious at the Battle of Hastings in 1066, William the Conqueror was able to assert personal ownership over all the land of England and sovereignty over its people. All power emanated from the King, and all persons held their property and privileges at his sufferance.

Feudal society was organized along military lines in 1181. King Henry II, great grandson of the Conqueror, issued the Assize of Arms, which formalized the military duties of subjects. The first three articles of the decree specify what armament each level of society is to maintain—ranging from the holder of a knight's fee, who must equip himself with a hauberk, a helmet, a shield and a lance, down to the poorest freeman armed only with an iron headpiece and a lance. The philosophy of the law is expressed in the fourth article, which is as follows:

> Moreover, let each and every one of them swear that before the feast of St. Hilary
> he will possess these arms and will bear allegiance to the lord king, Henry, namely the son
> of the Empress Maud, and that he will bear these arms in his service according to his order

---

[6] Scott, *Leading Senator Admits Gun Law Mistake!*, Mar. 1970 Guns & Ammo., 46, 47.

[7] For an earlier article which discusses the "collectivist" versus the "individualist" approach to the Second Amendment, *see* Feller & Gotting, *The Second Amendment: A Second Look*, 61 Nw. U.L. Rev. 46 (1966-67). The authors conclude: "[T]he 'right of the people' refers to the collective right of the body politic of each state to be under the protection of an independent, effective state militia". *Id.* at 69. (citation omitted). *But see* Hays, *The Right to Bear Arms, a Study in Judicial Misinterpretation*, 2 Wm. & Mary L. Rev. 381 (1960). Hays contends that the right to bear arms is an individual one.

and in allegiance to the lord king and his realm. And let none of those who hold these arms sell them or pledge them or offer them, or in any other way alienate them; neither let a lord in any way deprive his men of them either by forfeiture or gift, or as surety or in any other manner.[8]

The remainder of the statute prescribes rules and procedures governing its administration. The Assize of Arms marked the beginning of the militia system; its clear purpose was to strengthen and maintain the King's authority.

In 1215, the rebellious Norman barons forced King John to sign the Magna Carta, a document justly regarded as the foundation of Anglo-American freedom. The Great Charter consists of sixty-three articles which set forth in great detail certain restrictions on the King's prerogative. Its introductory article concludes, "Ye have also granted to all the free men of Our kingdom, for Us and Our heirs forever, all the liberties underwritten, to have and to hold to them and their heirs of Us and Our heirs."[9] Implicit in this statement is the fact that sovereignty is deemed to be vested in the office of kingship, and that the King is restricting his powers in favor of his subjects. Roscoe Pound makes this comment on the Magna Carta:

> The ground plan to which the common-law polity has built ever since was given by the Great Charter. It was not merely the first attempt to put in legal terms what became the leading ideas of constitutional government. It put them in the form of limitations on the exercise of authority, not of concessions to free human action from authority. It put them as legal propositions, so that they could and did come to be a part of the ordinary law of the land invoked like any other legal precepts in the ordinary course of orderly litigation. Moreover, it did not put them abstractly. In characteristic English fashion it put them concretely in the form of a body of specific provisions for present ills, not a body of general declarations in universal terms. Herein, perhaps, is the secret of its enduring vitality.[10]

Centuries were to pass before an English sovereign would again proclaim the doctrine of unrestricted royal power which William the Conqueror had established by force of arms, and which King John had lost in the same manner.

Even though medieval England had not yet developed firearms, the government found it necessary to severely restrict such weapons as did exist. In 1328 Parliament passed the celebrated Statute of Northhampton, which made it an offense to ride armed at night, or by day in fairs, markets, or in the presence of king's ministers.[11]

The fifteenth century dynastic struggle known as the War of Roses virtually destroyed the feudal system, and prepared the way for a new consolidation of royal power beginning with the coronation of Henry Tudor as King Henry VII in 1485. The Tudors maintained a large degree of national unity. Their task was made easier by practical applications of gunpowder. The royal cannon made resistance by the nobility futile.

Perhaps because of the weakness of their hereditary claims, the Tudor monarchs attempted to control and manipulate Parliament, rather than assert the royal prerogative in defiance of

---

[8]   THE ASSIZE OF ARMS, ¶ 4 (1181), in 2 ENGLISH HISTORICAL DOCUMENTS 416 (D. Douglas & G. Greenaway ed. 1953).

[9]   MAGNA CARTA: TEXT AND COMMENTARY 34 (A.E.D. Howard ed. 1964).

[10]   R. POUND, THE DEVELOPMENT OF CONSTITUTIONAL GUARANTEES OF LIBERTY 18-19 (1957).

[11]   STATUTE OF NORTHHAMPTON, 2 Edw. 3, c.3 (1328).

Parliament. It was even admitted that Parliament could regulate the succession to the throne, acting in conjunction with the reigning monarch, of course. In the reign of Elizabeth, it was declared to be high treason to deny that Parliament and the Queen could "make laws and statutes of sufficient force and validity to limit and bind the crown of this realm, and the descent, limitation, inheritance, and government thereof."[12]

The long war with the Hapsburg Empire that began at the time of the Spanish Armada contributed to an upsurge of national sentiment. Faith in the English militia was vindicated as free men had held their own against the massive, professional standing armies of the Spanish King. Englishmen came to believe the militia was the best security for their country and their liberties.

At the death of Elizabeth I in 1603, King James VI of Scotland ascended the English throne as James I. The advent of the House of Stuart marked the beginning of a century of religious and political struggle between Crown and Parliament. Out of this struggle, what we know as the English Constitution emerged. The monarchy was finally and firmly restricted, but preserved, the supremacy of Parliament was established, the common law became a strong, independent force, and the liberties of the people were encased in a Bill of Rights.

Although a model constitutional monarch in some respects, in the realm of political theory, James I challenged the sensibilities of the nation. He boldly proclaimed the divine right theory of government—that kings hold their thrones by the will of God alone, and not by the will of peoples or parliaments. Typical of his sentiment are these excerpts from his speech to Parliament on March 21, 1610:

> The State of MONARCHIE is the spremest thing upon earth: For Kings are not onely GODS Lieutenants upon earth, and sit upon GODS throne, but even by GOD himselfe they are called Gods.... In the Scriptures Kings are called Gods, and so their power after a certaine relation compared to the Divine Power.

The King concluded that "to dispute what GOD may doe, is blasphemie,"   and thus it is "sedition in Subjects, to dispute what a King may do in the height of his power."[13] Here was a King not restricted by any human law.

Neither the legal profession nor Parliament was willing to accept such a boundless royal prerogative. Having grown up in the civil law tradition of Scotland, James I was indifferent to the common law, but the English lawyers argued that, while the King had many privileges at common law, he was limited by and subordinate to it. When James I asserted that Parliament existed only by "the grace and permission of our ancestors and us,"[14] the House of Commons passed the famous Protestation of December 18, 1621, which asserted:

> That the Liberties, Franchises, Privileges and Jurisdictions of Parliament, are the ancient and undoubted birthright and inheritance of the subjects of England; and that the arduous and urgent affairs concerning the King, State and defence of the realm, and of the Church of England, and the making and maintenance of laws, and redress of michiefs and grievances, which daily happen within this realm, are proper subjects and matter of counsel and debate in Parliament: and that in the handling and proceeding of those businesses every member

---

[12]   Treasons Act, 13 Eliz. 1, c.1 (1571).

[13]   KING JAMES I, THE WORKES OF THE MOST HIGH AND MIGHTIE PRINCE JAMES 529, 531 (1916).

[14]   1 PARL. HIST. ENG. 1351 (1621).

of the House hath, and of right ought to have, Freedom of Speech, to propound, treat, reason and bring to conclusion the same....[15]

The King's response was to walk into the House of Commons and to tear from the Journal the page containing these words.

The leading legal theorist of the time was Sir Edward Coke, whose writings and leadership were to enhance the prestige of the common law, and bring it into alliance with Parliament against the monarchy. In response to an inquiry from James I, Coke and his colleagues declared:

> That the King by his proclamation cannot create any offence which was not an offence before, for then he may alter the law of the land by his proclamation in a high point; for if he may create an offence where none is, upon that ensues fine and imprisonment ...; That the King hath no prerogative, but that which the law of the land allows him....[16]

The common law courts asserted jurisdiction to inquire into the legality of acts of servants of the Crown, and thus began the doctrine of the rule of law.

In response to the wars waged by James I's improvident heir, Charles I, Parliament enacted the Petition of Right in 1628, inspired   and drafted largely by Coke. The petition was an assertion of the power of Parliament and the common law, and contained a long list of grievances. The abuses of the King's military power—billeting, martial law, imprisonment without trial, and forced loans—were particularly resented. Charles I had no choice but to sign the petition, since he needed revenues from Parliament, but he secretly consulted his judges who assured him that his signature would not be binding. Soon afterward, in 1629, the King dissolved Parliament and began the long period of personal rule which was to end in the Great Rebellion.

Charles I was short of money, and revived an ancient tax; his judges upheld the legality of this action in the famous Ship Money case of 1635. The King also wished to strengthen the Church of England, the mainstay of the monarchy. The ecclesiastical canons of 1640 emphatically affirmed the theory of Divine Right of Kings and, in addition, promulgated the doctrine of nonresistance:

> For subjects to bear arms against their kings, offensive or defensive, upon any pretence whatsoever, is at least to resist the powers which are ordained of God; and though they do not invade but only resist, St. Paul tells them plainly they shall receive to themselves damnation.[17]

This doctrine of "nonresistance" was to have an important role in religion and politics in both England and America, for the next century and a half.

Faced with a Scottish rebellion, Charles I was forced to summon the English Parliament in 1640 in order to obtain the resources necessary to put down the insurrection. After eleven years of personal royal government, Parliament trusted neither the King nor his leading minister, the Earl of Strafford. Parliament demanded a wide array of religious and political concessions, including the

---

[15]   *Id.* at 1361.

[16]   7 THE REPORTS OF SIR EDWARD COKE, KNT 76 (G. Wilson trans. 1777).

[17]   Constitutions and Cannons Ecclesiastical, Treated Upon by the Archbishops of Canterbury and York (1640), in 1 SYNODALIA 390-91 (E. Cardwell ed. 1842).

removal of Strafford as governor of Ireland and the disbanding of the strong army he had created there. When the King acceded to these demands, Ireland rebelled.

Charles I was now desperate. Scotland and Ireland were in open rebellion, and the Parliament of England was dominated by the King's enemies. The King had made numerous concessions, but to no avail. Strafford wanted to bring John Pym, the parliamentary leader, to trial for treasonable dealings with the Scottish army invading England, but Pym struck first with a bill of attainder against Strafford. The main charge was the creation of a powerful army in Ireland for the purpose of crushing opposition in England. The bill of attainder passed, and the King was forced to send his ablest servant to the scaffold in 1641.

Still unsatisfied, Parliament presented its Nineteen Propositions as an ultimatum to the King in 1642. The Propositions, if acceded to, would have established a very limited monarchy with the King surrendering the power of the sword and Parliament obtaining complete control over the militia. Instead, the King raised the royal standard at Nottingham and proclaimed Parliament to be in rebellion. Thus began the Civil Wars, which resulted in the decapitation of Charles I and the proclamation of a republic in 1649.

Oliver Cromwell and the Puritans came to power by force of arms and the creation of a disciplined standing army. Cromwell soon quarreled with Parliament and assumed the role of a military dictator. The soldiers supported their leader because Parliament proposed to disband much of the army thus depriving them of their livelihood, and also because they feared that Parliament might once again come under the control of the Anglicans, who would revive persecution of the Puritan sects.

It was soon proposed that Cromwell be made king, but only because that office would have definite constitutional restrictions. Finally Cromwell assumed the title of Lord Protector in 1653, under a written constitution that gave him virtually royal power. Although Cromwell's government brought domestic peace and ruled efficiently, it did not gain in popularity. The Lord Protector's government was created and maintained by bayonets, and the people came to hate it. The end of the Protectorate and its legacy have been described by historian Eric Sheppard as follows:

> The great soldier's death in 1658, while the army he had made was still fighting victoriously in Flanders, marked the beginning of the end of that army's rule; its leaders soon had no choice but to accept the inevitable, and in May 1660 the red coats of the New Model were arrayed on Blackheath to do honor to the monarch whom nine years before it had hunted into exile. A few months later, setting an example which has since been followed by all the great armies of England, it ... laid down its arms and passed silently and peacefully into the pursuits of peace, leaving behind it, in the minds of the governing class and the people, besides a deservedly high military reputation, a legacy of hatred and distrust of all standing armies which has endured to our own day.[18]

The mood of England at the restoration of Charles II, son of the martyred Charles I, was one of relief and enthusiasm. An act was swiftly passed which recited that "the people of this kingdom lie under a great burden and charge in the maintenance and payment of the present army," and provided that it should be disbanded with "all convenient speed."[19]

---

[18]   E. SHEPPARD, A SHORT HISTORY OF THE BRITISH ARMY (4th ed. 1959).

[19]   Disbanding Act, 12 Car. 2, c. 15 (1660).

Once again reliance for the country's security was placed in the militia system, which had fallen into disuse after two decades of professional armies, civil wars and military government. Statutes were passed in 1661 and 1662 declaring that the King had the sole right of command and disposition of the militia, and providing for its organization.[20] Winston Churchill makes this comment on the Cavalier Parliament, which had restored the monarchy:

> It rendered all honour to the King. It had no intention of being governed by him. The many landed gentry who had been impoverished in the royal cause were not blind monarchists. They did not mean to part with any of the Parliamentary rights which had been gained in the struggle. They were ready to make provision for the defence of the country by means of militia; but the militia must be controlled by the Lord-Lieutenants of the counties. They vehemently asserted the supremacy of the Crown over the armed forces; but they took care that the only troops in the country should be under the local control of their own class. Thus not only the King but Parliament was without an army. The repository of force had now become the county families and gentry.[21]

The revival of the militia did not mean that the King was forbidden to raise and maintain armies. He had no means of doing so, however, because Parliament held the purse strings, and the quartering of soldiers had been condemned since the days of the Petition of Right.

Foreign wars made the development of a standing army inevitable, and it reached 16,000 men by the end of the reign of Charles II. It was done with the consent of Parliament, and English country gentlemen were secure in their control of the domestic armed power—the militia. In addition, guns were taken out of the hands of the common people. Among the conditions of a 1670 statute was one that no person, other than heirs of the nobility, could have a gun unless he owned land with a yearly value of £100.[22] The protection of the people's liberties was thus committed entirely to Parliament and other legal institutions. The possibility of a citizen army, such as that created by Oliver Cromwell, was precluded.

In the reign of Charles II, religious controversy dominated politics. The Cavalier Parliament wished to maintain the established Anglican Church and persecute dissenters, Catholic and Puritan alike. Parliament was also alarmed by the prospect that the King's Catholic brother, the Duke of York, would succeed to the throne. A parliamentary attempt to exclude the Duke failed, but in 1673 and 1678, two Test Acts were passed, which barred Catholics from all civil and military offices and from both Houses of Parliament.[23]

In 1685, the Catholic Duke of York ascended to the throne of James II. The new King quieted the fears of his subjects by proclaiming his intention to maintain church and state as they were by law established. The people were also comforted by the fact that the heirs to the throne were his Protestant daughters, Mary and Anne, and his Protestant nephew, William of Orange, stadtholder of the Dutch Republic and Mary's husband. Because of the Test Acts, James II inherited an entirely Protestant government.

---

[20] First Militia Act, 13 Car. 2, Stat. I, c. 6 (1661); Second Militia Act, 14 Car. 2, c. 3 (1662).

[21] 2 W. CHURCHILL, A HISTORY OF THE ENGLISH-SPEAKING PEOPLES 336 (1956).

[22] Game Preservation Act, 22 Car. 2, c. 25, § 3 (1670).

[23] Test Act. 25 Car. 2, c. 2. (1673); Parliamentary Test Act, 30 Car. 2, Stat. 2, c. 1 (1678) (an exemption allowed the Duke of York to retain his seat in the House of Lords).

At the same time a rebellion, led by the Duke of Monmouth, broke out in the western counties. The King successfully crushed the uprising, but in the process succeeded in doubling his standing army to 30,000 men, granting commissions to catholic officers, and bringing in recruits from Catholic Ireland. In addition he quartered his new army in private homes. These arbitrary actions were in direct violation of previous parliamentary proclamations.

James II then asked Parliament to repeal the Test Acts and the Habeas Corpus Act, which Parliament refused to do. The King also asked the representatives of the nation to abandon their reliance on the militia, in favor of standing armies:

> My Lords and Gentlemen,
>
> After the storm that seemed to be coming upon us when we parted last, I am glad to meet you all again in so great Peace and Quietness. God Almighty be praised, by those Blessing that Rebellion was suppressed: But when we reflect, what an inconsiderable Number of Men began it, and how long they carried [it] on without any Opposition, I hope every-body will be convinced, that the Militia, which hath hitherto been so much depended on, is not sufficient for such Occasions; and that there is nothing but a good Force of well disciplined Troops in constant Pay, that can defend us from such, as, either at Home or Abroad, are disposed to disturb us...[24]

John Dryden, the poet, shared the King's attitude toward the militia when he wrote these timeless words:

> The country rings around with loud alarms,
> And raw in fields the rude militia swarms;
> Mouths without hands; maintained at vast expense,
> In peace a charge, in war a weak defence;
> Stout once a month they march, a blustering band, And
> ever, but in times of need, at hand.
> This was the morn when, issuing on the guard,
> Drawn up in rank and file they stood prepared
> Of seeming arms to make a short essay,
> Then hasten to be drunk, the business of the day.[25]

Parliament adjourned in 1686 without resolving any of the basic issues. The King kept his army and pursued his policies through extra-parliamentary means.

To get rid of the Test Act, and to revive the royal prerogative at the same time, the King arranged a collusive lawsuit. A coachman in the service of a Roman Catholic officer brought suit under the Test Act to recover the statutory reward for discovering violators, and the officer pleaded a royal dispensation in defense. The King's judges in *Godden v. Hales*[26] upheld the validity of the dispensation and gave judgment for the defendant. Lord Chief Justice Herbert stated:

---

[24] 9 H.C. JOUR. 756 (1685).

[25] J. DRYDEN, CYMON AND IPHIGENIA, IN THE POETICAL WORKS OF JOHN DRYDEN 641 (W. Christie ed. 1893).

[26] Godden v. Hales, 89 Eng. Rep. 1050 (ex. 1686), *as reported in*, 11 STATE TRIALS 66 (T. Howell comp. 1811).

We are satisfied in our judgments before, and having the concurrence of eleven out of twelve, we think we may very well declare an opinion of the court to be, that the King may dispense in this case: and the judges go upon these grounds;

    1. That the kings of England are sovereign princes.

    2. That the laws of England are the king's laws.

    3. That therefore 'tis an inseparable prerogative in the kings of England, to dispense with penal laws in particular cases and upon particular necessary reasons.

    4. That of those reasons and those necessities the king himself is sole judge: And then, which is consequent upon all,

    5. That this is not a trust invested in or granted to the king by the people, but the ancient remains of the sovereign power and prerogative of the kings of England; which never yet has taken from them, nor can be.[27]

Thus armed with the law, the King proceeded to dispense with statutes as he saw fit. He replaced Protestants and Catholics at high posts in government, particularly at important military garrisons. The army was further enlarged and 13,000 men were stationed at Hounslow Heath, just outside London, in order to hold the city in subjection if necessary. How far James II planned to carry his religious and political program is unknown, but his powerful standing army made many Protestants fearful and uneasy about the future.

With the birth of a son, who would take precedence over the King's Protestant daughters in the succession, fear led to revolution.   Leading subjects sent a secret invitation to William of Orange to come to England in defense of the liberties of the people and his wife's right to the Crown. When William landed with a large Dutch army, the English army and government deserted James II who fled to France. Thus the Glorious Revolution of 1688 was accomplished. James II had believed that his enemies were paralyzed by the Anglican doctrine of nonresistance, but he had so alienated his subjects that he was deposed without being able to put up any resistance himself.

William and Mary were offered the Crown jointly after they accepted the Declaration of Rights on February 13, 1689. The Declaration was later enacted in the form of a statute, known as the Bill of Rights.[28] The document is divided into two main parts: 1) a list of allegedly illegal actions of James II, and 2) a declaration of the "ancient rights and liberties" of the realm.

The sections of the first part of the statute that are relevant to the right to bear arms are the allegations that James II

did endeavor to subvert and extirpate the Protestant Religion and the Laws and Liberties of this Kingdom ...

    5. By raising and keeping a Standing army within this Kingdom in Time of Peace without Consent of Parliament and quartering Soldiers contrary to Law.

    6. By causing several good Subjects, being Protestants, to be disarmed at the same Time when Papists were both armed and employed contrary to Law.[29]

It should be pointed out that the King did not disarm Protestants in any literal sense; the reference is to his desire to abandon the militia in favor of a standing army and his replacement of Protestants by Catholics at important military posts.

---

[27]   *Id.* at 1199.

[28]   Bill of Rights, 1 W. & M., sess. 2, c. 2 (1689).

[29]   *Id.*

The parallel sections of the declaration of rights part of the statute are:

> 5. That the raising or keeping a Standing Army within the Kingdom in Time of Peace unless it be with the Consent of Parliament is against Law.
> 6. That the Subjects which are Protestants may have Arms for their Defence suitable to their Conditions, and as allowed by Law.[30]

The purpose, and meaning of, the right to have arms recognized by these provisions is clear from their historical context. Protestant members of the militia might keep and bear arms in accordance with their militia duties for the defense of the realm. The right was recognized as a restriction on any future monarch who might wish to emulate James II and abandon the militia system in favor of a standing army without the consent of Parliament. There was obviously no recognition of any personal right to bear arms on the part of subjects generally, since existing law forbade ownership of firearms by anyone except heirs of the nobility and prosperous landowners.

In summary, the English Bill of Rights represents the culmination of the centuries old problem of the relationship of sovereignty and armed force. The king could have an army, but only with the express consent of Parliament. The king could not, however, dismantle and disarm the militia. There was no individual right to bear arms; the rights of subjects could be protected only by the political process and the fundamental laws of the land.

III. England and Her Colonies

The revolutionary settlement that followed the accession of William and Mary gave the English people permanent security. England, however, had become the center of an Empire, and the relationship between England and the outlying territories raised legal and political problems.

When William and Mary, and, later, Queen Anne, all died without heirs, the Crown passed to the distantly-related House of Hanover in Germany. Uprisings led by the son and grandson of James II were suppressed in 1715 and in 1745, and Parliament felt it necessary to deprive the people entirely of the right to bear arms in large parts of Scotland.[31]

The history of the English colonies in America was closely intertwined with that of the Mother Country. The New England colonies had been settled by Puritan refugees from the early Stuart kings. When Cromwell and the Puritans came to power in England, thousands of royalists fled to the southern colonies, swelling their populations.

The foundation of government in the colonies was the charter granted by the king. An important feature of a charter was the provision securing for the inhabitants of the colony the rights of Englishmen. For example, the 1606 Charter of Virginia contains this passage:

> Also we do ... DECLARE ... that all and every the Persons being our Subjects, which shall dwell and inhabit within every or any of the said several Colonies and Plantations, and every of their children, which shall happen to be born within any of the
> Limits and Precincts of the said several Colonies and Plantations, shall HAVE and enjoy all Liberties, Franchises, and Immunities, within any of our other Dominions, to

---

[30] *Id.* Securing the Peace in Scotland Act.

[31] 1 Geo. 1, Stat. 2, c. 54 (1715).

all Intents and Purposes, as if they had been abiding and born, within this our Realm of *England*, or any other of our said Dominions.[32]

During the seventeenth century and the first half of the eighteenth century, the North American colonies were essentially self-governing republics following the political and legal model of England. In 1720, Richard West, counsel to the Board of Trade, gave this description of the state of law in the colonies:

> The Common Law of England is the Common Law of the Plantations, and all statutes in affirmance of the Common Law, passed in England antecedent to the settlement of a colony, are in force in that colony, unless there is some private Act to the contrary; though no statutes, made since those settlements, are there in force unless the colonies are particularly mentioned. Let an Englishman go where he will, he carries as much of law and liberty with him, as the nature of things will bear.[33]

The legal relationship of Britain and the colonies became more than an academic problem after the end of the Seven Years' War in 1763. That war, known in America as the French and Indian War, brought large British armies to colonies which had hitherto known no armed force but the colonial militia. The cost of the war was enormous, and the British government decided that the colonies should share it.

In his efforts to tax and govern the colonies, George III acted in two capacities: as King, armed with the prerogatives of his office, and as the agent of the British Parliament which at that time was under his personal control. The colonists acknowledged the authority of the King, but only in accordance with their charters and with the same restrictions that limited his power in Britain. Many of the colonists denied the authority of the British Parliament to regulate their internal affairs in any way.

Colonial resistance forced the British government to abandon the Stamp Tax, but Parliament passed the Declaratory Act in 1766 entitled "An Act for the better securing the Dependency of his majesty's dominions in *America* upon the Crown and parliament of *Great Britain*."

> Whereas several of the Houses of Representatives in his Majesty's Colonies and Plantations in *America*, have of late, against Law, claimed to themselves or to the General Assemblies of the same, the sole and exclusive Right of imposing Duties and Taxes upon his Majesty's Subjects in the said Colonies and Plantations; and have, in pursuance of such Claim, passed certain Votes, Resolutions and Orders, derogatory to the Legislative Authority of Parliament, and inconsistent with the Dependency of the said Colonies and Plantations upon the Crown of *Great Britain* be it declared ... That the said Colonies and Plantations in *America* have been, are, and of Right ought to be, subordinate unto, and dependent upon, the Imperial Crown and Parliament of *Great Britain*; and that the King's Majesty, by and with the Advice and Consent of the Lords Spiritual and Temporal, and Commons of *Great Britain* in Parliament assembled, had, hath, and of Right ought to have, full Power and Authority to make Laws and Statutes of sufficient Force and Validity to bind

---

[32]   VA. CHARTER (1606), in 7 THE FEDERAL AND STATE CONSTITUTIONS, COLONIAL CHARTERS, AND OTHER ORGANIC LAWS OF THE STATES, TERRITORIES, AND COLONIES 3788 (F. Thorpe ed. 1909) [hereinafter cited as CONSTITUTIONS].

[33]   1 G. CHALMERS, OPINIONS OF EMINENT LAWYERS ON VARIOUS POINTS OF ENGLISH JURISPRUDENCE 194, 195 (1814).

the Colonies and People of *America*, Subjects of the Crown of *Great Britain*, in all Cases whatsoever.[34]

The colonists were free-born Englishmen and they were not willing to accept inferior status. They could not admit the authority of Crown and Parliament to bind them "in all cases whatsoever." They fell back on the doctrine of fundamental law as expressed in 1764 by James Otis:

> 'Tis hoped it will not be considered as a new doctrine, that even the authority of the Parliament of *Great-Britain* is circumscribed by certain bounds, which if exceeded their acts become those of mere *power* without *right*, and consequently void. The judges of England have declared in favour of these sentiments, when they expressly declare; that *acts of Parliament against natural equity are void*. That *acts against the fundamental principles of the British constitution are void*. This doctrine is agreeable to the law of nature and nations, and to the divine dictates of natural and revealed religion.[35]

The concept of fundamental law was developed and grounded squarely on the English legal tradition. In 1772, Samuel Adams wrote in response to another writer in the *Gazette*:

> Chromus talks of *Magna Carta* as though it were of no greater consequence that an act of Parliament for the establishment of a corporation of button-makers. Whatever low ideas he may entertain of the *Great Charter* ... it is affirm'd by Lord Coke, to be declaratory of the principal grounds of the fundamental laws and liberties of England. "It is called *Charta Libertatum Regni, the Charter of the Liberties of the kingdom*, upon great reason ... because *liberos facit, it makes and preserves the people free*." ... But if it be declaratory of the principal grounds of the fundamental laws and liberties of England, it cannot be altered in any of its essential parts, without altering the constitution.... Vatel tells us plainly and without hesitation, that "the supreme legislative cannot   change the constitution."
> ... If then according to Lord Coke, *Magna Charta* is declatory of the principal grounds of the *fundamental* laws and liberties of the people, and Vatel is right in his opinion, that the supreme legislative cannot change the constitution, I think it follows, whether Lord Coke has expressly asserted it or not, that an act of parliament made against Magna Charta in violation of its essential parts, is void.[36]

This statement of fundamental law later influenced the intellectual foundation of judicial review in the United States.

In order to sustain his claim of full and unrestricted sovereignty, George III sent large standing armies to the colonies. America was outraged. The colonists drew their arguments from Whig political theorists on both sides of the Atlantic who maintained that standing armies in time of peace were tools of oppression, and that the security of a free people was best preserved by a militia.

The American colonists, who had always relied on their own militia, hated and feared standing armies even more than their English brethren. In quartering his redcoats in private homes, suspending charters and laws, and eventually imposing martial law, George III was doing in America

---

[34]   Declaratory Act, 6 Geo. 3, c. 12 (1766).

[35]   J. OTIS, THE RIGHTS OF THE BRITISH COLONIES ASSERTED AND PROVED 72-73 (1764).

[36]   S. ADAMS, *Candidus Letters* (1772), in 2 THE WRITINGS OF SAMUEL ADAMS 324-26 (H. Cushing ed. 1906).

what he could not do in England. The royal prerogative had virtually ended in England with the Revolution of 1688, but the King was reviving it in America.

The Fairfax County Resolutions, drawn up under the leadership of George Washington and passed on July 18, 1774, reflect the colonial attitude in the year prior to the outbreak of war. Of particular interest is the following paragraph:

> *Resolved*, That it is our greatest wish and inclination, as well as interest, to continue our connection with, and dependence upon, the *British* Government; but though we are its subjects, we will use every means which Heaven hath given us to prevent our becoming its slaves.[37]

In October of the same year, the First Continental Congress assembled and stated the position of the colonies in these resolutions:

> *Resolved*, ... 1. That they are entitled to life, liberty, & property, and they have never ceded to any sovereign power whatever, a right to dispose of either without their consent.
>
> *Resolved*, ... 2. That our ancestors, who first settled these colonies, were at the time of their emigration from the mother country, entitled to all the rights, liberties, and immunities of free and natural-born subjects, within the realm of England.
>
> *Resolved*, ... 3. That by such emigration they by no means forfeited, surrendered, or lost any of those rights, but that they were, and their descendants now are, entitled to the exercise and enjoyment of all such of them, as their local and other circumstances enable them to exercise and enjoy.
>
> *Resolved*, ... 4. That the foundation of English liberty, and of all free government, is a right in the people to participate in their legislative council: and as the English colonists are not represented, and from their local and other circumstances, cannot properly be represented in the British parliament, they are entitled to a free and exclusive power of legislation in their several provincial legislatures, where their right of representation can alone be preserved, in all cases of taxation and internal polity, subject only to the negative of their sovereign, in such manner as has been heretofore used and accustomed....[38]

After stating these general principles, the Congress listed specific rights that had been violated by George III, including the following:

> *Resolved*, ... 9. That the keeping a Standing army in these colonies, in times of peace, without the consent of the legislature of that colony, in which such army is kept, is against law.[39]

---

[37] Fairfax Co. Resolutions, (1774) in A. E. D. Howard, THE ROAD FROM RUNNYMEDE: MAGNA CARTA AND CONSTITUTIONALISM IN AMERICA 435 (1968).

[38] 1 JOURNALS OF THE CONTINENTAL CONGRESS 1774-1789, 67-68 (Oct. 14, 1774) (W. C. Ford ed. 1904-1907).

[39] *Id.* at 70.

The colonists were asserting, in effect, that the restrictions on royal power that had been won by Parliament in its long struggle against the Stuart kings were binding against the sovereign, in favor of the colonial legislatures as well as Parliament. In order to make that claim good, the colonists were forced to take up arms.

IV. Popular Sovereignty and the New Nation

America's long war in defense of the rights of Englishmen began in 1775. Although many colonists still hoped for a reconciliation with the mother country, it was necessary to set up state governments in the interim. In Connecticut and Rhode Island, all that was necessary was to strike the King's name from the colonial charters, which continued to serve for many years as state constitutions.

In other states, written constitutions were drawn up. They generally had these features: 1) an assertion that political power derives from the people; 2) provision for the organization of the government with a three-fold separation of powers; 3) a powerful legislature with authority to pass all laws not forbidden by the Constitution; and 4) a specific bill of rights restricting governmental power in the same way that the English Bill of Rights restricted the King. It is important to emphasize that the concept of enumerated powers had not yet been   developed, and that rights were, as always before, conceived to be in the nature of restrictions on power, not as individual freedoms.[40]

The Declaration of Independence substituted the sovereignty of the people for that of the King, and appealed to the "Laws of Nature and of Nature's God," but it did not proclaim a social or legal revolution. It listed the colonists' grievances, including the presence of standing armies, subordination of civil to military power, use of foreign mercenary soldiers, quartering of troops, and the use of the royal prerogative to suspend laws and charters. All of these legal actions resulted from reliance on standing armies in place of the militia.

Although America repudiated the British King, it did not repudiate British law. The Constitution of Maryland, for example, declared:

> That the inhabitants of Maryland are entitled to the common law of England, and the trial by jury according to the course of that law, and to the benefit of such of the English statutes as existed on the fourth day of July, seventeen hundred and seventy six, and which, by experience, have been found applicable to their local and other circumstances, and have been introduced, used and practiced by the courts of law or equity, ...[41]

---

[40]   For example, the Virginia Bill of Rights, adopted June 12, 1776, declared: "That a well-regulated militia, composed of the body of the people, trained to arms, is the proper, natural, and safe defence of a free State; that standing armies, in time of peace, should be avoided, as dangerous to liberty; and that in all cases the military should be under strict subordination to, and governed by the civil power." VA. CONST., Bill of Rights, § 13 (1776) in 7 CONSTITUTIONS 3814.

The comparable provision in Massachusetts was as follows: "The people have a right to keep and to bear arms for the common defence. And as, in time of peace, armies are dangerous to liberty, they ought not to be maintained without the consent of the legislature; and the military power shall always be held in an exact subordination to the civil authority, and be governed by it." MASS. CONST., Declaration of Rights, art. 17 (1780) in 3 CONSTITUTIONS 1892. (Considered in its context, the meaning of the "right to keep and bear arms" is clear. The words "for the common defence" makes it obvious that a collective right is intended. The people of Massachusetts did not want to risk a second British occupation.)

[41]   MD. CONST., Declaration of Rights, art. 3 (1851), in 3 CONSTITUTIONS 1713.

The War for Independence was fought by fourteen different military organization—the Continental Army under Washington, and the thirteen colonial militias. The debate over the relative merits of standing armies and the militia continued even during the fighting. A defender of standing armies, Washington wrote to the Continental Congress in September of 1776 as follows:

> To place any dependence upon Militia, is, assuredly, resting upon a broken staff. Men just dragged from the tender Scenes of domestick life; unaccustomed to the din of Arms; totally unacquainted   with every kind of military skill, which being followed by a want of confidence in themselves, when opposed to Troops regularly train'd, disciplined, and appointed, superior in knowledge and superior in Arms, makes them timid, and ready to fly from their own shadows....
>
> The Jealousies of a standing Army, and the Evils to be apprehended from one, are remote; and, in my judgment, situated and circumstanced as we are, not at all to be dreaded; but the consequence of wanting one, according to my Ideas, formed from the present view of things, is certain, and inevitable Ruin; for if I was called upon to declare upon Oath, whether the Militia have been most serviceable or hurtful upon the whole; I should subscribe to the latter.[42]

To maintain the supremacy of civil power over that of the military Article II of the Articles of Confederation provided that each state would retain "its sovereignty, freedom, and independence."[43] A provision that "every state shall always keep up a well regulated and disciplined militia, sufficiently armed and accoutred" was included in Article VI.[44] In contrast, the military powers of the United States rested in Congress were strictly limited; Congress could not maintain standing armies without the consent of nine of the thirteen states.

The government of the United States under the Articles of Confederation was weak. Experience was to show that it needed to be strengthened in its military powers.

V. Forging a More Perfect Union

When the War for Independence ended, the government of the Confederation was faced with one gigantic, insoluble problem—money. As troublesome as foreign and domestic bondholders were, there was one stronger pressure group that simply could not be ignored: the former soldiers who had been promised back pay and large pensions. Organized under the name of the Society of Cincinnati, these veterans were viewed with suspicion by many Americans, who nurtured fears of standing armies.

The danger to civil authority from the military was not entirely imaginary. In the summer of 1783 there was a direct attempt to coerce the Confederation into paying what had been promised to the army. Originally intended as a peaceful protest march on the capitol in Philadelphia, the ex-soldiers were soon "mediating more violent measures,"   including "seizure of the

---

[42]   Letter from George Washington to the President of Congress, Sept. 24, 1776, in 6 THE WRITINGS OF GEORGE WASHINGTON 110, 112 (J. Fitzpatrick ed. 1931-1944).

[43]   *See generally* M. JENSEN, THE NEW NATION: A HISTORY OF THE UNITED STATES DURING THE CONFEDERATION, 1781-1789 (1950).

members of Congress."[44] Alarmed, Congress adjourned and fled to Trenton, New Jersey. The soldiers eventually gave up, and the officers who led them escaped.

Following the abortive demonstrations in Philadelphia in the summer of 1783, Madison and other leaders felt the need to reorder the nation's military structure.

The other important military event that precipitated demands for a stronger national government was Shays' Rebellion in Massachusetts in 1786. Oppressed by debt, farmers in the western part of the state seized military posts and supplies and defied the state government. Although the insurrection was suppressed fairly easily and Shays himself pardoned, exaggerated reports of the uprising circulated among the states, and conservatives were aghast. Madison, in writing the introduction to his notes on the Federal Convention, lists Shays' Rebellion as one of the "ripening incidents" that led to the Convention.[45]

Thomas Jefferson, in contrast, was not alarmed by the apparent dangers of anarchy, and he criticized the clamor of the Federalists. Just after receiving a copy of the proposed Constitution, he wrote from Paris:

> ... We have had 13 states independent 11 years. There has been one rebellion. That comes to one rebellion in a century & a half for each state. What country before ever existed a century & a half without rebellion? & what country can preserve its liberties if their rulers are not warned from time to time that their people preserve the spirit of resistance? Let them take arms. The remedy is set them right as to facts, pardon & pacify them. What signify a few lives lost in acentury or two? The tree of liberty must be refreshed from time to time with the blood of patriots & tyrants. It is natural manure. Our Convention has been too much impressed by the insurrection of Massachusetts: and in the spur of the moment they are setting up a kite to keep the hen yard in order.[46]

Whatever the merits of Jefferson's beliefs, they were not shared by the majority of the Convention, which wished to prevent insurrections by strengthening the military powers of the general government.   The new military powers of Congress were listed in Article I, Section 8 of the proposed constitution, and include the following authority:

> To raise and support Armies, but no Appropriation of Money to that Use shall be for a longer Term than two Years;
> To provide and maintain a Navy;
> To make Rules for the Government and Regulation of the land and naval Forces;
> To provide for calling forth the Militia to execute the Laws of the Union, suppress Insurrections and repel Invasions;
> To provide for organizing, arming, and disciplining, the Militia, and for governing such Part of them as may be employed in the Service of the United States, reserving to the States respectively, the Appointment of the Officers, and the Authority of training the Militia according to the discipline prescribed by Congress;

---

[44]   Debates of the Congress of the Confederation (June 2, 1783), in 5 THE DEBATES IN THE SEVERAL STATE CONVENTIONS ON THE ADOPTION OF THE FEDERAL CONSTITUTION 93 (J. Elliot ed. 1836-1845) [hereinafter cited as STATE DEBATES].

[45]   DRAFTING THE FEDERAL CONSTITUTION: A REARRANGEMENT OF MADISON'S NOTES GIVING CONSECUTIVE DEVELOPMENT OF PROVISIONS IN THE CONSTITUTION OF THE UNITED STATES 10 (A. Prescott ed. 1941) [hereinafter cited as MADISON REARRANGED].

[46]   Letter from Thomas Jefferson to William Stephen Smith, Nov. 13, 1787, in 4 THE WORKS OF THOMAS JEFFERSON 362 (P. Ford ed. 1892-1899).

The spirited debate over these provisions in the Federal Convention reflects the purposes and fears of the framers of the Constitution.

There was universal distrust of standing armies. For example, in June of 1787, Madison stated:

> ... A standing military force, with an overgrown Executive will not long be safe companions to liberty. The means of defence agst. foreign danger, have been always the instruments of tyranny at home. Among the Romans it was a standing maxim to excite a war, whenever a revolt was apprehended. Throughout all Europe, the armies kept up under the pretext of defending, have enslaved the people. It is perhaps questionable, whether the best concerted system of absolute power in Europe cd. maintain itself, in a situation, where no alarms of external danger c. tame the people to the domestic yoke. The insular situation of G. Britain was the principal cause of her being an exception to the general fate of Europe. It has rendered less defence necessary, and admitted a kind of defence wch. c. not be used for the purpose of oppression.[47]

The defense "which could not be used for the purpose of oppression" was the militia, which was still revered on both sides of the Atlantic, even with its shortcomings.

Yet, despite the preference for the militia, it was generally agreed that Congress must have authority to raise and support standing armies in order to protect frontier settlements, the national government, and the nation when threatened by foreign powers. However, a few members were still fearful. Elbridge Gerry and Luther Martin, both of whom later opposed the Constitution, moved that a definite limit—two or three thousand men—be placed on the size of the national standing army. Voting by states, as always, the Convention unanimously rejected the motion. The judgment of Congress and the two year appropriation limitation were thought to be sufficient safeguards.[48]

The proper extent of federal authority over the militia was much more heatedly debated. The subject was introduced by George Mason, author of the Virginia Bill of Rights, who later opposed the Constitution, but who now maintained that uniformity of organization, training and weaponry was essential to make the state militias effective. His hope was that the need for a standing army would be minimized; perhaps only a few garrisons would be required. Mason's opinions were shared by Madison, who gave this analysis:

> The primary object is to secure an effectual discipline of the Militia. This will no more be done if left to the states separately than the requisitions have been hitherto paid by them. The states neglect their militia now, and the more they are consolidated into one nation, the less each will rely on its own interior provisions for its safety, and the less prepare its militia for that purpose; in like manner as the militia of a state would have been still more neglected than it has been, if each county had been independently charged with the care of its militia. The discipline of the militia is evidently a *national* concern, and ought to be provided for in the *national* Constitution.[49]

---

[47] 1 THE RECORDS OF THE FEDERAL CONVENTION OF 1787, at 465 (M. Farand ed. 1911).

[48] MADISON REARRANGED 513-26.

[49] *Id.* at 522.

Despite such explanations, there were still opponents to the militia clauses. Gerry, for example, declared:

> This power in the United States, as explained, is making the states drill sergeants. He had as lief-let the citizens of Massachusetts be disarmed as to take the command from the states and subject them to the general legislature. It would be regarded as a system of despotism.[50]

Later, as the Convention moved toward resolution of the issue, Gerry marshalled his final arguments. One can sense his feeling of outrage, as he solemnly warned of the dangers of centralized military power: "Let us at once destroy the state governments, have an executive for life or hereditary, and a proper Senate; and then there would be some consistency in giving full powers to the general government...."[51] But as the states are not to be abolished, he wondered at the attempts that were made to give powers inconsistent with their existence. He warned the Convention against pushing the experiment too far. Some people will support a plan of vigorous government at every risk. Others, of a more democratic cast, will oppose it with equal determination; and a civil war may be produced by the conflict.

Madison rose immediately and answered Gerry in these words:

> As the greatest danger is that of disunion of the states, it is necessary to guard against it by sufficient powers to the common government; and as the greatest danger to liberty is from large standing armies, it is best to prevent them by an effectual provision for a good militia.[52]

The last discussion of the militia clauses took place on September 14, 1787, just before the Convention finished its work. Mason moved to add a preface to the clause that allowed federal regulation of the militia, in order to define its purpose. His proposed addition was "that the liberties of the people may be better secured against the danger of standing armies in time of peace." The motion was opposed as "setting a dishonourable mark of distinction on the military class of citizens," and was rejected.[53]

Thus ended the Convention's debate over the relative merits and difficulties of standing armies and the militia. The debate was soon to be revived, however, as the new nation prepared to consider the proposed new form of government.

VI. The Ratification Controversy and the Bill of Rights

The new Constitution was signed on September 17, 1787 and the contest over its ratification soon began. The controversy was carried on mainly through the printed media. It was an unequal contest because the proponents of the new government, who now called themselves Federalists, controlled most of the newspapers. The Antifederalists resorted mainly to pamphlets and handbills.

---

[50]   *Id.* at 521.

[51]   *Id.* at 523-24.

[52]   *Id.* at 524.

[53]   *Id.* at 525.

Because the Antifederalist effort was decentralized and local in nature, it is difficult to generalize about the arguments used against the Constitution. The unifying theme, to the extent there was one, was that the new government would overreach its powers, destroy the states, deprive the people of their liberty, and create an aristocratic or monarchical tyranny. In finding evidence of such dangers, the Anti-federalists often made inconsistent interpretations of what the Constitution provided. In the case of the militia powers, for example, it was said that Congress would disarm the militia in order to remove opposition to its standing army; at the same time it was argued that Congress would ruthlessly discipline the militia and convert it into a tool of oppression.

Bearing in mind the inconsistency of the Anti-federalist position, some of the pamphlets and articles will be examined in order to show how the fears of military power existed. One of the most scurrilous critics of the Constitution was "Philadelphiensis." His identity is uncertain, but he is believed to have been Benjamin Workman, a radical Irishman and a tutor at the University of Pennsylvania. His comments include the following:

> Who can deny but the *president general* will be a *king* to all intents and purposes, and one of the most dangerous kinds too; a king elected to command a standing army? Thus our laws are to be administered by this *tyrant*; for the whole, or at least the most important part of the executive department is put in his hands.
>
> The thoughts of a military officer possessing such powers, as the proposed constitution vests in the president general, are sufficient to excite in the mind of a freeman the most alarming apprehensions; and ought to rouse him to oppose it at *all events*. Every freeman of America ought to hold up this idea to himself, *that he has no superior but God and the laws*. But this tyrant will be so much his superior, that he can at any time he thinks proper, order him out in the militia to exercise, and to march when and where he pleases. His officers can wantonly inflict the most disgraceful punishment on a peaceable citizen, under pretense of disobedience, or the smallest neglect of militia duty.[54]

Another anonymous writer, Brutus, appealed to history as proof that standing armies in peacetime lead to tyranny:

> The same army, that in Britain, vindicated the liberties of that people from the encroachments and despotism of a tyrant king, assisted Cromwell, their General, in wresting from the people that liberty they had so dearly earned....
>
> I firmly believe, no country in the world had ever a more patriotic army, than the one which so ably served this country in the late war. But had the General who commanded them been possessed of the spirit of a Julius Caesar or a Cromwell, the liberties of this country ... [might have] in all probability terminated with the war.[55]

Still another unknown, styling himself "A Democratic Federalist," asserted that the Revolution had proved the superiority of the militia over standing armies:

> Had we a standing army when the British invaded our peaceful shores? Was it a standing army that gained the battles of Lexington and Bunker Hill, and took the ill-fated Burgoyne? Is not a well-regulated militia sufficient for every purpose of internal defense?

---

54 'Philadelphiensis' *Letter*, Independent Gazetteer (Phila.), Feb. 7, 1788.

55 'Brutus' *Letter*, N.Y. Journal, Jan. 24, 1788.

And which of you, my fellow citizens, is afraid of any   invasion from foreign powers that our brave militia would not be able immediately to repel?[56]

Some writers, such as "Centinel," feared that national control over the militia would transform that bulwark of democracy into a tool of oppression:

> This section will subject the citizens of these states to the most arbitrary military discipline: even death may be inflicted on the disobedient; in the character of militia, you may be dragged from your families and homes to any part of the continent and for any length of time, at the discretion of the future Congress; and as militia you may be made the unwilling instruments of oppression, under the direction of government; there is no exemption upon account of conscientious scruples of bearing arms, no equivalent to be received in lieu of personal services. The militia of Pennsylvania may be marched to Georgia or New Hampshire, however incompatible with their interests or consciences; in short, they may be made as mere machines as Prussian soldiers.[57]

Other Antifederalist propagandists believed that the true motive for assertion of national control over the militia was not to use it, but to destroy it, and thus eliminate any opposition to the new standing army. The Bostonian who used the pseudonym "John De Witt" asked these questions about the militia clauses:

> Let us inquire why they have assumed this great power. Was it to strengthen the power which is now lodged in your hands, and relying upon you and *you solely* for aid and support to the civil power in the execution of all the laws of the new Congress? Is this probable? Does the complexion of this new plan countenance such a supposition? When they unprecedently claim the power of raising and supporting armies, do they tell you for what purposes they are to be raised? How they are to be employed? How many they are to consist of, and where stationed? Is this power fettered with any one of those restrictions, which will show they depend upon the militia, and not upon this infernal engine of oppression to execute their civil laws? The nature of the demand in itself contradicts such a supposition, and forces you to believe that it is for none of these causes—but rather for the purpose of consolidating and finally destroying your strength, as your respective governments are to be destroyed. They well know the impolicy of putting or keeping arms in the hands of a nervous people, at a distance from the seat of a government, upon whom they mean to exercise the powers granted in that government....
>
> It is asserted by the most respectable writers upon government, that a well regulated militia, composed of the yeomanry of the country, have ever been considered as the bulwark of a free people. Tyrants have never placed any confidence on a militia composed of freemen.[58]

Anonymous pamphleteers and propagandists were not the only persons concerned about standing armies and the militia. Richard Henry Lee, in a letter that was widely circulated in Virginia, combined the contradictory arguments that the militia would be abandoned in favor of a standing

---

[56] 'A Democratic Federalist' *Letter*, Pa. Packet (Phila.), Oct. 23, 1787.

[57] 'Centinel' *Letter*, Independent Gazetteer (Phila.), Nov. 8, 1787.

[58] 'John De Witt' *Letter*, Am. Herald (Boston), De. 3, 1787.

army, and that the militia would be strengthened and forged into an instrument of tyranny. He foresaw that a small proportion of the total militia would be made into a select unit, much like a standing army, while the rest of the militia would be disarmed:

> Should one fifth, or one eighth part of the men capable of bearing arms, be made a select militia, as has been proposed, and those the young and ardent part of the community, possessed of but little or no property, and all the others put upon a plan that will render them of no importance, the former will answer all the purposes of any army, while the latter will be defenceless.[59]

A necessary premise underlying Anti-federalist attack on the militia clauses of the Constitution was that these clauses operated to place exclusive jurisdiction over the militia in the hands of the general government. Though the Federalists denied this premise, it was affirmed even by Luther Martin and Elbridge Gerry, who had been members of the Federal Convention, but who now opposed the Constitution. Martin is particularly interesting because he advanced all of the contradictory arguments used by the antifederalists. Speaking on November 29, 1787 to the Maryland legislature, he said:

> ... Engines of power are supplied by the standing Army—unlimited as to number or its duration, in addition to this Government has the entire Command of the Militia, and may call the whole Militia of any State into Action, a power, which it was vainly urged ought never to exceed a certain proportion. By organizing the Militia Congress have taken the whole power from the State Governments; and by neglecting to do it and encreasing the Standing Army, their power will increase by those very means that will be adopted and urged as an ease to the People.[60]

Martin later invoked the opposite approach, that the militia would be subject to ruthless discipline and martial law, and would be marched to the ends of the continent in the service of tyranny. In a letter published on January 18, 1788, Martin wrote that the new system for governing the militia was "giving the states the last coup de grace by taking from them the only means of self preservation."[61]

Elbridge Gerry, like many of the pamphleteers, viewed centralized military power as inseparable from monarchy:

> By the edicts of authority vested in the sovereign power by the proposed constitution, the militia of the country, the bulwark of defence, and the security of national liberty is no longer under the control of civil authority; but at the rescript of the Monarch, or the aristocracy, they may either be employed to extort the enormous sums that will be necessary to support the civil list—to maintain the regalia of power—and the splendour of the most useless part of the community, or they may be sent into foreign countries for the fulfilment of treaties, stipulated by the President and two thirds of the Senate.[62]

---

[59] R. H. LEE, OBSERVATIONS LEADING TO A FAIR EXAMINATION OF THE SYSTEM OF GOVERNMENT PROPOSED BY THE LATE CONVENTION 24-25 (1787).

[60] 3 THE RECORDS OF THE FEDERAL CONVENTION OF 1787, at 157 (M. Farrand ed. 1911).

[61] Martin, *Letter*, Md. Journal, Jan. 18, 1788.

[62] E. GERRY, OBSERVATIONS ON THE NEW CONSTITUTION AND ON THE FEDERAL AND STATE CONVENTIONS 10 (1788).

The supporters of the proposed constitution were well-prepared to meet these and similar arguments. They had the support of America's two national heroes, George Washington and Benjamin Franklin, and this helped make the Constitution respectable, as well as alleviating fears. Articles favoring the Constitution, such as the *Federalist Papers*, were often reprinted in distant states. Intelligent and well-educated, the proponents of the new government carefully and consistently answered the arguments of their rivals.

To the general argument that there were not sufficient restrictions on the power of the proposed general government, the federalists replied that no bill of rights was necessary. This was because the Constitution would establish a novel type of government, one of enumerated powers; restrictions were necessary only where full sovereignty was conferred. In Federalist Number 84, Alexander Hamilton made the argument in these words:

> It has been several times truly remarked that bills of rights are, in their origin, stipulations between kings and their subjects, abridgements of prerogative in favor of privilege, reservations of rights not surrendered to the prince Such was MAGNA CHARTA, obtained by the barons, sword in hand from King John. Such were the subsequent confirmations of that charter by succeeding princes. Such was the Petition of Right assented to by Charles I, in the beginning of his reign. Such, also, was the Declaration of Right presented by the Lords and Commons to the Prince of Orange in 1688, and afterwards thrown into the form of an act of parliament called the Bill of Rights. It is evident, therefore, that, according to their primitive signification, they have no application to constitutions professedly founded upon the power of the people, and executed by their immediate representatives and servants.[63]

To particular criticism of the military clauses of the proposed Constitution, both Hamilton and Madison replied in detail in the Federalist Papers.

Hamilton denied that a standing army was unnecessary, citing recent experience:

> Here I expect we shall be told that the militia of the country is its natural bulwark, and would be at all times equal to the national defence. This doctrine, in substance, had like to have lost us our independence. It cost millions to the United States that might have been saved....
>
> The American militia, in the course of the late war, have, by their valor on numerous occasions, erected eternal monuments to their fame; but the bravest of them feel and know that the liberty of their country could not have been established by their efforts alone, however great and valuable they were. War, like most other things, is a science to be acquired and perfected by diligence, by perseverance, by time, and by practice.[64]

Hamilton did not, however, go so far as to say that standing armies were a good thing. Instead, he argued that a strong militia would minimize the need for them.[65]

---

[63]   THE FEDERALIST No. 84, at 536 (H. Lodge ed. 1888) (A. Hamilton).

[64]   *Id.* No. 25 at 150 (A. Hamilton).

[65]   Hamilton explained: "If a well-regulated militia be the most natural defence of a free country, it ought certainly to be under the regulation and at the disposal of that body which is constituted the guardian of the national security. If standing armies are dangerous to liberty, an efficacious power over the militia, in the body to whose care the protection of the state is committed ought, as far as possible, to take away the inducement and the pretext to such unfriendly institutions. If the federal government can command the aid of the militia in those emergencies which call for the military arm in support of the civil magistrate, it can the better

Madison also addressed himself to the fear that the new national government would disarm the militia and destroy state government. He first argued that the states would still have concurrent power over the militia, thus denying that the proposed Constitution gave exclusive jurisdiction over the militia to the general government. He also pointed out that the militia, comprised of half a million men, was a force that could not be overcome by any tyrant.[66]

The arguments of the federalists appear to have quieted the fears of their countrymen, since the early state conventions were all easy victories for the new Constitution. Between December 7, 1787 and January 9, 1788, Delaware, Pennsylvania, New Jersey, Georgia and Connecticut all ratified unconditionally and overwhelmingly; the vote was unanimous in three of these states. In Massachusetts, the contest was close. On February 6, 1787, the state convention ratified the new Constitution by a narrow margin.

On the other hand, Maryland overwhelmingly approved the Constitution on April 28, 1787. South Carolina was next, on May 23, 1787. Eight states had now ratified the document and only one more was needed. All of the ratifications, except Massachusetts, had been by majorities of two-thirds or more. The remaining states were to see close contests, and all of them would suggest that a Bill of Rights be added to the Constitution.

New Hampshire, on June 21, 1787, became the ninth state to approve the new form of government, thus assuring that the proposed Constitution would go into effect. The New Hampshire convention proposed some amendments in its ratifying resolution. Among the proposals were a three-fourths vote requirement for keeping standing armies, a flat prohibition on quartering troops, and a prohibition against Congressional disarmament of the militia. Although no records were kept of the debates, it seems likely that the delegates feared that New England's experiences with General Gage's redcoats would be repeated.

As yet undecided, Virginia was vital to the Union as the largest, richest, and most populous state. The Virginia convention was also important because it was the only one in which the military clauses of the Constitution were extensively discussed.

The main protagonist of the Virginia debates was Patrick Henry, backwoods lawyer, ardent republican, and incomparable orator. By means of the rhetorical question, Henry was able to capture the fears and emotions which led to the adoption of the Second Amendment:

> A standing army we shall have, also, to execute the execrable commands of tyranny; and how are you to punish them? Will you order them to be punished? Who shall obey these orders? Will your mace-bearer be a match for a disciplined regiment? In what situation are we to be? ...
>
> Your militia is given up to Congress, also, in another part of this plan: they will therefore act as they think proper: all power will be in their own possession. You cannot force them to receive their punishment: of what service would militia be to you when most probably, you will not have a single musket in the state? for, as arms are to be provided by Congress, they may or may not furnish them....
>
> By this, sir, you see that their control over our last and best defence is unlimited. If they neglect or refuse to discipline or arm our militia, they will be useless: the states can do neither—this power being exclusively given to Congress....

---

dispense with the employment of a different kind of force. If it cannot avail itself of the former, it will be obliged to recur to the latter. To render an army unnecessary will be a more certain method of preventing its existence than a thousand prohibitions upon paper." *Id.* No. 29, at 169 (A. Hamilton).

[66]   *Id.* No. 46, at 297-99 (J. Madison).

... If we make a king, we may prescribe the rules by which he shall rule his people, and interpose such checks as shall prevent him from infringing them; but the President, in the field, at the head of his army, can prescribe the terms on which he shall reign master, so far that it will puzzle any American ever to get his neck from under the galling yoke....[67]

While other critics lacked Henry's oratorical talents, they also feared disarmament of the militia by the new national government. George Mason, for example, spoke as follows:

... There are various ways of destroying the militia. A standing army may be perpetually established in their stead. I abominate and detest the idea of government, where there is a standing army. The militia may be here destroyed by that method which has been practised in other parts of the world before; that is, by rendering them useless—by disarming them. Under various pretences, Congress may neglect to provide for arming and disciplining the militia; and the state governments cannot do it, for Congress has an exclusive right to arm them ...[68]

Mason then went on to cite the case of a former British governor of Pennsylvania who had allegedly advised disarmament of the militia as part of the British government's scheme for "enslaving America." The suggested method was not to act openly, but "totally disusing and neglecting the militia."[69] Mason said:

... This was a most iniquitous project. Why should we not provide against the danger of having our militia, our real and natural strength, destroyed? The general government ought, at the same time, to have some such power. But we need not give them power to abolish our militia ...[70]

In these words lie the origin of the Second Amendment. The new government should be allowed to keep its broad general military powers, but it should be forbidden to disarm the militia.

Madison, leader of the Federalist forces, still argued that the militia clauses were adequate as written. He said the states and national government would have concurrent power over the militia. In response to a question, he explained why the general government was to have power to call out the militia in order to execute the laws of the union:

... If resistance should be made to the execution of the laws, he said, it ought to be overcome. This could be done only in two ways—either by regular forces or by the people. If insurrections should arise, or invasions should take place, the people ought unquestionably to be employed, to suppress and repel them, rather than a standing army. The best way to do these things was to put the militia on a good and sure footing, and enable the government to make use of their services when necessary.[71]

---

[67] Spoken at the Virginia Convention 3 STATE DEBATES 51-59.

[68] *Id.* at 379.

[69] *Id.* at 380.

[70] *Id.*

[71] *Id.* at 378.

It is interesting to note that Madison uses the words "people" and "militia" as synonymous, as does the Second Amendment, which he was later to draft.

The Federalists still maintained that a bill of rights was unnecessary where there was a government of enumerated powers. Governor Randolph, who had attended the Philadelphia Convention and had refused to sign the Constitution, but who was now supporting its adoption, spoke as follows:

> On the subject of a bill of rights, the want of which has been complained of, I will observe that it has been sanctified by such reverend authority, that I feel some difficulty in going against it. I shall not, however, be deterred from giving my opinion on this occasion, let the consequence be what it may. At the beginning of the war, he had no certain bill of rights; for our charter cannot be considered as a bill of rights; it is nothing more than an investiture, in the hands of the Virginia citizens, of those rights which belonged to British subjects. When the British thought proper to infringe our rights, was it not necessary to mention, in our Constitution, those rights which ought to be paramount to the power of the legislature? Why is the bill of rights distinct from the Constitution? I consider bills of rights in this view—that the government should use them, where there is a departure from its fundamental principles, in order to restore them.[72]

This statement is very important, because it clearly explains how men in the eighteenth century conceived of a right. A right was a restriction on governmental power, necessitated by a particular abuse of that power.

The Virginia convention, however, decided that it would be wise to impose restrictions on the power of the general government before abuses occurred. So the delegates appended to their ratification resolution a long document recommended to the consideration of the Congress. This document is divided into two distinct parts: a declaration of principles and specified suggested amendments to the Constitution designed to secure these principles.

The declaration of principles tells much about the social and political philosophy of eighteenth century Americans. The theory of government as a social compact is affirmed. There are five provisions that relate directly to the background of the Second Amendment.

The third principle condemns the Anglican doctrine of nonresistance as "absurd, slavish, and destructive of the good and happiness of mankind."[73] This is not surprising, since Virginia had recently disestablished the Anglican Church, and had taken up arms to resist the authority of the head of that church.

The seventh principle is "that all power of suspending laws or the execution of laws by any authority, without the consent of the representatives of the people in the legislature is injurious to their rights, and ought not to be exercised."[74] The attempt to assert such power had cost James II his throne and George III his American colonies, even though both Kings had been backed by powerful standing armies.

The seventeenth, eighteenth and nineteenth principles are as follows:

---

[72] *Id.* at 466.

[73] J. MADISON, THE DEBATES IN THE FEDERAL CONVENTION OF 1787 660 (G. Hunt & J.B. Scott ed. 1920).

[74] *Id.* at 661.

Seventeenth, That the people have a right to keep and bear arms; that a well regulated Militia composed of the body of the people trained to arms is the proper, natural and safe defence of a free State. That standing armies in time of peace are dangerous to liberty, and therefore ought to be avoided, as far as the circumstances and protection of the Community will admit; and that in all cases the military should be under strict subordination to and governed by the Civil power.

Eighteenth, That no Soldier in time of peace ought to be quartered in any house without the consent of the owner, and in the time of war in such manner only as the laws direct.

Nineteenth, That any person religiously scrupulous of bearing arms ought to be exempted upon payment of an equivalent to employ another to bear arms in his stead.[75]

These words encapsulate the Whig point of view in the long debate over the relative merits of standing armies and the militia. The specific amendments that were proposed to protect these principles were:

Ninth, That no standing army or regular troops shall be raised or kept up in time of peace, without the consent of two thirds of the members present in both houses.

Tenth, That no soldier shall be inlisted for any longer term than four years, except in time of war, and then for no longer term than the continuance of the war.

Eleventh, That each State respectively shall have the power to provide for organizing, arming and disciplining it's own Militia, when soever Congress shall omit or neglect to provide for the same. That the Militia shall not be subject to Martial law, except when in actual service in time of war, invasion, or rebellion; and when not in the actual service of the United States, shall be subject only to such fines, penalties and punishments as shall be directed or inflicted by the laws of its own State.[76]

It is important for our purposes to note that there is no mention here of any individual right.

The Purpose of the Second Amendment

There might never have been a federal Bill of Rights had it not been for one alarming event that is almost forgotten today. As part of the price of ratification in New York, it was agreed unanimously that a second federal convention should be called by the states, in accordance with Article V of the Constitution, to revise the document. Governor Clinton wrote a circular letter making this proposal to the governors of all the states.

Madison feared that a new convention would reconsider the whole structure of government and undo what had been achieved. Professor Merrill Jensen, in *The Making of the American Constitution*, analyzes the situation as follows:

The Bill of Rights was thus born of Madison's concern to prevent a second convention which might undo the work of the Philadelphia Convention, and also of his concern to save his political future in Virginia. On the other side such men as Patrick Henry

---

[75] *Id.* at 662.

[76] *Id.* at 663.

understood perfectly the political motives involved. He looked upon the passage of the Bill of Rights as a political defeat which would make it impossible to block the centralization of all power in the national government.[77]

Madison had outmaneuvered the anti-federalists by drafting the Bill of Rights very soon after the First Congress met.

Madison's original draft of the provision that eventually became the Second Amendment read:

> The right of the people to keep and bear arms shall not be infringed; a well armed but well regulated militia being the best security of a free country; but no person religiously scrupulous of bearing arms shall be compelled to render military service in person.[78]

There was debate in Congress over the religious exemption, and it was removed. Otherwise, there was general discussion of standing armies and the militia, and widespread support for the proposal. It became part of the Constitution with the rest of the Bill of Rights on December 15, 1791.

Considering the immediate political context of the Second Amendment, as well as its long historical background, there can be no doubt about its intended meaning. There had been a long standing fear of military power in the hands of the executive, and, rightly or wrongly, many people believed that the militia was an effective military force which minimized the need for such executive military power. The proposed Constitution authorized standing armies, and granted sweeping Congressional power over the militia. Some even feared disarmament of the militia. The Second Amendment was clearly and simply an effort to relieve that fear.

Neither in the Philadelphia Convention, in the writings of the pamphleteers, in the newspapers, in the convention debates, nor in Congress was there any reference to hunting, target shooting, duelling, personal self-defense, or any other subject that would indicate an individual right to have guns. Every reference to the right to bear arms was in connection with military service.

Thus the inevitable conclusion is that the "collectivist" view of the Second Amendment rather than the "individualist" interpretation is supported by history. It thus becomes necessary to examine the decisions of the Supreme Court in order to determine whether that body has expanded the right to bear arms beyond what was intended in 1789.

VII. Supreme Court Interpretation of the Second Amendment

The Second Amendment has been directly considered by the Supreme Court in only four cases: *United States v. Cruikshank*,[79] *Presser v. Illinois*,[80] *Miller v. Texas*[81] and *United States v. Miller*.[82]

In *Cruikshank*, the defendants had been convicted of conspiracy to deprive negro citizens of the rights and privileges secured to them by the Constitution and laws of the United States, in

---

[77]   M. JENSEN, THE MAKING OF THE AMERICAN CONSTITUTION 149 (1964).

[78]   1 ANNALS OF CONG. 434 (1789).

[79]   92 U.S. 542 (1875).

[80]   116 U.S. 252 (1886).

[81]   153 U.S. 535 (1894).

[82]   307 U.S. 174 (1939).

violation of the criminal provisions of the Civil Rights Act of 1870. Among the rights violated were the right to peaceably assemble and the right to keep and bear arms for a lawful purpose.

Chief Justice Waite, speaking for the majority, held that the rights violated by the defendants were not secured by the Constitution or laws of the United States, and thus the judgment of conviction was affirmed. The chief justice began with a long discussion of the nature of the federal system in general, and the attributes of state and national citizenship in particular. The only rights protected by the national government were those necessary for participation in that government. The right to petition Congress would be such a right, but a person must look   to his state government for protection of similar rights in other situations.

In particular reference to the Second Amendment, the opinion states:

> The second and tenth counts are equally defective. The right there specified is that of "bearing arms for a lawful purpose." This is not a right granted by the Constitution. Neither is it in any manner dependent upon that instrument for its existence. The second amendment declares that it shall not be infringed; but this, as has been seen, means no more than that it shall not be infringed by Congress. This is one of the amendments that has no other effect than to restrict the powers of the national government, leaving the people to look for their protection against any violation by their fellow-citizens of the rights it recognizes, to what is called, in *The City of New York v. Miln*, 11 Pet. 139, the "powers which relate to merely municipal legislation, or what was, perhaps, more properly called internal police," "not surrendered or restrained" by the Constitution of the United States.[83]

The only dissenter in *Cruikshank* was Justice Clifford, who found the indictment vague on its face. He thus concurred in the result reached by the majority without discussing any constitutional issues.

The next, and undoubtedly the most important Second Amendment case was *Presser v. Illinois*[84] decided in 1886. Herman Presser, a German-American, was the leader of *Lehr und Wehr Verein*, a fraternal, athletic and paramilitary association incorporated under Illinois law. He was convicted for parading and drilling with men under arms, in violation of an Illinois statute, and was fined ten dollars.

On appeal to the United States Supreme Court, it was contended that the Illinois statute conflicted with the military powers given to Congress by the Constitution, with federal statutes passed in pursuance of those powers, and with various other parts of the Constitution, including the Second Amendment. The Supreme Court unanimously rejected all of these claims and affirmed the conviction.

It should be emphasized that *Presser* was argued and decided as a case presenting broad issues of the relationship of state and federal military power, and that the Second Amendment was only one aspect of that question. In reference to the Illinois statute, the Court observed:

> We think it clear that the sections under consideration, which only forbid bodies of men to associate together as military organizations, or to drill or parade with arms in cities and towns unless authorized by law, do not infringe the right of the people to keep and bear arms. But a conclusive answer to the contention that this amendment

---

[83]   92 U.S. at 553 (1875).

[84]   116 U.S. 252 (1886).

prohibits the legislation in question lies in the fact that the amendment is a limitation only upon the power of Congress and the National government, and not upon that of the States.[85]

The Court cited *Cruikshank* in support of this proposition. The inapplicability of the Second Amendment to the states was a sufficient ground for rejecting Presser's Second Amendment contentions, but the Court did not stop there. It preferred to discuss the problem further and make clear the nature of the right protected by the Second Amendment.

> It is undoubtedly true that all citizens capable of bearing arms constitute the reserved military force or reserve militia of the United States as well as of the States, and, in view of this prerogative of the general government, as well as of its general powers, the States cannot, even laying the constitutional provision in question out of view, prohibit the people from keeping and bearing arms, so as to deprive the United States of their rightful resource for maintaining the public security, and disable the people from performing their duty to the general government.[86]

One view of the Second Amendment suggests that this dicta constitutes the first step toward incorporating the right to bear arms into the Fourteenth Amendment,[87] apparently forgetting that the Court was laying the Second Amendment "out of view." The Court had stated that the Illinois law does not have the effect of depriving the federal government of its military capacity.

To further clarify its view that the Second Amendment is concerned only with military matters, the opinion focuses on *Presser*:

> The plaintiff in error was not a member of the organized volunteer militia of the State of Illinois, nor did he belong to the troops of the United States or to any organization under the militia law of the United States. On the contrary, the fact that he did not belong to the organized militia or the troops of the United States was an ingredient in the offence for which he was convicted and sentenced. The question is, therefore, had he a right as a citizen of the United States, in disobedience of the State law, to associate with others as a military company, and to drill and parade with arms in the towns and cities of the State? If the plaintiff in error has any such privilege he must be able to point to the provision of the Constitution or statutes of the United States by which it is conferred.[88]

The obvious implication here is that any right to bear arms by virtue of the Second Amendment, even if asserted against the national government, is contingent upon military service in accordance with statutory law. This implication is confirmed later in the opinion, as the Court declared:

> The right to voluntarily associate together as a military company or organization, or to drill or parade with arms, without, and independent of, an act of Congress or law of the State authorizing the same, is not an attribute of national citizenship. Military organization

---

[85]   *Id.* at 264-65.

[86]   *Id.* at 265.

[87]   *See generally* H. Black, The Bill of Rights, 35 N.Y.U.L. REV. 865 (1960).

[88]   *Id.* at 266.

and military drill and parade under arms are subjects especially under the control of the government of every country. They cannot be claimed as a right independent of law.[89]

Thus the *Presser* case clearly affirms the meaning of the Second Amendment that was intended by its framers. It protects only members of a state militia, and it protects them only against being disarmed by the federal government. There is no individual right that can be claimed independent of state militia law. Furthermore, the dicta relating to preservation of the nation's military capacity could not be used as the basis for questioning any regulation of private firearms, unless such a regulation violated an act of Congress; Congress is obviously the best judge of the proper means of preserving the nation's military capacity.

The third, and least important, of the Second Amendment cases was *Miller v. Texas*.[90] A convicted murderer asserted that the state had violated his Second and Fourth Amendment rights. The Supreme Court unanimously dismissed the claim in one sentence, relying on the inapplicability of these provisions to the states, and citing *Cruikshank* and other cases.

The fourth and last time that the Supreme Court considered the Second Amendment was in *United States v. Miller*.[91] The result reached by Justice McReynolds for a unanimous Court was obviously correct, but the opinion is so brief and sketchy that it has undoubtedly caused much of the uncertainty that exists today about the meaning of the Second Amendment.

Defendants Miller and Layton were indicted for violation of the National Firearms Act of 1934,[92] which was designed to help control gangsters, and which infringed the right to keep and bear sawed off shotguns, among other arms. The District Court of the United States for the Western District of Arkansas sustained a demurrer and quashed the indictment, holding the 1934 Act unconstitutional on Second Amendment grounds. The government appealed to the Supreme Court, which reversed and remanded.

When *Miller* was argued before the High Court, there was no appearance for the defendants. With only one side presenting a case, it is easy to understand why the Court viewed the issues as rather simple, and not needing very much analysis.

The Court began by observing that the National Firearms Act was a valid revenue measure, and not a usurpation of the police powers of the states. The opinion then addresses itself to the Second Amendment issue:

> In the absence of any evidence tending to show that possession or use of a "shotgun having a barrel of less than eighteen inches in length" at this time has some reasonable relationship to the preservation or efficiency of a well regulated militia, we cannot say that the Second Amendment guarantees the right to keep and bear such an instrument. Certainly it is not within judicial notice that this weapon is any part of the ordinary military equipment or that its use could contribute to the common defense.[93]

It is this paragraph that is the source of the uncertainty and confusion arising from the *Miller* case. The Court was merely correcting the error of the district judge, but it made the mistake of

---

[89]   *Id.* at 267.

[90]   153 U.S. 535 (1894).

[91]   307 U.S. 174 (1939).

[92]   National Firearms Act *as amended* 26 U.S.C. §§ 5801-5872 (1972).

[93]   307 U.S. at 178.

looking at the weapon, rather than the person, in determining that the Second Amendment is not applicable.

Fortunately, however, Justice McReynolds went on and partially clarified the ambiguity in the above paragraph. He cited the militia clauses of the Constitution and said:

> With obvious purpose to assure the continuation and render possible the effectiveness of such forces the declaration and guarantee of the Second Amendment were made. It must be interpreted and applied with that end in view.[94]

These words alone undercut any individual right interpretation of the Second Amendment.

Justice McReynolds then proceeded to give a brief history of the militia, stressing its function as a military force. He then considered the relevance of state interpretations of the right to bear arms, and noted:

> Most if not all of the States have adopted provisions touching the right to keep and bear arms. Differences in the language employed in these have naturally led to somewhat variant conclusions concerning the scope of the right guaranteed.[95]

He concluded that such decisions did not support the trial judge's ruling. He then referred the reader to "some of the more important opinions" concerning the militia. First among these opinions was *Presser v. Illinois*.[96]

Thus, in spite of some ambiguity in the Court's opinion in *Miller*, there is no reason to suppose that there was any change in the established view that the Second Amendment defines and protects a collective right that is vested only in the members of the state militia.

VIII. Conclusion

In the last angry decades of the twentieth century, members of rifle clubs, paramilitary groups and other misguided patriots continue to oppose legislative control of handguns and rifles. These ideological heirs of the vigilantes of the bygone western frontier era still maintain that the Second Amendment guarantees them a personal right to "keep and bear arms."[97] But the annals of the Second Amendment attest to the fact that its adoption was the result of a political struggle to restrict the power of the national government and to prevent the disarmament of state militias.[98] Not unlike their English forbears, the American revolutionaries had a deep fear of centralized executive power, particularly when standing armies were at its disposal. The Second Amendment was adopted to prevent the arbitrary use of force by the national government against the states and the individual.

---

[94] *Id.*

[95] *Id.* at 182.

[96] 116 U.S. 252 (1886).

[97] A recent call to action was made by an organization which calls itself the *Sheriff's Posse Comitatus*. This group, dismayed over claimed violations of the Second Amendment promises to "come together and do something about it." Its propaganda concludes rather ominously, "The PEOPLE are the rightful masters to both congress and courts, not to over throw (sic) the Constitution, but to over throw (sic) the men who pervert the Constitution." *Flyer, Sheriff's Posse Comitatus*, Petaluma, California, 1975.

[98] *See* notes 60-66 and accompanying text.

Delegates to the Constitutional Convention had no intention of establishing any personal right to keep and bear arms. Therefore the "individualist" view of the Second Amendment must be rejected in favor of the "collectivist" interpretation, which is supported by history and a handful of Supreme Court decisions on the issue.

As pointed out previously, the nature of the Second Amendment does not provide a right that could be interpreted as being incorporated into the Fourteenth Amendment. It was designed solely to protect the states against the general government, not to create a personal right which either state or federal authorities are bound to respect.

The contemporary meaning of the Second Amendment is the same as it was at the time of its adoption. The federal government may regulate the National Guard, but may not disarm it against the will of state legislatures. Nothing in the Second Amendment, however, precludes Congress or the states from requiring licensing and registration of firearms; in fact, there is nothing to stop an outright congressional ban on private ownership of all handguns and all rifles.

[Originally published as Report of the Subcommittee on the Constitution of the Committee on the Judiciary, United States Senate, 97th Cong., 2d Sess., The Right to Keep and Bear Arms 171-175 (1982) ("Other Views"). Reproduced in the 1982 Senate Report, pg. 171-175, with permission. The article reproduced in the Senate Report is an abridgement of an article appearing elsewhere. No reference to the original is provided. Only the Introduction and Part 2 were included by the Subcommittee, and footnotes were omitted.]

THE ASSOCIATION OF THE BAR
OF THE CITY OF NEW YORK
42 West 44th Street, New York, N.Y. 10036

Gun Control Legislation

By THE COMMITTEE ON FEDERAL LEGISLATION

INTRODUCTION

Since the enactment of the Gun Control Act of 1968 there has been a substantial increase in the incidence of gun-related crimes and it has become evident that the existing system of law is inadequate. Efforts have been underway in both Houses of Congress to enact further gun control legislation and the Executive Branch has indicated support for stronger gun control. Both the Subcommittee on Crime of the House Committee on the Judiciary and the Subcommittee on Crime and Juvenile Delinquency of the Senate Committee on the Judiciary have accumulated a substantial factual record on which to base legislation.

We believe that the contribution of handguns to the current increase in homicide and other violent crimes requires immediate and comprehensive action. In our opinion, the continued existence of an unwarranted supply of handguns is an underlying factor in the decline of our major urban centers. This Committee does not find any substantial justification for the continued widespread public possession of handguns, and, accordingly, we strongly endorse the legislative proposals calling for a prohibition on the manufacture, importation, sale, and private possession of handguns.[1] Whether or not our recommendations are politically feasible at this moment in time, we are of the firmly held conviction that a complete ban on handguns should be the ultimate objective of any new federal gun control legislation.

This report is divided into four parts. Part I describes the current federal law and the congressional proposals for change. Part II examines the constitutional bases for Congress legislating a prohibition on the manufacture, importation, sale, and private possession of handguns. Part III discusses the need for adopting far reaching gun control legislation. Our recommendations are contained in Part IV.

II. *GUN CONTROL AND THE CONSTITUTION*

To determine whether a federal statute restricting handguns would be constitutional, two questions must be answered: (A) Is there a constitutional right to possession of handguns which cannot be infringed by legislation, and (B) does regulation of handguns fall within the scope of any of the subjects on which Congress is empowered by the Constitution to legislate? A review of the relevant decisions demonstrates that Congress may constitutionally enact legislation restricting and prohibiting the possession of handguns by private citizens.[10]

A. *Is There a Constitutional Right to Possess Handguns?*

Debates on the merits of gun control legislation are regularly punctuated by claims of a constitutional right to possess firearms. The source of these claims is the Second Amendment to the Constitution, which provides:

> "A well regulated Militia, being necessary to the security of a free State, the right of the people to keep and bear Arms, shall not be infringed."

Although spirited controversy as to the meaning of the Second Amendment continues unabated among commentators,[11] courts over a long period of time have consistently given the amendment a very narrow construction. The Second Amendment as so interpreted places no restrictions on Congress' ability to regulate handguns.

A constitutional provision concerning the right to "bear Arms" is directed at checking power. The question is what the framers of the Constitution intended. There are basically three relationships which could have been intended to be affected: (1) the individual against the world; (2) the populace against the government, whether state or federal; and (3) the state government against the federal government. The first possibility, that the framers were concerned with the right of individuals to protect their homes and their persons from whatever depredations might confront them, appears to be without historical support.[12] The amendment itself speaks of the "security of a free State." The disputes have centered around the second and third possibilities.

The initial question is the proper interpretation of the term "Militia." The practice in Europe of maintaining large standing armies while prohibiting the general populace from having guns led to a preference in colonial America for the militia as the primary military force. This force would be drawn from the people and would be active only in time of military need.[13]

Some have argued that the militia was regarded as the populace at large—or at least those members of the populace capable of bearing arms.[14] To these commentators, militia meant the "unorganized militia," so that the Second Amendment must be read as permitting the populace to maintain arms as a check against excesses of any or all government. This position is sometimes characterized as more extreme than it really is. The framers of the   Constitution need not have created a "right to revolution" or a license to band together in paramilitary organizations to have established a check on the government by permitting the populace to keep and bear arms.[15] Whatever the merits of the "unorganized militia" analysis may be, however, it has never found judicial favor.

The federal courts have long regarded the Second Amendment as concerned only with the "organized militia" maintained by the states. In 1875, the Supreme Court ruled in *United States v. Cruickshank*[16] that the Second Amendment restricted Congress alone and not state governments. More recently, in *United States v. Miller*,[17] the Supreme Court held that Congress could regulate firearms so long as there was no evidence of a relationship between the regulation and the preservation or efficiency of the state militia. The Court said that Miller could not attack his indictment for interstate shipment of a sawed-off shotgun under the Second Amendment:

> "In the absence of any evidence tending to show that possession or use of a 'shotgun having a barrel of less than eighteen inches in length' at this time has some reasonable relationship to the preservation or efficiency of a well regulated militia, we

cannot say that the Second Amendment guarantees the right to keep and bear such an instrument. Certainly it is not within judicial notice that this weapon is any part of the ordinary military equipment or that its use could contribute to the common defense."[18]

Some have argued that the *Miller* case should be read narrowly, since evidence of a military use can be shown as a matter of fact for most kinds of weapons.[19] However, federal courts after *Miller* have read the decision as requiring a showing that the challenged legislation actually interfered with the state militia. Under this standard, Second Amendment challenges to federal gun control legislation uniformly have been rejected.[20]

Further, even if the Second Amendment were to be interpreted to refer to an "unorganized militia," it would not follow that Congress would be barred from regulating the ownership of handguns. Such regulation would still be constitutional unless handguns were regarded as "Arms" within the meaning of the Second Amendment. It appears instead that the "Arms" of the militia were understood to consist of rifles and muskets.

In addition to the constitutional provisions and old state statutes quoted in *United States v. Miller*[21] and other secondary sources,[22] there are a number of early cases considering whether handguns are "arms" within the meaning of the Second Amendment. While the decisions are not uniform, the weight of authority is that handguns do not constitute such "Arms."[23]

This position is most effectively expressed in *State v. Workman*,[24] where the Supreme Court of Appeals of West Virginia wrote:

> "...in regard to the kind of arms referred to in the amendment, it must be held to refer to the weapons of warfare to be used by the militia, such as swords, guns, rifles, and muskets,—arms to be used in defending the state and civil liberty,—and not pistols, bowie-knives,   brass knuckles, billies, and such other weapons as are usually employed in brawls, street fights, duels, and affrays, and are only habitually carried by bullies, blackguards, and desperadoes, to the terror of the community and the injury of the state."[25]

Thus, in our view, the Second Amendment poses no barrier to congressional efforts to reduce "the terror of the community and the injury of the state" by prohibiting the private possession of handguns.

B. *Does Congress Have Power to Regulate the Manufacture, Possession and Sale of All Handguns?*

While several congressional powers could be invoked in support of gun control legislation,[26] justification is ordinarily found under Congress' power to regulate interstate and foreign commerce.[27] There can be no serious dispute that certain kinds of gun-related activities—for example, interstate sales of firearms—can be regulated under the commerce clause. The disagreements arise over how far Congress may go in regulating local gun activity under its power to regulate matters "affecting" commerce.

In *United States v. Bass*,[28] the Supreme Court recently avoided a constitutional issue concerning 18 U.S.C. § 1202, which prohibits the transportation, receipt or possession of guns by felons, by holding that proof that the prohibited conduct in each case was in commerce or affected commerce was required by the statute. Prior courts of appeals decisions had differed as to whether that statute was a constitutional exercise of the commerce power without such proof.[29]

However, in *Perez v. United States*,[30] a case decided shortly before the *Bass* case, the Supreme Court had laid the groundwork for the power to create a federal criminal law under the commerce clause. The *Perez* case concerned the constitutionality of a provision in Title II of the Consumer Credit Protection Act, 18 U.S.C. §§ 891 *et seq.*, making loan sharking a federal crime. In holding that Perez had been lawfully convicted despite the absence of proof of the effect of his conduct on commerce, the Court cited a variety of reports and statistical studies providing evidentiary support for the congressional finding that, in the aggregate. loan sharking had an effect on commerce. It concluded, therefore, that Congress could prohibit the practice regardless of the extent to which the activities of each particular loan shark may have affected commerce.

An examination of *Perez* and its progeny, and of other federal criminal legislation regulating local activity, points out what may have led the Supreme Court to take a very narrow position in the *Bass* case, namely the lack of any substantial legislative findings. In *Perez*, the Court put great emphasis on the findings made by Congress of the impact of loan-sharking on interstate commerce, even as a local activity, and on the very substantial evidence which was available to Congress to support those findings. In *Bass*, in contrast, there was virtually no legislative history to guide the Court in its interpretation of congressional intentions.

The implication of the limitation on Congress' attempted exercise of　　　power in the *Bass* case is that if gun control legislation is supported by substantial documentation and carefully drawn congressional findings concerning the effects of the proscribed activity on interstate commerce generally, the Supreme Court would sustain the exercise of power under the commerce clause even if the activity of specific individuals were purely local in nature.

In a number of cases involving federal gun control legislation arising after *Bass*, courts have followed *Perez* to uphold the power of Congress to regulate firearms felonies without a showing in each case of a nexus with interstate commerce.[31] In *United States v. Nelson*,[32] the Fifth Circuit affirmed a conviction under 18 U.S.C. § 922(a)(6), which prohibits the making of false statements in connection with the acquisition of a firearm, in spite of a failure to show a nexus between the defendant's false statements to the gun dealer and interstate commerce. Although the individual activity was clearly local, the court found that under *Perez* the Congress does have the power to regulate an intrastate activity, an isolated instance of which may have no direct connection with interstate commerce, because that intrastate activity in the aggregate does impose a burden on interstate commerce.[33]

The decision in *Nelson* leaves open the question whether Congress has the power under the *Perez* theory to regulate possession of a firearm. It could be argued that the manufacture and sale of firearms presents a stronger case for federal regulation since a potential impact on interstate commerce is discernable, while possession of a firearm could be an entirely and perpetually local activity in a given instance. Such an argument ignores the aggregate effect on commerce of a substantial number of people possessing firearms. In an analogous situation, regulation of the possession of narcotics and other controlled substances under 21 U.S.C. §§ 841 and 844, and predecessor statutes, courts have upheld the regulation without a showing in each case of a nexus with interstate commerce.

In *Deyo v. United States*,[34] for example, the Ninth Circuit affirmed a conviction for possession and sale of a drug against the contention of the defendant that the conviction was invalid because there had been no proof of a connection between the defendant's activities and interstate commerce.

The court described at length the congressional findings supporting federal control of the possession of these drugs. The court concluded that effective interstate regulation was not possible if intrastate transactions were not also regulated.[35]

The conclusion to be drawn from the narcotics possession cases is that if it can be shown through proper congressional findings that possession of handguns as a class of activity has an effect on interstate commerce, then individual possession could be legitimately proscribed without any showing in each case of a nexus with interstate commerce, notwithstanding that a particular weapon had never been in interstate commerce. Indeed it is the possession of handguns that can be viewed as being responsible for their manufacture, importation and sale. Thus, if undertaken after congressional findings of effect on interstate commerce based on substantial investigation, federal legislation banning the manufacture, sale and possession of handguns would in our view be authorized by the commerce clause.